D1624582

The Saga of the Spirit

The Saga of the Spirit

A Bibilical, Systematic, and Historical Theology of the Holy Spirit

Morris A. Inch

BAKER BOOK HOUSE
Grand Rapids, Michigan 49506

ISBN: 0-8010-5037-5

Library of Congress
Card Catalog Number: 84-72984

Printed in the United States of America

My wife, Joan, deserves special recognition for having prepared the manuscript draft on a borrowed manual typewriter, while we were serving a short term at the Jos ECWA Seminary in Nigeria. She also managed to keep up a positive spirit and encouraging attitude. The publication of the book will serve as a continuing reminder to us of the cherished nationals and expatriots who serve throughout Nigeria, and it is to them we make this dedication.

Contents

Preface

W. H. Griffith Thomas attempted to pull together the delicate weave of biblical, systematic, and historical theology in regard to the Holy Spirit in lectures given at Princeton Seminary in 1913. His subsequent publication, *The Holy Spirit of God*, remains a landmark for those who aspire to such an inclusive work. But, in the interim, this study of the Holy Spirit has progressed, opening new vistas and encouraging additional speculation. Whatever the original strengths and weaknesses of Thomas' work, there remains an unfinished task that invites new efforts to probe the sometimes enigmatic subject of the Holy Spirit.

The project is no less imposing than when Thomas attempted it. One must devise a means to survey the topic from each perspective and still keep the results within a reasonable length. This requires being selective, sacrificing otherwise legitimate considerations and abbreviating what could have been a more extensive discussion at some point or another. Given the difference in individual priorities, some sections of this book will seem much too brief and others unnecessarily long.

We begin with biblical theology. Here we seek to discover the teaching within the historical setting of the text itself. We assume first one vantage point and then another—the giving of the Law, the establishment of Israel as a nation, the people in captivity, and the advent of Christ. Each adds to what went before, resulting in a biblical mosaic of the Spirit in operation.

We then turn to systematic theology. Here we construct our own organization of biblical teaching on the Holy Spirit. The topic unfolds with the identity of the Spirit, the world, life together, life alone, and the powers. It is a somewhat novel arrangement, but it has precedents at critical points.

We conclude with historical theology. One can seem to do no better than select significant and somewhat typical episodes in this instance. The selection differs substantially from that of Thomas, as does the treatment as such. We hope to illustrate that by taking a cross section of history at any given point in time, we will discover the Spirit at work, thereby enriching our understanding of the ways of God with the affairs of men.

The saga of the Spirit never comes to an end. One simply stops recording it. This is little more than a progress report, as each person sees it from his or her own unique perspective. If this book helps others better to understand, appreciate, and act upon the Spirit's presence with us, it has fulfilled its purpose.

PART 1

Biblical Theology

Geerhardus Vos writes: "Biblical Theology occupies a position between Exegesis and Systematic Theology in the encyclopaedia of theological disciplines. It differs from Systematic Theology not in being more Biblical, or adhering more closely to the Scriptures, but in that its principle of organizing the Biblical material is historical rather than logical. Whereas Systematic Theology takes the Bible as a completed whole and endeavers to exhibit its total teaching in an orderly, systematic form, Biblical Theology deals with the material from the historical standpoint, seeking to exhibit the organic growth or development of the truths of Special Revelation from the primitive pre-redemptive Special Revelation given in Eden to the close of the New Testament canon."[1]

Although biblical theology may be said to have a logical order, it is an order discovered in a historical setting rather than a device used to structure the biblical teaching for the sake of convenience. It resembles the order found in nature as one strolls through the forest, rather than the artificial order seen while walking into a plant nursery. The histori-

1. Geerhardus Vos, *Biblical Theology*, p. 5.

cal feature provides the key to understanding what is being said about the topic.

Biblical theology is also fragmentary as compared to systematics, since it takes a particular perspective instead of a comprehensive view. It is characterized by restraint, a focus on what appears relevant at the moment, even when this has some larger significance or application.

We may also describe biblical theology as progressive. Each instance builds upon what went before—clarifying some point at issue, elaborating on a previously mentioned point, or extending into an area as yet untouched. Taken together, these are like so many building blocks going into a construction, whereby the later units are placed upon the firm base of the former.

However, biblical revelation does not proceed with equally measured steps but with major leaps or epochs. These significant events provide an opportunity to recast the past in the light of God's most recent initiative and to appraise what the future may hold in store. For instance, the Gospels are products of the early church as it reflected back on the salient features of Jesus' life and ministry, in connection with its ongoing needs and in preparation for the return of Christ. Of more immediate concern to our study, we take the Pentateuch as essentially Mosaic in character, recalling the time of beginnings and the patriarchs upon deliverance from Egypt, and with the conquest of Canaan still in the future. Here is where we elect to begin our study of biblical theology: with the post-exodus experience of Israel.[2]

---

2. Such Old Testament theologies as the following prove a helpful resource for this and subsequent Old Testament considerations: Gerhard Hassel, *Old Testament Theology: Basic Issues in the Current Debate;* David Hinson, *Theology of the Old Testament;* Edmond Jacobs, *Theology of the Old Testament;* Walter Kaiser, *Toward an Old Testament Theology;* John McKenzie, *A Theology of the Old Testament;* Th. C. Vriezen, *An Outline of Old Testament Theology.* Chester Lehman's *Biblical Theology* includes New Testament times as well. Some of the New Testament theologies that are available include Rudolf Bultmann, *Theology of the New Testament;* Hans Conzelmann, *An Outline of the Theology of the New Testament;* Donald Guthrie, *New Testament Theology;* Gerhard Hassel, *New Testament Theology: Basic Issues in the Current Debate;* Joachim Jeremias, *New Testament Theology;* Werner Kummel, *The Theology of the New Testament According to Its Major Witnesses;* George Ladd, *A Theology of the New Testament;* Elmer Martens, *God's Design: A Focus on Old Testament Theology;* Stephen Neill, *Jesus Through Many Eyes: Introduction to the Theology of the New Testament;* Charles Ryrie, *Biblical Theology of the New Testament.* George Montague's *The Holy Spirit: Growth of a Biblical Tradition* may be singled out for its comprehensive treatment of the Holy Spirit from the biblical theology perspective.

1

Sinai

Although scholars delight in debating the date of the exodus and the circumstances surrounding it, the fact is generally accepted. The *fact* is that Israel, this subject people, threw off the yoke of Egyptian oppression in order to assemble at the foot of the sacred mountain and assume their covenant relationship with the Almighty. This was in keeping with God's earlier charge to Moses, "When you have brought the people out of Egypt, you shall worship God at this mountain" (Exod. 3:12).

1 Description

The traditional site for Mount Sinai is a granite ridge, the peaks of which reach about 8,000 feet above sea level. The most conspicuous peak, Jebel Musa (Mountain of Moses), looks out toward a wide plain approximately four miles in length and up to a mile in width—providing a plausible place for the people of Israel to have encamped. Nestled on the lower slopes of the ridge is the sixth-century Monastery of St. Catherine, housing a priceless library, where the fourth-century Codex Sinaiticus (ancient Greek manuscript of the New Testament) was discovered.

It was at this location, if tradition is accurate, that Moses received the tablets from God and set forth the covenant. One could hardly overestimate its significance for posterity. Three major religious faiths in particular are rooted in this ancient event: Judaism, Christianity, and Islam. The world at large has also felt its impact.

I recall reclining at dusk on a rock crevice overlooking St. Catherine's. The sun was sliding behind the high walls which cradle the monastery, so that the line of shade was rapidly escaping behind me. The wind was picking up, and as it twisted through rock formation, it created an eerie sound resembling a muffled human voice. Here, I thought, it all began. Here the people waited while the thunder grew louder, the lightning flashed, and the clouds drew close around the sacred mountain (Exod. 19:16). Here Moses scaled to the top to meet with the Almighty, to return with the provisions of the covenant.

This is where our study properly begins, not necessarily in person but vicariously through the sacred text of Scripture. As best we can, we shall have to recover from antiquity what happened here and how the saga of the Spirit got under way. There are no subsequent developments which can be understood apart from this original setting.

2 Historical Setting

Israel migrated to Egypt in order to escape the famine which ravished the land. Joseph, who had by that time assumed an influential position in the court, was able to extend Pharaoh's favor to his kin. All went well for the time being. The people of Israel grew in numbers and prospered in the land.

However, "a new king rose over Egypt, who did not know Joseph" (Exod. 1:8). The former association and commitments were either forgotten or ignored. This cleared the way for initiating a radically new and adverse policy so far as Israel was concerned. The king had apparently been worried over the growing prosperity and strength of the people of Israel. He likely thought that they might turn against him at some critical moment and prove his downfall. In any case, the possibility was not to be taken lightly. He appointed severe taskmasters to afflict Israel with hard labor and build the storage cities of Pithom and Raamses (Exod. 1:9–11).

Some suppose that Israel had previously served as a mercenary force to repel potential invaders. If so, this would help explain Pharaoh's concern. It would also accentuate the desperate situation of the people, having lost royal sponsorship to assume abject slavery.

The king went still further in his policy of oppression, ordering the Hebrew midwives to put to death any male children who were born to their people. When the midwives refused to obey, they gave as a reason that the Hebrew women were more vigorous than the Egyptians and gave birth before they arrived to help them. Thereupon Pharaoh commanded all the people that when a son was born he should be cast into the Nile and only the daughters be allowed to live (Exod. 1:15–22).

". . . the sons of Israel sighed because of the bondage, and they cried out; and their cry for help because of their bondage rose up to God" (Exod. 2:23). God heard their petition, remembered His covenant with the Hebrew patriarchs, and solicited Moses to deliver the people from their grievous oppression. Although Moses had been raised in the royal court as the adopted child of Pharaoh's daughter, when he witnessed an Egyptian mercilessly beating a Hebrew, he struck him down and hid his body in the sand. He subsequently fled to Midian when the matter became known.

Here Moses married and settled in the land. One day as he pastured the flock of Jethro, his father-in-law, he witnessed a burning bush that was not being consumed by the flames. When he turned aside to observe the astonishing phenomenon more closely, a voice addressed him out of the bush and said, "I am the God of your father, the God of Abraham, the God of Isaac, and the God of Jacob" (Exod. 3:6). Moses hid his face, for he was afraid to look upon God. The voice continued on, describing the affliction in Egypt, the people's cry for deliverance, and God's intent to answer their request through Moses.

The remainder is also a matter of record: how Moses protested his unsuitability for the task, how God encouraged him, the struggle with a reluctant Pharaoh, the plagues upon Egypt, the escape of Israel, and the destruction of the pursuing Egyptian forces.

Finally, as God had promised that they would, Israel made its way to the site where Moses had received his commission, in order to assume their rightful role as the people of God. They were free at long last.

This account provides the traditional setting for the Pentateuch (the first five books of the Bible). Qualifications aside, Gleason Archer observes: "The atmosphere of Exodus through Numbers (not to exclude Genesis as part of the corpus) is unmistakably that of the desert, not of an agricultural people settled in their ancestral possessions for nearly a thousand years (as Wellhausen supposed)."[1] It is also a theological unit, to be understood against its historical background.

3 Liberation

God's Spirit is first set forth in the role of delivering the people from bondage. Subsequently, Isaiah would recall how Israel had "rebelled and grieved His Holy Spirit," until under the chastening of the Almighty they "remembered the days of old, of Moses. Where is He who brought them up out of the sea with the shepherds of His flock? Where is He who put His Holy Spirit in the midst of them, Who caused His glorious arm to go at the right hand of Moses . . . ?" (Isa. 63:10–12). The prophet had no difficulty in sweeping aside whatever else had become associated with the notion of the Spirit to identify the preliminary motif.

There are two aspects to this liberation: external deliverance and internal appropriation. The former is depicted by the chronicles as past, the latter as in progress. God had by His Spirit liberated the people in Egypt, but they still needed to be weaned away from its influence—in order to experience their destiny as the people of God.

Isaiah painfully recalls how they rebelled and grieved the Holy Spirit. The people of Israel complained against Moses and Aaron in the wilderness: "Would that we had died by the Lord's hand in the land of Egypt, when we sat by the pots of meat, when we ate bread to the full; for you have brought us out into this wilderness to kill this whole assembly with hunger" (Exod. 16:3). Nor were they persuaded to occupy Canaan, the Promised Land. They trembled at the report that there were giants in the land, and by way of comparison they "became like grasshoppers" in their sight (Num. 13:33). All night long they cried and wept, and in the morning they threatened to replace Moses and Aaron with a captain who would lead them back to Egypt.

In all this, they grieved the Holy Spirit, for they had set themselves in opposition to His task of liberation. The past seemed more appealing, and the future too threatening, for them to allow Him to finish His work in their lives.

The Almighty complained to Moses: "How long will this people spurn Me? And how long will they not believe in Me, despite all the signs which I have performed in their midst? I will smite them with pestilence and dispossess them, and I will make you into a nation

---

1. Gleason Archer, *A Survey of Old Testament Introduction*, p. 106.

greater and mightier than they" (Num. 14:11–12). But Moses interceded on behalf of the people, and God spared their lives—according to His great mercy and for the glory of His name. Yet, none of them would enter into the land of promise except Joshua and Caleb.

We sense in the severity of God's judgment the resolute purpose of the Spirit to complete the work of liberation assigned to Him. We may expect Him to leave no stone unturned in order to achieve His goal. He is no more content to leave man in spiritual bondage than in physical captivity. They are equally repugnant to Him, and He is from the outset portrayed as the liberating Spirit.

The apostle Paul would sum up matters at a much later date, when he declares that "where the Spirit of the Lord is, there is liberty" (2 Cor. 3:17). He makes no exceptions, and he intends none. Wherever the Spirit is, there is liberty, and (by implication) without the Spirit, there is no liberty. What masquerades as freedom amounts to slavery in another form. We exchange masters in search for a liberty that is the domain of the Spirit.

Much of what we observed to the present seems familiar to those of us who have benefited from the biblical legacy. We take for granted what had still to be engrained in the understanding of ancient Israel out of the crucible of life. The saga of the Spirit was in the making, but there was as yet a long way to go.

4 Spirit and Word

We observe from the start the close association between the liberating intent and power of the Spirit and the role of God's Word in bringing deliverance. In the beginning, the earth was "formless and void, and darkness was over the surface of the deep; and the Spirit of God was moving over the surface of the waters. Then God said, 'Let there be light'; and there was light" (Gen. 1:2–3). There the two are seen virtually as a composite in bringing about God's purpose in the creation.

This association between Spirit and Word is reenforced time and again. When God placed man in the Garden, He charged him not to eat of the tree of the knowledge of good and evil: ". . . for in the day that you eat from it you shall surely die" (Gen. 2:17). But man chose rather to believe Satan's lie, and he took of the forbidden fruit—which solicited Dietrich Bonhoeffer's pointed comment: "Man renounces life from this Word and snatches it for himself."[2] He anticipates a new freedom by

2. Dietrich Bonhoeffer, *Creation and Fall/Temptation*, p. 73.

substituting his own word for God's Word, only to fall prey to an oppressive slavery.

Illustrations could be multiplied, but for our immediate purposes it is more important to point out how the Spirit and Word relate to Moses. When the patriarch was overwhelmed with his responsibility to govern Israel, the Almighty charged him, "Gather for Me seventy men from the elders of Israel, whom you know to be elders of the people and their officers and bring them to the tent of meeting, and let them take their stand there with you. Then I will come down and speak with you there, and I will take of the Spirit who is upon you, and will put Him upon them; and they shall bear the burden of the people with you, so that you shall not bear it all alone" (Num. 11:16–17). Thus would they share with Moses in his role as agent of the Spirit in declaring God's Word to the people.

Nehemiah reflects back on God's provision in addressing the Almighty: "And Thou didst give Thy good Spirit to instruct them, Thy manna Thou didst not withhold from their mouth, and Thou didst give them water for their thirst" (Neh. 9:20). Jesus similarly picked up a reference from Deuteronomy in reaffirming that "man does not live by bread alone, but man lives by everything that proceeds out of the mouth of the Lord" (Deut. 8:3; *cp.* Matt. 4:4). The Word of God is no less sustenance than bread and water. Thereby are men delivered from bondage into life and service.

Moses was the fountainhead of the prophets, that distinguished assembly of persons who spoke out for God. He, like those who followed him, challenged the waywardness of men with the unfailing word of liberty and life over against that of bondage and death. They had to decide whether to receive the enablement of the Spirit or grieve Him by their resistance.

All this should remind us of the significance of revelation in the biblical way of thinking. Kenneth Hamilton elaborates: "That God, the Infinite Spirit, is unknowable in Himself is an affirmation made by Christian theology throughout its history. But that our approach to Him is one of 'going towards' or of engaging on 'a quest' for Him is utterly alien to the whole perspective of the Christian faith. For the biblical foundation on which Christian theology is built states with unmistakable clarity that, though we can never approach nearer to Him by our own volition or through our own wisdom, He has come to us."[3] He has

3. Kenneth Hamilton, *Words and the Word*, p. 70.

come to us—and spoken with us—in order that we might know His way and walk in it.

Revelation consists of a divine self-disclosure. It resembles what one being volunteers to share with another, rather than what we can intuit or pry loose by some means. It requires a divine initiative, without which it would be impossible to know of the mysterious ways of God.

We hasten to add that revelation is not simply from God but about His activity. It asserts what God has been up to, is currently engaged in, and may be counted upon doing. It describes the sovereign activity of God in the course of history. It also warns man against seeking to oppose His righteous purposes, but instead to cooperate in whatever way possible.

This is obviously a historical perspective, related to the actual events which people experience. It is lineal rather than cyclic, after the pattern of the ancient nature cults. The fathers pass on their legacy to their sons, and the latter to their sons after them—whether for good or evil. We may add that God tempers the results so as to encourage man to rise above the circumstances of the past, but not to obliterate the past or its effect on subsequent generations.

Hamilton adds: "On the other hand, the historical view does not place restrictions on what the real world can contain."[4] We have to cope with a reductionist mentality that wants to reduce the real world to less than reality. This approach ignores the mighty acts of God; it wants to silence the Word of God and to eliminate the presence of the Spirit of God. In their place, such reductionism offers the paltry gods of our own making, powerless as they are to rescue us from bondage.

The combination of Spirit and Word reminds us that there are certain events of prime importance to mankind. Over all opposition, they are like giant steps forward—toward the eventual success of God's purpose. They give meaning to all the rest, whatever intervenes. The exodus was such an event, as we have been assured of by the Word of God.

We may also suppose that events of such a nature may, as accomplished by the Spirit and attested by the Word, have a liberating dimension to them. They provide the opportunity for us to break away from all that hinders us and to engage with confidence in what lies before. Although it is presumption on our part to push ahead of them, it is a lack of faithfulness to lag behind. Moses attempted to convey this to the people of Israel, and subsequent generations would think back upon their struggle as a warning and admonition.

---

4. *Ibid.*, p. 58.

5 Birthright

Moses leveled his attack against the bondage of the spirit, which persisted with the people after their physical deliverance. He could achieve his purposes only at the expense of challenging the religious-political establishment, still fresh in the minds of those he sought to lead. Wallis Budge suggests: "The three main elements of the Egyptian religions were a solar monotheism, a fertility cult and a hog-wild cult of anthropomorphic divinity."[5] It is not surprising that the biblical account of creation strikes at all these elements. It portrays the sun as "the greater light" (Gen. 1:16) created by *the* Almighty rather than divine or even symbolic divinity, the earth's bounty as freely given for man's benefit (Gen. 2:16) instead of something he must petition the gods for, and man as assigning the animals their names (Gen. 2:19) in contrast to rendering them worship.

The reference to "the beginning" (Gen. 1:1) would seem to correspond to what the ancient Egyptians referred to as "the time of the gods." In the beginning, according to the polemic biblical account, there was none but the Almighty. Amon could not be found, nor Osiris, nor Ptah. We sense in this connection the words of the Shema: "Hear, O Israel! The Lord is our God, the Lord is one! And you shall love the Lord your God with all your heart and with all your soul and with all your might" (Deut. 6:4–5). This is proper in the first place because there is no other. The rival gods are but the creation of man, subsequent to primeval time.

Those who translate the text to read "wind of God" rather than "Spirit of God" can make a plausible case (Gen. 1:2).[6] However, the close association of wind, breath, and spirit suggests that we respect their composite usage, and in this we have adequate biblical precedent. Psalm 33:6 testifies that "By the word of the Lord the heavens were made, and by the breath of His mouth all their host." Elihu's couplet is strikingly to the point: "The Spirit of God has made me, and the breath of the Almighty gives me life" (Job 33:4).

The Spirit (wind) of God is portrayed as bringing order out of chaos. This might include such things as allowing the light to break through the dense cloud cover enveloping the earth, dividing between the atmospheric and terrestrial water and then between the terrestrial water

5. E. A. Wallis Budge, *Egyptian Religion*, p. 6.

6. See the rationale developed by Harry Orlinsky, *Biblical Culture and Bible Translation*, pp. 400–408.

and land, and the fashioning of plant and animal life. He is displayed as designing the delicate balance of life with regard to the earth.

In Hebraic thought, the ideas of creation and preservation are closely linked if not inseparable. The psalmist writes, ". . . Thou dost take away their spirit, they expire, and return to their dust. Thou dost send forth Thy Spirit, they are created; and Thou dost renew the face of the ground" (Ps. 104:29–30). Where the Spirit is, there is purposeful design and life; should the Spirit absent Himself, life would return to the formless dust from which it was derived.

We note in passing how the Spirit advocates a purposeful variety. Karl Barth comments that "because God is, and is its Creator, the creature may say after Him: I am also, and to his fellow creature: Thou art also, and of this creature: he, or she, or it is also."[7] This preserves the unique worth of each of God's creatures, as they complement and enrich one another in the grand design of things.

"Then the Lord God formed man of dust from the ground, and breathed into his nostrils the breath of life; and man became a living being" (Gen. 2:7). God created man from the dust of the ground, from the dry red earth rather than the fertile, black, muddy soil inundated by the Nile and associated with the favor of the gods. It is as though the author wanted, once and for all time to cast off the ties with Egypt (its gods, enticements, and slavery), and raise up in its place a free people, whose sole trust resided in the Almighty. Frail people though they were, from dust to dust, their lives and destiny were in the hands of an all-sufficient God.

God breathed into man the breath of life and man became "the living one." (A comparable word is found in the Egyptian writings concerning metamorphosis of the dead in the other world—from a lifeless body to a living being.) With the breath of God, man began to live, as the climax to creation and in the image of God. All this implies that life depends ultimately upon God, rather than on ruthless rulers, their emissaries, or the peculiar set of circumstances we face.

The condition for freedom is now all too evident. It involves a choice between God and freedom—or the chariots of Egypt and slavery. Where the Spirit of God may be found, there is genuine liberty, such freedom as the world cannot give and certainly cannot take away. This freedom ties back into "the time of the gods" according to Egyptian thinking, to primeval time. It extends to the time when God set the course of life,

7. Karl Barth, *Church Dogmatics*, Vol. III, Part I, p. 345.

and before men tampered with it. Such freedom captures the essential character of life as the Spirit endowed it.

The most significant thing said about man as he was constituted is that he was created in the image of God (Gen. 1:26–27). To be created in the image of God means that man resembles God in *some* respects. It does not imply that man resembles God in all respects or that he is necessarily identical to God in any respect. Most obvious, man resembles God in his ability to comprehend truth and act on moral precepts, making it possible to commune with God and superintend the creation. According to Leon Wood, still another "noteworthy factor true of man at his formation was that he was susceptible to the control of the Spirit who had formed him, without the hindrance of sin's influence that exists for regenerated man today."[8]

This perspective on man in retrospect must have clashed with the vacillating experience of the people of Israel. They had been slow to believe and hesitant to claim their birthright of freedom. Others had been quick to intimidate them and to deny its existence. But, in the face of every opposition, Moses held firm to the idea that they had been born free. This was God's purpose for them from the beginning, and His persisting resolve—as evidenced by their recent deliverance from Egypt.

6 Providence

Scripture traces the results of man's defection after the fall. As time passed, man seemed to get progressively worse. "Then the Lord saw that the wickedness of man was great on the earth, and that every intent of the thoughts of his heart was only evil continually" (Gen. 6:5). The Almighty had announced: "My Spirit shall not strive with man forever," and He was deeply grieved with man (Gen. 6:3, 6).

These words testify to God's providential concern for man, expressed by the disposition and activity of His Spirit. The apostle Paul would warn his readers not to "grieve the Holy Spirit of God" (Eph. 4:30), which they were calculated to do by resisting His work in their lives. Do not presume on God's gracious concern, as if there were no limit to it, no matter how much we abuse our privileges or oppress others. The Spirit does not take such behavior lightly, nor can we count on Him to overcome our rebellion.

8. Leon Wood, *The Holy Spirit in the Old Testament*, p. 37.

God proceeded to make a covenant with Noah and his posterity, and declared that the rainbow would serve as a sign to successive generations that "never again shall the water become a flood to destroy all flesh" (Gen. 9:15). Rabbinic scholars have speculated that the bow is turned toward heaven so that it would not appear that God would shoot arrows at them. As Nachmanides observes: "It is indeed the way of warriors to invert the instruments of war which they hold in their hands when calling for peace from their opponents."[9]

The promise was made to all peoples, and not to Israel alone, thus assuring us of God's interest in the entire human race. The Spirit was never conceived of as a partisan agent of a tribal god, but the universal benefactor of a sovereign deity.

Maimonides wrote that according to Jewish thought the Gentiles are obligated to observe a minimum of seven precepts: "(a) to establish courts of justice, (b) to abstain from idolatry, (c) blasphemy, (d) incest, (e) murder, (f) robbery, and (g) eating flesh cut from living animals."[10] He reasoned further that Israel was obligated in addition to be a hallowed people. But he left no doubt that the devout Gentile, who observed the Noahic Covenant by abiding by the precepts implied in it, would benefit not only in this life but also inherit a portion in the life to come.

The Noahic Covenant supports the integrity of respective cultures as a basis for serving the Almighty. The Gentile need not become a Jew, nor exchange his cultural pattern for some other Gentile alternative. He need only discover what it means to walk with God within his own familiar cultural setting.

This or any other covenant underscores the central feature of grace in man's relationship to God. We deserve far less than the covenant offers us, if anything at all. It is unmerited favor, the righteousness of Noah not to the contrary. Although we may accept its provisions, we have no right to demand them. We ought not to think of God's grace as cheap. God accepts us in order to make us more acceptable. The covenant signals the beginning of the Spirit's work with its recipients, but they must expect to be pliable or cast aside.

Man ought to respond to the covenant not in resentful compliance but love. God deserves our love, not simply for what He does on our behalf, but for who He is. The rabbis could hardly make reference to

9. Nachmanides, *Commentary on the Torah: Genesis*, p. 137.
10. Maimonides, *The Commandments*, p. 9.

God without adding the words, "Blessed be He," as if to bear witness to the fact that to know Him is to love Him.

In the biblical setting, love is an active word, involving not sentiment alone but obedience. Suppose there were two sons, each of whom received a request from their father. One heartily acknowledged his filial duty but failed to carry through on it; the other complained (not the desired response) but did as he was directed. Which of these can be said to have loved his father? The latter, according to rabbinic thinking.

Love ought not to waver with the changes in circumstances. The Mishnah teaches, "It is incumbent on a man to bless [God] for the evil in the same way as the good."[11] Job reasoned with his wife, "Shall we indeed accept good from God and not accept adversity?" (Job 2:10). To this the text adds: "In all this Job did not sin with his lips."

To sum up, the Noahic Covenant illustrates the manner in which the Spirit works with reference to divine promise. It suggests that the Spirit is disposed to reconcile man to God by means of grace (unmerited favor), irrespective of ethnic origin, supposing he responds to the provisions of the covenant, as motivated by love. Any particular covenant implies or makes explicit the conditions on which man may expect the blessing of God as ministered by the Spirit of God.

The Abrahamic Covenant is a further evidence of God's providential concern for man, for Israel in particular but for all people as a result. God instructed Abram, "Go forth from your country, and from your relatives, and from your father's house, to the land which I will show you; and I will make you a great nation, and I will bless you, and make your name great, and so you shall be a blessing; and I will bless those who bless you, and the one who curses you I will curse. And in you all the families of the earth shall be blessed" (Gen. 12:1–3). Then, Abram responded as God had enjoined him to do, and so claimed the promise of the Almighty.

The covenant with Abram (thereafter, Abraham) involved a people, a land, and an extended blessing. God promised Abram a people so numerous as to be compared with the sand along the seashore (Gen. 32:12). They would be a holy people, set aside as a testimony to God's faithfulness and as the agent of God's blessing.

Holiness is associated primarily with God, with the accent on His awesome majesty and untarnished purity. "Holy, Holy, Holy, is the Lord of hosts," and in His presence man cries out, "Woe is me, for I am

---

11. *Ibid.*, p. 5.

ruined! Because I am a man of unclean lips, and I live among a people of unclean lips" (Isa. 6:3, 5).

Holiness may be derived by persons or—in a more qualified sense—by things, as they participate with God in His purpose. So far as man is concerned, holiness especially implies being just, truthful, and merciful. It also precludes idolatry, as Moses warned: "For you are a holy people to the Lord your God; the Lord your God has chosen you to be a people for His own possession out of all the peoples who are on the face of the earth" (Deut. 7:6). It is in this connection, with the sanctifying work of the Spirit, that we have the first references in Scripture to the *Holy* Spirit (Ps. 51:11; Isa. 63:10–12).

The covenant made a heavy demand on Abraham. He was required to leave his country, kindred, and father's house for a destination yet to be specified. It was a historical incident, but one that, according to J. H. Hertz, has contained significance to Abraham's posterity: "A similar call comes to Abraham's descendants in every age and clime, to separate themselves from all associations and influences that are inimical to their Faith and Destiny."[12] While the covenant applied to a particular land, it implied that the people take every step necessary to assure their role as a peculiar people.

The peculiar nature of the people was tied to their being a blessing to all the families of the world. They were to become God's hand reaching toward a fallen world and God's redemptive means as served by the Spirit.

Through these and many other ways, we see God's providential concern expressed for humankind. His Spirit grieves over us when we turn to evil ways, strives with us to bring us back into the way of God, and negotiates with us through covenantal promises to provide such grace as is necessary to realize our calling as the people of God. Man resembles the prodigal son referred to by Jesus (Luke 15:11–32), beloved of God but wasting his inheritance in "a far country" (KJV). The Spirit calls to mind the more pleasant circumstances in the Father's home and urges us to reconsider—for the glory of God and our own eternal welfare.

7 Vassal Treaty

All roads in the Pentateuch may be said to proceed from and to Sinai. We have made the return trip to that imposing scene at the foot of the

12. J. H. Hertz (ed.), *The Pentateuch and Haftorahs*, p. 45.

Holy Mount. Here we pause long enough to draw together such strands as we have previously introduced and add what is yet lacking from the liberation theme. Here we attempt to get the saga of the Spirit in sharper focus, thereby setting the foundation for what will follow.

The promises of God are never simply history divulged beforehand.[13] They lack the eventual context or circumstances within which fulfillment takes place. The present instance is a case in point. God had promised to bless Abraham's posterity, and that promise is picked up in the Mosaic Covenant, as Israel is set apart for God's redemptive purpose.

The Mosaic Covenant reflects the pattern of an ancient vassal treaty.[14] There is reference made to the deliverance from Egypt, which was to incite reverence for the Almighty. This was coupled with appreciation for God's rich provision in the exodus. The body of the treaty consists of instructions which the people must heed if they are to enjoy God's continued favor. There follows the recital of potential blessings and cursings, depending upon whether or not the people are obedient. The final element consists of the provision for renewing the covenant. The covenant obligations do not change so far as its basic content is concerned, but there is anticipated such change as necessary in order to relate abiding terms to new situations.

Salvation history, in the strictest sense, begins with the Mosaic Covenant (*cp*. Heb. 1:1). There were intimations earlier, but Moses was the fountainhead of the prophets, and salvation history is said to convene with the prophets. Thus may salvation history be distinguished from history in general.

"God's activity in history, aimed at the creation of a consecrated people of God, was discerned not only in isolated marvelous events, but also in the emergence of specially equipped men and women whose leadership in word and deed, by wars of liberation without and by the establishment of the will of God in the social and moral order within, dragged the dullness of the people with them, again and again smashing and sweeping away all the obstacles, which the incursion of heathen morals and ways of thought raised against them."[15] This comment by

---

13. A. Berkeley Mickelsen elaborates the distinction of promise (in terms of prediction) from history written before the event in *Interpreting the Bible*, pp. 289–92.

14. Meredith Kline analyzes Deuteronomy accordingly: preamble (1:1–5), historical prologue (1:6–4:49), stipulations (5–26), curses and blessings or ratification (27–30), and succession arrangements or continuity (31–34) in his *Treaty of the Great King*, p. 28.

15. Walther Eichrodt, *Theology of the Old Testament*, II, p. 50.

Walther Eichrodt suggests the tortuous route salvation history had to take, faced with opposition from without and with vacillation from within.

The more insidious threat was from within. There was the temptation to be like the other nations in order to win their acceptance. There was the nostalgic feeling for the old ways, and the tendency to slip back into them. God's people were often their own worst enemy.

These people were blessed with heroic leaders, but they were not demigods; their human frailty was all too evident for us to make such a mistaken identification. In a peculiar sense, they were men and women of God, endued by His Spirit for some special tasks, and they often seemed to rise to an occasion out of what had previously been a very ordinary pattern of life. They were in God's place, at God's time, for God's purpose.

Eichrodt adds: "In the activity of these mediators and instruments of the divine covenant purpose of salvation the Israelite people recognized afresh the interruption of God's transcendent life into the paltry patchwork of this world."[16] Perhaps more clearly than the heroic figures themselves, they could see the horizons extend to reveal the hand of God at work in the affairs of men. This was not necessarily a break with the commonplace, but could be when the commonplace took on uncommon significance. It occurred when the vassal people sensed something of their role as the people of God—when heaven seemed to brush earth, and they felt an inexplicable response as if on cue.

We recall how all this began in a specific sense with Moses, on whom the Spirit rested for his task (Num. 11:17). The Spirit instructed the people through Moses. We call this teaching *Torah*. (The popular notion of Torah as law is misleading.) Rabbi Meir reflects on the student of Torah: "He is called friend, beloved [of God], lover of God, lover of mankind; and it clothes him with humility and reverence, and fits him to become righteous, saintly, upright, and faithful; and it keeps him far from sin and brings him to virtue, and from him men employ counsel and sound knowledge, understanding, and might."[17] It is an instruction suited to free men, assuming a covenant relationship with the Almighty.

The Torah rests on two great principles: the love of God and of one's fellowman (Exod. 20:1–17; *cp.* Matt. 22:36–40). Although the love of

16. *Ibid.*
17. Maimonides, *The Commandments*, p. 17.

God may be variously understood, it involves openness: the willingness, indeed, compelling desire, to allow God's inscrutable will to be achieved in one's life. Such love does not have to know the future, so long as it can be assured that the future lies in God's hands.

Love of one's fellowman must be viewed in a reciprocal setting. It allows one to "be there" for another, and the other to "be there" for him. This love involves being as quick to accept a service voluntarily made as to offer a service to another in need. As a giving to—and receiving from—others, it signifies, in the deepest sense of the word, being a covenant community.

Brevard Childs concludes that the Torah encompasses Israel's "whole life, defining her relations to God and to her neighbors, and the quality of her existence."[18] Nothing remains outside of the purview of Torah, and there is nothing unconditioned by its pervasive presence. Dissect Hebrew life at any point and we discover the principle of Torah at work.

The concepts of covenant and Torah are so closely related as often to be thought identical. But covenant is the more inclusive designation, embracing teaching within the sovereign act of God's grace. The covenant is first and foremost an act of grace, which is to protect the Torah from legalism. Conversely, the presence of Torah guards the covenant from antinomianism. The two, whether taken separately or together, should be recognized as a means whereby men are freed to serve the Almighty, and as an instrument employed by the Spirit.

8 Theistic Humanism

It is the purpose of the covenant not only to glorify God's name, but to enhance human life. This is vividly illustrated in the rabbinic suggestion that the Sabbath is the best of days in which to enjoy marital relations. One honors the Creator by relishing His creation.

Rabbi Yechiel Eckstein challenges the Christian's stress on the burden associated with covenantal responsibility: "For when seen from within, this yoke or burden is one that the observant Jew accepts willingly, out of abiding love and immeasurable joy. He regards the Torah and its laws as God's precious gift to Israel, as the concrete manifestation of his goodness and love for his people. The law purifies him, enables his

18. Brevard Childs, *The Book of Exodus*, p. 367.

spirit, and sanctifies his daily life."[19] He then concludes: "Rather than a burden, it is the Jew's greatest delight."

The problem with man is that he attempts to grasp life for himself instead of accepting it from God's gracious hand. He discovers that the more he grasps, the less he has as a result. His is a futile effort to capture what God wants to bestow upon him as a gift.

The people of Israel had gone through a rather thoroughly dehumanizing experience in slavery, and the covenant was meant to offer them a new lease on life. It was nothing less than a humanistic manifesto, even though we cannot limit it to that alone. Not only had they been born free, but now they were made free.

What had they lost, and what did they hope to regain as the covenant people? What some have chosen to call "creatureliness." Ray Anderson describes its basic character: "From a phenomenological perspective, this creatureliness exists as a state of being common to all who have been given a *nephesh*, or creaturely soul by the Creator. All creatures who have this breath of life exist on a continuum, with an indeterminate number of variations, but with a common creaturely existence."[20] It is what distinguishes animated life forms from material objects. The slave exists to please his master; the free person enjoys a life of his own in conjunction with others.

"Creatureliness" implies more than this minimal definition so far as man is concerned. The psalmist concluded that God has made man a little lower than Himself (or the angels?), and "dost crown him with glory and majesty"—so that he might rule over the work of His hands (Ps. 8:5–6). There is a mark of nobility in man's character that we dare not ignore. To treat him with less respect is to reject the purpose for which God intended him and the Spirit strives to enable him.

Anderson allows that "Human beings are creaturely beings. Of that there can be little doubt. What is debatable is the assertion that *being* human is the result of more than that which creaturely existence can produce and sustain."[21] Scripture clearly teaches that man's creatureliness originates with God and is sustained by Him. Man does not live of himself.

We can readily understand why such a perspective would be identified as "*theistic* humanism." The notion and character of man as crea-

---

19. Yechiel Eckstein, *What Every Christian Should Know About Judaism*, p. 24.
20. Ray Anderson, *On Being Human*, p. 22.
21. *Ibid.*, p. 33.

ture are derived from revelation rather than perception. What we see of man in his fallen state may not coincide with the state in which he was created (Heb. 2:8).

The Israelites were enjoined not to "wrong a stranger or oppress him, for you were strangers in the land of Egypt" (Exod. 22:21). Since they had experienced the bitter lot of the oppressed, they ought to empathize with that of others. They should learn that the covenant was for them and for those with whom they came in contact, a mandate for man to reach out to achieve his human potential by the grace of God.

9 Two Ways

The covenant also introduces the classic doctrine of the Two Ways, so aptly described by the psalmist: "How blessed is the man who does not walk in the counsel of the wicked,/nor stand in the path of sinners,/nor sit in the seat of scoffers!" (Ps. 1:1). He delights himself in the law of the Almighty, and meditates upon it day and night. He resembles a tree aptly planted by a stream, which yields its fruit at the appointed season, and whose leaves do not shrivel up and die. He prospers in whatever he sets out to do (vv. 2–3).

"The wicked are not so," but rather resemble the chaff which the wind scatters in every direction. For this reason, the wicked shall not stand in the judgment, nor sinners in the assembly of the righteous. For the Almighty knows the way of the righteous, but the way of the ungodly shall perish (vv. 4–6).

When Joshua had gathered the people of Israel at Shechem, he renewed the covenant with them, having set certain of the company in front of Mount Gerizim, and others before Mount Ebal, in order to recite the blessings and curses (Josh. 8:32–35). This vividly displayed the difference between the way of the righteous and that of the wicked. Gerizim retains to this day an impressive stand of trees—suggesting how the righteous prosper—and Ebal's rocky slope reminds us of the barren nature of a wicked life.

It is hard to imagine a geographical area as a whole which would reenforce this contrast between the Two Ways as does the Promised Land. It consists largely of a slender strip of fertile ground, nourished by both the northern tributaries and the dew from the ocean. As the terrain drops off quickly in marginal areas, there appear sections which are virtually uninhabitable, where the inhabitants are confronted day by day with a drama of life and death, vacillating according to the fortunes of weather. Here the rains push life into the arid lands, only to be thrust back by the hot winds blowing in from the wilderness.

The covenant set Two Ways before the people: the way of obedience and divine blessing, and the way of disobedience and a barren existence. Orlinsky argues: "It was unthinkable that God, the incomparable, would fail to protect a law-abiding Israel and make it prosper; had He not already demonstrated by His acts His interest in Israel? But if Israel failed to heed God's commandments, then He could punish and even destroy her."[22]

This is not to suggest that God would utterly destroy the people of promise, no matter how we understand the words of the apostle Paul: "God has not rejected His people whom He foreknew . . ." (Rom. 11:2). God is more resolute in His purpose with Israel than we might at first be led to believe.

But the people must not presume upon the long-suffering of God. There was a limit with the striving of the Spirit with man, one which might be passed over without notice by those foolish enough to court the wrath of God. The wise man learned to walk humbly before the Almighty and with regard for his fellowman. This was the calling and character of a covenant people.

Summary

As our first vantage point from which to view the activity of the Spirit, we elected the lofty height of Mount Sinai. From there we reflected upon the deliverance of Israel from Egypt, not a physical liberation alone but an ongoing spiritual emancipation. Both were, when considered individually or in combination, the work of God's Spirit.

From the outset, there was the closest association of the Spirit and the Word of God. Both were present in the creation narrative and at critical points thereafter—being particularly evident with the ministry of Moses. The patriarch introduced the school of the prophets, those fearless few who delivered the liberating Word of God to an often wayward people. We have elsewhere noted: "The prophets moved earth by way of heaven."[23] They thought in terms of the progressive revelation of God's involvement in the world, and they

22. Orlinsky, *Biblical Culture and Bible Translation*, p. 27

23. Morris Inch, *Understanding Bible Prophecy*, p. 45.

were confident of the power of God to liberate man from bondage to service.

Man was born free. Long before man enslaved his fellowman, he had been created free. What God had made free, we ought not to suppose that the gods of Egypt could reverse. The Genesis narrative virtually bristles with this polemic, underscoring the inventive diversity that results from creation. Freedom in the Spirit is a freedom to develop one's unique qualities, and so to enrich the rest of creation.

In spite of a good beginning, man has fallen victim to bondage. But he has also experienced God's providential concern for him in his desperate need. This concern has surfaced with the Noahic and Abrahamic Covenants, the first with the nations and the second with regard to Abraham's posterity—but with the benefit of all mankind in view. Thus we trace the Spirit's continuing ministry to man, by way of divine promise and enablement.

The Mosaic Covenant is both another evidence of God's providential concern and a critical chapter as well. It takes the form of an ancient vassal treaty, in deference to the Great King who has delivered Israel from bondage and may rightfully anticipate their grateful obedience and service. The covenant sets forth such stipulations as the people are expected to abide by, and what they may expect if faithful (or unfaithful) to its precepts. By way of the covenant, the Spirit is peculiarly associated with the chosen people, to correct them as they err and confirm them in the ways of righteousness.

The covenant fosters what we have designated a "theistic humanism." One cannot profess to love God and hate his fellowman. Neither can he hope to love his fellowman as he ought without recourse to the Almighty. Man is a peculiarly noble creature in God's design, meant to exercise his stewardship over creation. The covenant anticipates no less.

This brought us to consider the concept of the Two Ways: that of the righteous and that of the wicked. The covenant contrasts these so as not to leave the matter in doubt. The way of the righteous will prosper; the way of the wicked will prove defective.

We return to Paul's comment that "where the Spirit of the Lord is, there is liberty" (2 Cor. 3:17). His conviction was grounded in the early experience of the Hebrew people, providing a solid foundation on which to lay subsequent considerations. The continuity with regard to the saga of the Spirit runs from beginning to end.

2

Zion

We move our observation post from "the Mountain of God" to "the gates of Zion," from the wilderness of Sinai to the City of David. Time has passed, and the people of Israel have now settled down, struggling to survive among often-hostile neighbors. They have made the transition from nomadic existence in the wilderness to an agricultural economy. They have wrestled with the issues of governance and diplomacy. For better or worse, they have arrived in the Promised Land.

10 Reflection

The ancient Jebusite city was contained on a spur flanked by the Tyropeon and Kidron valleys. Exceedingly small by modern standards, it had an approximate circumference of 4,200 feet. The temple mount extended to the north, and the Gihon springs provided an abundant source of water.

In Jerusalem today, one cannot get the full effect of the site as a fortified city. The Tyropeon has been filled in and the general topography sufficiently altered so that we do not see it as it once appeared. But, with the use of a little imagination, one can reconstruct the rocky spur, isolated on two sides by steep valleys and heavily fortified on the third.

This was described as the "city of God," and as especially dear to the heart of God. The psalmist exclaimed, "The Lord loves the gates of Zion/More than all the other dwelling places of Jacob" (Ps. 87:2). Although it resembled other fortified areas of Canaanite times, its defense lay with the Almighty (v. 5). Surely we have selected a choice location from which to view the continuing saga of the Spirit.

11 Historical Setting

On this occasion, our historical setting is a period of time rather than a specific date. It may be further characterized as a point of reference that remained throughout the period. Zion continued as the sometimes-disputed center of religious life even when the nation was divided into separate political entities. Those scattered to the extent of Palestine and abroad still looked to Jerusalem as the holy city. From time to time, pilgrims made their way "up to Jerusalem" to renew their faith and reinforce their identity as the people of God.

Slavery in Egypt, the wilderness wandering, and the conquest soon ceased to be memories of the living and became the reports of others, passed down from one generation to the next. Israel had to focus its attention on the current demands for survival among threatening nations, complicated by internal strife. The needs of the people often went neglected in deference to personal and partisan interests. As idolatry stalked the efforts of the covenant people, the Promised Land proved difficult to gain and still more difficult to hold and benefit from.

Between the time of the patriarchs and the monarchy was what has been called the "distressing days of the judges," which seems the more striking because it was meant to be an era of divine rule (a theocracy). Leon Wood elaborates: "A description of this form of government may be worded succinctly: it is that form in which God is the supreme Ruler. It is not a democracy, in which the people rule; it is not a monarchy in which an earthly king rules; it is a theocracy in which God rules."[1]

Of course, the concept of theocracy was not new. It was implied in creation and made explicit in the vassal treaty with Israel. What was changed is that the people had now made their way into the land and needed to set up a political system to manage their life together. This was further complicated by the fact that they had not dispensed with the traditional inhabitants, who continued to foster strife.

---

1. Leon Wood, *Distressing Days of the Judges*, p. 25.

This was a turbulent time, in which Israel experienced one wave of oppression after another, interspersed with deliverance at the hand of one of the judges. We read of Othniel that "the Spirit of the Lord came upon him, and he judged Israel" (Judg. 3:10); that "the Spirit of the Lord came upon Gideon; and he blew a trumpet, and the Abiezrites were called together to follow him" (6:34); that "the Spirit of the Lord came upon Jephthah" (11:29); and, regarding Samson, that "the Spirit of the Lord began to stir him in Mahaneh-dan, between Zorah and Eshtaol" (13:25). Thus does the Spirit make His appearances as the agent of the theocracy, a role which continues to predominate throughout the era that followed.

Eventually the people asked for a king to be appointed over them. Samuel took this request as a personal affront, but the Almighty counseled him, "Listen to the voice of the people in regard to all that they say to you, for they have not rejected you, but they have rejected Me from being king over them" (1 Sam. 8:7). Their request for a king, logical as it may have seemed otherwise, was a repudiation of God's sovereign rule.

Although Samuel acceded to the people's request, he warned them of dire consequences: a military draft, servitude, a wide confiscation of land, taxation, and the loss of personal liberty (1 Sam. 8:11–17). Since they had been concerned only about what gains might be achieved from the monarchy, they were reminded of what they would lose.

Saul was appointed king and then David, through whom the monarchy took on its classic form. The king was charged with implementing the goals of the society, maintaining order in the process, and regulating its foreign relations. He assumed these obligations within the scope of the covenant, as a faithful administrator of its provisions.

The Hebrew monarchy involved more than the king and his subjects. It consisted of a finely tuned balance of power, in which the prophets, cultus, and sages played their roles. As storm clouds gathered, the prophets assumed the role of watchman, and reminded the people of the high and uncompromising demands of the Almighty. What the prophets warned of soon came to pass with the fall of the northern kingdom to Assyria and, at a later time, the southern kingdom to Babylon. The former glory of Zion faded until it was all but eclipsed by the captivity, but during that time it afforded a point of continuity from which to view the saga of the Spirit.

12 Case of the Judges

The advent of one biblical epoch never fully eclipses what went before. It rather embodies salient features of the previous era in the process of developing what may be added to it. The time of the judges provides a striking case in point. We have seen the work of the Spirit in liberating the covenant people and the reminder that if they are to continue to enjoy the blessing of God, they must abide by the provisions of the covenant. We discover that this theme is picked up with the judges, who called the people again to repentance and restoration when they saw them fall away into bondage.

Israel had been called as the people of God to abide by His will and serve His purposes, and such a high calling immediately encountered testing. The Canaanite religion was notorious for its indulgence of human vice. It sought to insure the fertility of the land through cultic prostitution, not even ruling out human sacrifice as a means of obtaining the favor of the gods.

Those who live in an urban environment can little appreciate the strength that such a faith had upon this agrarian culture. Wood adds: "The Canaanites believed that the farmer was completely at the mercy of this god [Baal] in respect to both crops and livestock; and they apparently were willing to pass this belief along to the Israelites, fresh from their wilderness conditions. If the Israelites were to expect produce from Canaanite soil, they would not only have to plant and cultivate seed in the right manner but worship the god of the soil as well."[2] There appears to have developed a breach between the official stance of the new immigrants (as the people of God) and the practice of individuals and groups who readily compromised the provisions of the covenant to accommodate the demands of Baal.

Such was the setting for the judges of Israel and their labors. They were instruments of God's sovereign rule in the midst of turbulent times for the people of promise. They were leaders who threw off the oppression of the enemy, called the people to repentance, and served an uneasy peace. These judges were a varied lot as well: Gideon, the youngest of his family; Deborah, a nondescript woman in a patriarchal society; Jephthah, of illegitimate birth and a bandit chieftain; and Samson, a man of undisciplined passion. But they had a task in common and were endowed alike by the Spirit to fulfill that task.

The pattern was set with Othniel of whom it was said, "And the Spirit of the Lord came upon him, and he judged Israel" (Judg. 3:10). The Book of Judges consists primarily of a series of cycles wherein the defection of the people is followed by their oppression under the heel of

2. *Ibid.*,p. 144.

their enemies, their petition to the Almighty for rescue, deliverance at the hand of the judges, and a period of peace—which invites the people to return to their evil ways and starts the cycle all over again.

We pick up the cycle after the death of Othniel: "Now the sons of Israel again did evil in the sight of the Lord" (Judg. 3:12). The account contrasts with the success under Joshua, and its primary purpose was to show why the people had not experienced the blessings available to them. These accounts were told and retold as a means of warning and encouragement, lest they fall into a similar condition or so as not to utterly despair of their situation.

How had the Israelites sinned? They had at the outset failed to occupy the land fully. This was done in direct violation of the directive God had given to them (Exod. 23:23; 34:11–16; Deut. 7:1–5), and amounted to defection by the vassal people. It also suggests that their confidence in God was wavering in the face of obstacles encountered with possession of the land.

Their courting of Baal was only a step removed. Man is inclined to worship something—if not the Almighty, then an alternative. Baal presented an attractive substitute for those so recently turned to an agrarian life, under the apprenticeship of the Canaanites.

Israel's respect for the rights of others diminished accordingly, seeking one lower level after another. Sexual sins abounded, and the guilty were defended rather than suffering the reproach of society. There was no civil authority to check the rampant degeneration, and "everyone did what was right in his own eyes" (Judg. 21:25).

". . . So the Lord strengthened Eglon the king of Moab against Israel, because they had done evil in the sight of the Lord" (Judg. 3:12). This was God's doing, as a reproach for the sins of a wayward people: "For whom the Lord loves He reproves, even as a father, the son in whom he delights" (Prov. 3:12).

The expedition against Israel represented an alliance of Moab, Ammon, and Amalek. The Israelites had reason to recall what Amalek had done to them as they made their way toward the Promised Land—how he "met you along the way and attacked among you all the stragglers at your rear when you were faint and weary; and he did not fear God" (Deut. 25:18). Moab, for its part, had enticed Israel to engage in idolatry, which brought down a plague upon them (Num. 25:1–9). The Ammonites were neighbors and kinsmen of the Moabites. The alliance recalled the ominous evil out of Israel's past: their own defection, the persecution of others, and the swift judgment of the Almighty.

Eglon set up his administration at "the city of the palms" (Jericho), and from there exercised rule over the people. The subjugation was especially grievous for Israel. Although they could anticipate as the covenant people the noblest position among the nations, instead they found themselves in bondage to some petty rulers of the area. In their plight, they knew where to turn. Theirs was a desperation that rekindled a lingering faith. Not despair alone or faith alone, but the two coupled together, began to turn the situation around.

"But when the sons of Israel cried to the Lord, the Lord raised up a deliverer for them . . ." (Judg. 3:15)—when they were ready to confess their sin and repent of it and when they were prepared to renew the covenant and trust the enabling work of the Spirit. The deliverances under the judges were, in a sense, miniature reproductions of the liberation from Egypt, but here there was greater emphasis on the culpability of the people and the conditions for restoration.

It seems best to cast the Spirit with reference to the cycle of deliverance as a whole, rather than as related to deliverance alone. He works redemptively with the sometimes grim realities of a prodigal people of God, sometimes to chastise, on other occasions to console, and to deliver when the time was ripe.

13 The Monarchy

Immediately after Samuel had anointed the new king, it was said that the "Spirit of the Lord came mightily upon David from that day forward . . ." (1 Sam. 16:13). To this was added the observation that "the Spirit of the Lord departed from Saul, and an evil spirit from the Lord terrorized him" (v. 14). The mantle of the Spirit had been passed from one to the other, so as to extend the rule of God by means of the monarchy.

While the monarchy had come into being at the request of a rebellious people, God embraced it within the scope of the covenant. He engaged in the selection and training of the king, developed auxiliary means (such as the prophetic office, cultus, and the sages), and worked with the nation at large—in terms of domestic and international policies. All of this reminds us of the sanctifying work of the Spirit in fostering a people of God.

One would not want to minimize the role which the monarch played in Israel. An evil king could bring disaster crashing down upon the nation; a good king could raise the nation to divine favor and prosperity.

The king, along with his associates, was responsible for advancing the covenantal ideals throughout the domain. This promotion characteristically involved an emphasis on righteousness and justice, from which we must deduce that these are priority concerns of the Spirit.

"Do two men walk together unless they have made an appointment [agreement]?" (Amos 3:3). This rhetorical question assumes a negative response. Prodigal man cannot walk with a righteous God.

The covenant people were to learn the Almighty's ways through the vicissitudes of life, turning to Him freshly each morning, walking circumspectly through the day, and returning thanks for His sustaining grace at day's end. Righteousness related essentially to bringing one's life into accord to the will of God, by being sensitive to the leading of the Spirit of God.

Justice is closely associated with righteousness, as it applies particularly to how we treat others. The covenant people were not to have two rules, one for the rich and the other for the poor, but to treat both alike. They were to show no partiality, to resist special interests, and to oppose such power structures as would help some to profit at the expense of others. The idea of justice involves more than simply abiding by the letter of the law. It requires creative approaches to meeting the needs of the impoverished, the widowed, the infirm, and the dispossessed. We are exhorted to ". . . let justice roll down like waters and righteousness like an ever-flowing stream" (Amos 5:24).

The Israelites were also to apply the ideals of righteousness and justice to their international relations. This involved at the outset the recognition that their ultimate defense resided not in the effectiveness of their arms but in their trust in the Almighty. The psalmist confided, "Some boast in chariots, and some in horses;/But we will boast in the name of the Lord, our God" (Ps. 20:7).

The Hebrew nation was no exception when it came to balancing its ideals over against the hard realities of international affairs. How were they to weigh the appeal to human rights as compared to national security? With emphasis on the former, realizing that God was their refuge and strength, for one cannot expect to reap good by promoting evil.

Where then was the place of national honor? Clearly subjected to the honor which Israel might bring to the Almighty, with the understanding that God would reciprocate. He honors those who honor Him.

David was the paradigm by which the succeeding kings of Judah and Israel were measured. It was said of Solomon that he "did what was evil in the sight of the Lord, and did not follow the Lord fully, as David his father had done" (1 Kings 11:6). According to George Riggan, "The rule of Yahweh and that of the king, however, were never regarded as identical."[3] Even David presumed on his royal office and became self-seeking. His redeeming quality was a contriteness of heart that responded to words of admonition and diligently sought the forgiveness of God. A psalm of David implores God not to "Take Thy Holy Spirit from me" (Ps. 51:11), and another requests: "Teach me to do Thy will, for thou art my God; let Thy good Spirit lead me on level ground" (Ps. 143:10).

14 The Prophets

Although the prophets were not a new addition, the inception of the monarchy created the need for a differentiated and active school of prophets to help balance the power of the political leaders. These prophets acted as a check on political pragmatism and shoddy ethics and appealed to the binding character of the covenant.

Moses was, as previously mentioned, at the fountainhead of the prophetic office (Deut. 18:14–22). Peter Craigie explains: "The institution of this continued line of prophets was marked by the events at Horeb, when the people, afraid to listen directly to the voice of God, requested Moses to act as a mediator on their behalf. The divinely appointed prophet (v. 18) thus provided the Israelites with a way of knowing and understanding the course of human events that was totally at variance with the manner of their neighbors."[4] This has set the prophets apart as those who reveal the secret things of God.

Given the serious nature of declaring a message as the Word of God, the Deuteronomy text turns to distinguish between true and false prophets. The criteria for identifying the genuine prophet of God were that his words be in accord with what had already been revealed, and that they come to pass. Craigie adds: "Over the course of a prophet's ministry, in matters important and less significant, the character of the prophet as a true spokesman of God would begin to emerge clearly. And equally, false prophets would be discredited and dealt with under the law."[5]

The general absence of prophets from the times of the judges may at first seem strange. According to Norman Gottwald, "It becomes under-

---

3. George Riggan, *Messianic Theology and Christian Faith*, p. 25.
4. Peter Craigie, *The Book of Deuteronomy*, p. 262.
5. *Ibid.*, p. 263.

standable, however, when we consider that the judges themselves in a sense fulfill prophetic function, as well as the political. They rally the loyalties of the people to the God of Israel."[6] As an exception, Deborah was called a prophetess (Judg. 4:4), although her political role clearly predominated.

The prophets took on a major role with the monarchy (for the reason and in the way alluded to previously). For all of their variation, there was much in common in their message. Strictly speaking, the prophets were not religious innovators but advocates of the covenant. They took an uncompromising stand within the Mosaic tradition. J. Philip Hyatt elaborates: "The prophets believed that sin is a rebellion against a sovereign God and rises from corruption of the heart. Their view of sin was serious because their view of God's nature was serious. To them, sin often involves maltreatment of one's neighbor and wrong social relations, but it is basically an offence against God and a flouting of his authority."[7] Theirs was a religious theme that involved a rigorous social ethic.

Their faith was not simply a convenience that could be assumed or put away. The prophets *really* believed in God as sovereign over the world at large and the chosen people in particular. They lived before the awesome reality of the Almighty, and this permeated their life and ministry.

Predictably, the prophetic remedy was to turn from sin and be delivered by God. Things would not be restored to the way they had been previously; that would have been unrealistic to propose. Rather, God offered to pick up with the situation, from the point of repentance, with a redemptive solution.

The prophets dealt with revealed principles rather than blueprints for an ideal society. They offered no Platonic model, tucked away in the heavens, which they hoped could be duplicated. Their alternative was to observe the Decalogue in the changing conditions of life, with reverence for God and respect for one another.

The prophet did not limit his approach to the abstract, but pressed in terms of concrete instances. For example, he complained when a person was sold into slavery for incurring some insignificant debt or when his cloak (taken in pledge) was held back over the night—contrary to

6. Norman Gottwald, *All the Kingdoms of the Earth*, p. 50.

7. J. Philip Hyatt, *Prophetic Religion*, p. 176.

the provision of the Law (Amos 2:6, 8; Exod. 22:26). Such acts escaped neither the sharp eye of the prophet nor his equally sharp tongue.

As a result, the prophetic message was "a direct, relatively unambiguous declaration of man's responsibilities. It has little patience with subtleties, inferences, connotations, and the like. It tells it like the prophet sees it."[8] It measured the prevailing practices against the demands of the covenant.

The prophets understood history as the breaking in of God's kingdom into the affairs of man. It was a sort of divine leverage that would alter events when man allowed himself to be God's fulcrum. History is also moving toward its destiny with the Almighty, not in a uniform and harmonious way, but with both spirited leaps ahead and agonizing lapses. God resembles less an imminent force within the process than the One who stands beside, above, and before man in his struggle.

While Israel occupies center stage in this drama, all nations were (and are) involved. The prophet saw his task as no narrow, partisan effort, but God's will for all men. Even when a prophet labored exclusively with Israel, we must bear in mind his concern for the larger significance of Israel with regard to the family of nations.

Although the prophets often spoke of the future, their message had to do primarily with current affairs. They exhibited more interest in "telling forth" than in foretelling. Even when they focused on some future point of reference, it was not to satisfy the idle curiosity of their audience but to challenge their way of living in the light of what would come to pass.

We have belabored the role of the prophets because it was so clearly associated with the work of the Spirit. References abound. Micah declares that he was filled "with the Spirit of the Lord" (Mic. 3:8). Zechariah makes reference to "the words which the Lord of hosts had sent by His Spirit through the former prophets" (Zech. 7:12). A similarly sweeping reference to the Spirit's ministry through the prophets states, "Thou didst bear with them for many years,/And admonished them by Thy spirit through Thy prophets" (Neh. 9:30).

Also of interest are those texts which specifically tie the prophet's counsel to the king. Thus "the Spirit of God came on Azariah," and he brought words of encouragement to Asa (the king): "Listen to me, Asa, and all Judah and Benjamin: the Lord is with you when you are with Him. And if you seek Him, He will let you find Him; but if you forsake

---

8. Morris Inch, *Understanding Bible Prophecy*, p. 25.

Him, He will forsake you" (2 Chron. 15:1–2). The Spirit of the Lord likewise came upon Jahaziel, who also spoke out, "Listen, all Judah and the inhabitants of Jerusalem and King Jehoshaphat: thus says the Lord to you, 'Do not fear or be dismayed because of this great multitude, for the battle is not yours but God's'" (2 Chron. 20:14–15). When the Spirit came upon Zechariah, the son of Jehoiada, he admonished the people for their transgression, after which Joash the king commanded that he be stoned to death in the court of the temple (2 Chron. 24:20–21).

Leon Wood offers four categories for the prophetic teachings of Isaiah concerning the Spirit: those regarding attributes of the Spirit (Isa. 4:4; 11:2; 28:6); those related to the coming of Messiah (Isa. 11:2; 42:1; 61:1); those admonishing the people to be directed by the Spirit (Isa. 30:1; 32:15; 44:3); and those concerning the superintendence of the Spirit with the creation in general and man in particular (Isa. 34:16; 40:7; 40:13).[9] All of these passages suggest Isaiah's deep awareness of the work of the Spirit in and around him.

Joel promised a time when God would pour out His Spirit on all mankind, and their sons and daughters would prophesy, their old men dream dreams, and their young men see visions (Joel 2:28). He then repeated for emphasis, "I [God] will pour out My Spirit in those days" (v. 29). The Spirit within the prophet thus testified to what was yet to come to pass.

We conclude that the role of the Spirit during the monarchal period was most closely associated with the prophets and seen in their ministry. Holy Writ tersely announces "that no prophecy of Scripture is a matter of one's own interpretation, for no prophecy was ever made by an act of human will, but men moved by the Holy Spirit spoke from God" (2 Peter 1:20–21). The prophetic legacy was thus put under the aegis of the Spirit.

Prophecy does not come about as a result of man's insight into the nature of things, but as the Spirit of God reveals the things of God to serve the purposes of God. More particularly, prophecy explains the history of Israel in reference to its covenantal obligations. It traces the sovereign work of God through the vacillating behavior of the chosen people, and its portent for what the future held in store.

The prophetic message qualifies as *special* revelation in several ways. First, it was special in that it dealt with a covenant between God and a select people. Israel alone assumed the covenant obligation, the wider

9. Wood, *The Holy Spirit in the Old Testament*, p. 27, 28.

implication notwithstanding. The Israelites were *the* covenant people. Second, the prophetic message was also special revelation in that it detailed Israel's struggle with the obligations of the covenant. We read of the people's defection, the painful results, and their eventual captivity. We likewise read of their repentance, God's forgiveness, and their prospect for the future. There are no comparable records in history from which we can learn of man's willfulness and God's unrelenting faithfulness.

Finally, what makes the prophetic message most strikingly special is that it constitutes a *divine* commentary on the events which were transpiring. This elevates the words of the prophets to the Word of God. It accounts for the familiar prophetic formula, "Thus God says."

Abraham Herschel concludes, "'Know thy God' (I Chron. 28:9) rather than 'Know Thyself' is the categorical imperative of the biblical man. There is no self-understanding without God-understanding."[10] The Spirit directs our attention to the Almighty, to the world as God's domain, to His Word as the true account of it, and to ourselves as responsible for whatever has been revealed. He discourages such fantasy worlds as we may fashion to serve our personal interests and to ignore our responsibilities to others.

15 The Cultus

While the prophet presented God's Word to man, the priest interceded on his behalf with God. Here the cultus came into play as a complement to the prophetic office. Through ritual, devoutly understood and faithfully practiced, the covenantal truth was appropriated as a vital reality.

The cultic roots of Israel predate Moses' experience with the burning bush, but this was a pivotal point. Prior to that time, the cultus was primarily associated with the patriarchs, and—in terms of their encounters with God—the memorials raised to them and the stories concerning those episodes passed down from generation to generation. This is evidenced by the fact that when the Almighty spoke to Moses out of the burning bush, He identified Himself as "the God of Abraham, the God of Isaac, and the God of Jacob" (Exod. 3:6, 15).

The bush burned by "the mountain of God," and the Almighty promised Moses that "when you have brought the people out of Egypt, you

---

10. Abraham Herschel, *The Prophets*, p. 488.

shall worship God at this mountain" (Exod. 3:1, 12). At this time, Sinai assumed a central focus in the cultic activity of the people. Here they waited before the quaking mountain to receive the Decalogue and extended ritual instructions and to learn of the provisions of the vassal treaty. The sprinkling of blood upon the altar and people sealed the covenant and set the cultic order in motion.

The most obvious carry-over from Sinai into the land of promise was the ark of the covenant, containing the tablets of Moses. The ark was associated at first with the tabernacle and then with the temple, but always with the presence of God. It signified that God was pleased to dwell with the chosen people.

Immediately after the treaty was ratified, the people were instructed to build a portable tabernacle (Exod. 25:8). Bezalel was selected to oversee its construction, and endued by the Spirit for the task (Exod. 31:1–5). This suggests at the outset the concern of the Spirit with the cultus.

Solomon constructed the temple as a permanent accommodation for the ark and sacrificial complex. "And it came about when the priests came from the holy place, that the cloud filled the house of the Lord, so that the priests could not stand to minister because of the cloud, for the glory of the Lord filled the house of the Lord" (1 Kings 8:10–11). Thus was Solomon's provision sanctified for its cultic purpose.

All Israelite men were required to attend three festivals: the Passover and Feast of Unleavened Bread (Exod. 12:11–17), Feast of Weeks (Deut. 16:9–10), and Feast of the Tabernacles (Deut. 16:13). The first celebrated the deliverance from Egypt, the second the beginning of harvest, and the third the end of harvest season. These feasts could serve an additional purpose, as with the Feast of the Tabernacles (Booths), which recalled how Israel had lived in tents during its wilderness sojourn.

The most solemn occasion of the year was the Day of Atonement, its primary purpose being to make ritual propitiation for the congregation. But the most significant observance was the Sabbath. It alone was prescribed in the Decalogue as a day of rest. Paul Heinisch comments: "Man arranges his labors more or less for his own interests and profit; on the Sabbath the Israelite should abstain from all work to show that God has full and complete right to his time. The Sabbath rest thus was an acknowledgment of Yahweh as supreme Lord."[11] It, like

11. Paul Heinisch, *Theology of the Old Testament*, p. 209.

the other ritual responsibilities, reinforced the theocratic ideal of the covenant.

The primary cultic agency was the home. The relationship between parents and children suggested the obligation of the people to the Almighty, as well as His tender care for them. The ritual objects were many and varied: the prescribed food, the Sabbath lamp, the mezuzah attached to the doorpost—to mention a few. The theocratic teaching was felt through influence and example in the home before being inculcated by precept.

The Spirit appears in the midst of the cultus as the divine celebrant. Life is good—as it was declared in the creation narrative—in spite of the suffering that dogs its footsteps. No one knew this better than the people of God, encouraged to praise by the Spirit of God. Israel had special cause for thanksgiving. The chosen people had been delivered from the harsh circumstances of oppression, sustained in the wilderness wandering, settled into the Promised Land, and protected thereafter. The Psalms illustrate the broad scope of their experience as a people favored by God, not least of which was their opportunity to serve Him.

The notion of a festive spirit has often been lost sight of in our effort to reconstruct the experience of Israel. For instance, the Sabbath was not a drudgery to the righteous. Rather, they looked forward to it as an opportunity to worship the Almighty. It helped raise the mundane, the routine, and the oppressive to the realm of worship.

There was time to weigh the serious words of the prophet, but also to enjoy the blessings of God. To render thanks for life, friends, and opportunities. To let the Spirit elevate their spirits in praise to the Almighty. To rejoice over the presence and care of the God of Israel.

16 The Sage

If we have minimized the place of the Spirit with regard to the cultus, we have virtually ignored it in reference to the sage. Although the precise relationship between the wisdom of Israel and that of her neighbors has been lost to antiquity, we can assume its influence during Israel's sojourn in Egypt upon the Canaanites among whom they dwelt, and during their intercourse with the powers as they traded across the Fertile Crescent.

However, folk wisdom seems to appear spontaneously within traditional societies. It reflects the sage advice of the elders to their posterity:

the comment that bears repetition, qualifications, and expansion. The era of the patriarchs was no exception to the rule, and by the time Israel settled in Egypt, it no doubt already enjoyed a rich tradition of wisdom material. Whatever it added subsequently, it was qualified by the distinctive faith of the Hebrew.

Once the monarchy became firmly established, the sage appears to have assumed an advisory role in the royal court, following a practice familiar to them from the nations of antiquity. Leo Perdue speculates that there may have been royal schools for the training of the sages, seeing that "comparable literature from the other cultures of the ancient Near East was composed within the milieu of schools which was also used for the training of bureaucrats and officials, and it does seem reasonable to suggest that for the practical functioning of the kingdom of Israel, and, early on, even a small but important empire, trained officials were necessitated and it would seem plausible to suggest that such training occurred within a royal school which was partially responsible for the creating of wisdom literature."[12] This is not to say that wisdom was restricted to this source, but that it took on a bureaucratic function, which would have included both the compilation of past wisdom and the generation of new. Such may have been the nature of "the men of Hezekiah, king of Judah," who were said to have transcribed the proverbs of Solomon (Prov. 25:1).

Considerable speculation has revolved around the relationships among sage, scribe, priest, and prophet. We seem safe in affirming that during the monarchal period the wise men might likewise be scribes or, if not, closely aligned with them. There appears no such close association between sage and priest, although they appear quite compatible. The prophets did on occasion attack those who elevated wisdom over "the word of the Lord," much as they attacked promotion of the cultus as an end in and of itself (Jer. 8:8–9). Yet, as C. H. Bullock elaborates, "the fact that the prophets attributed wisdom to the Lord (Isa. 28:23–29; Jer. 10:12) and shared stylistic features with wisdom . . . would sustain the position that the prophets did not wholly reject wisdom."[13] Each played a complementary role in the monarchy, even when momentary tensions were created by their interplay.

Wisdom dealt characteristically with man's way with his world. In *Israelite Wisdom*, it is noted: "As is well known, wisdom searches for the

12. Leo Perdue, *Wisdom and Cult*, p. 141.

13. C. Hassell Bullock, *An Introduction to the Poetic Books of the Old Testament*, p. 25.

knowledge of order, or for those to whom this seems too rigid, for a certain regularity with the diversity of the phenomena of the world."[14] Thus, for example, we recall diversity and design from the creation account, whereby the Spirit brought order out of chaos. Wisdom literature in its simplest form amounts to recording what has been observed about one thing or another. Thus Job describes an ostrich (39:3–18), a horse (39:19–25), a hippopotamus (40:15–24), and a crocodile (41:1–34). These accounts may include appreciative comments, as the author marvels at the creative design of nature and the power of the Almighty.

The literature may take a more idealistic turn, discussing creation more in terms of its pristine nature. But even then the sage senses the disruption that has taken place and the brutal aspects of nature as we experience it. He is, if anything, a hard-line realist.

Wisdom theology emphasizes the immanence of God. It is not even the acts of God, let alone the words of God, that provide the focus—for to talk about the acts of God is to single them out from the remainder of life, and that is something the sages appear reluctant to do. As stewards of the creation, they record what the more disciplined and sensitive can observe around us, for their benefit and ours.

According to Gerhard Von Rad, "To a greater extent than modern man, ancient man was disturbed by the awareness of a superior force of contingent events. To him it was a threat to be ceaselessly determined and driven by events which defied all interpretation. Thus it is one of man's basic urges to limit as far as possible, with all the powers of the keenest observations, the sphere of contingency and, wherever possible, to wrest from the inscrutable contingent event some kind of meaning albeit a deeply hidden one."[15] In other words, the sage pressed for some causal relationship—carrying it back as far as he could, yielding his search momentarily, only to pick it up again at another time or in a different circumstance.

This quest tended to take an inductive route, although the sage's perception of man in the creation orbit provided a point of reference and confidence for his search. He knew who he was, even when the finer distinctions became lost in the maze of interwoven strands of experience. He could also readily accommodate the valid observations of his

---

14. John Gammie, et al. (eds.), *Israelite Wisdom*, p. 44.

15. Gerhard Von Rad, *Wisdom in Israel*, p. 9.

pagan contemporaries, because he understood that all truth was God's truth.

A related theological conviction had to do with "the proper time." The tree bears fruit in its time, the birds migrate according to their time, and the youth reaches his or her time for marriage. Moreover, ". . . there is a time for every event under heaven" (Eccles. 3:1): a time to give birth and to die, to plant and to harvest, to weep and to laugh, to be silent and to speak, to carry on war and to make peace. Von Rad adds that the sages "were of the opinion that men could easily be trained to ascertain the correct time for a project, even in difficult cases, by means of careful assessment of the circumstances and a close examination of the situation."[16] Their conclusion could be supported, if not from empirical evidence alone, then by the confidence that the Spirit's desire was to instruct the diligent in God's ways.

No text is more central to appreciating wisdom theology than "The fear of the Lord is the beginning of wisdom, and the knowledge of the Holy One is understanding" (Prov. 9:10). The wise man, when everything else has been said, fears God. He is diligent, temperate, and quick to help, for his ways will come under the careful scrutiny of the Almighty.

This leaves us to comment more pointedly on wisdom as it relates to the Spirit. One might argue that the sage added little to what we have already learned of the Spirit from other sources. Even if that were true, the sage provides a needed balance to the rest. He helps us understand how the Spirit sanctifies all of life for our use. He encourages us to accept everything from the hand of God and return thanks. Paul, schooled as he was in the traditions of his people, wrote that "in everything by prayer and supplication with thanksgiving let your requests be made known to God" (Phil. 4:6).

It follows from this way of thinking that life should be enjoyed quite naturally. One does not have to dwell on some obscure meaning to appreciate what God is about. Life is, in a sense, its own justification and cause for thanksgiving. This is a dimension of the Spirit's ministry that religious enthusiasts often corrupt. They think we must be constantly pumping up our religious emotion in order to be truly pious, and imagine this to be "life in the Spirit." The sage counsels that we let enthusiasm rise naturally out of the good life, without artificial stimulants.

16. *Ibid.*, p. 141.

The religious rationalist fares no better than the sage. The former's approach to life appears too abstract, irrelevant, and fragmentary. The sage was more practical, more concrete, and more involved.

There was an added note of optimism in the writing of the sage. This was a constrained optimism, unlike the unbridled optimism that ran rampant during the late nineteenth century in America, but an optimism nonetheless. The sage believed that such optimism was warranted from the very nature of things in God's world. He was not arguing that life was as it should be or that improvement was coming by leaps and bounds, but that God was at work in it. Man could benefit himself and others by joining with the Spirit in some constructive fashion. This was far better than trying to frustrate the purposes of God, a fruitless effort in any case and a painful one in addition.

Summary

Our vantage point from Zion has permitted us to observe the era of the monarchy and to recognize the Spirit at work as its theocratic agent. As we pulled apart the weave of the monarchy to look not only at the royal office, but the prophets, cultus, and sages as well, we discovered that these were orchestrated by the Spirit to help Israel realize its potential as the people of God. For example, the Spirit came upon Saul, but removed Himself after repeated provocation. He resided with David, who, for all of his shortcomings, became the paradigm for subsequent rulers. He was a man of contrite heart, who pleaded that the Spirit not forsake him.

The Spirit was especially identified with the prophets, who were said to be filled with the Spirit. On the basis that God had sent His Word by the Spirit through him, the prophet came to be known as a "man of the Spirit." In league with others or alone, he stood to balance the uncompromising demands of the covenant over against the political pragmatism of the monarchy. He sometimes paid for this with his life. As bad as circumstances might become, the prophet promised a time when the Spirit would be poured out on all mankind, and his faith outlived him.

The cultus provided us with a different insight into the Spirit. We saw Him as celebrant, leading the people in rituals of worship. We sensed that the Spirit was concerned not only with revealing what was unknown, but with helping the people rejoice over what was known. He was a festive Spirit as viewed through the cultus.

The wisdom of the sages broadened our outlook so as to see the Spirit in superintending life in all its dimensions—so that the wise man will cooperate, and the fool will make a shipwreck of his life. All ground is made holy by the step of a righteous man, for the Spirit sanctifies it accordingly.

The monarchy came into being at the request of a rebellious people, but the Spirit fine-tuned the monarchy to be responsive to the covenant of a vassal people with the Great King. He left, as it were, no stone unturned to achieve His driving purpose. He selected, educated, and set aside the rulers as seemed fitting; He schooled the prophets and dealt severely with those who were false; He directed the people in worship; He sanctified life in all aspects through the sages. The theocratic intent was everywhere evident when viewed from the gates of Jerusalem, from the favored perspective of Zion.

We left Sinai with an impression of the Spirit as involved in liberating the people of God from their bondage. We have added from Zion the notion of the Spirit as building up the household of faith. The former emphasizes a break from the old life; the latter accents the creation of a new. The two taken together suggest how the Spirit directs the people of God through history—as a pilgrimage of faith. Life involves change, and so to live is to change. We cannot decide between changing or not, but whether we shall become victims of change or catalysts in the process. The Spirit may be said to make the difference between failure and success. The people of God, when reliant on the Spirit of God, become effective instruments in achieving His benevolent purposes.

3

Rivers of Babylon

Those in captivity sat down "by the rivers of Babylon" to weep, as they remembered the glory of Zion. They asked themselves, "How can we sing the Lord's song/In a foreign land?" (Ps. 137:4). We have moved our observation post from Sinai to Zion, and now to the rivers of Babylon with the Jews in exile. We will pause here long enough only to consider the exile and sketch the intertestamental period.

17 Observation

Samuel Schultz comments that Nebuchadnezzar's "marked success had enlarged the small kingdom of Babylon to span the Near East from Susa to the Mediterranean, from the Persian Gulf to the upper Tigris, and from the Taurus Mountains down to the first cataract in Egypt. As an adventurous builder he made the city of Babylon the mightiest fortress in the world, adorned with unsurpassed splendor and beauty."[1] The famed hanging gardens, which Nebuchadnezzar built for his Median queen, were regarded by the Greeks as one of the seven wonders of the world.

1. Samuel Schultz, *The Old Testament Speaks*, p. 237.

The Jews of the exile lived to view such splendor and be reminded of their inability to contend with Babylon's might. They remembered the former glory of Zion, unimpressive by comparison but dear to their hearts. They tried to sing, but the words choked in their throats, as if out of place in a foreign land.

We could have hoped for higher ground from which to survey our topic, some lofty height, free from domination and secure from attack. But we have to settle for the alluvial plains of Babylon, surrounded on every side by alien captors.

18 Historical Setting

Israel was no stranger to oppression, having been a slave people before the exodus. It had failed to expel the people of the land during the conquest and experienced periodic subjection in the times of the judges. The monarchy struggled to sustain itself against the superpowers to the northeast and southwest, as well as the more immediate rivals in and about Palestine. The task was made more difficult by a separation of the kingdom into north and south. The fortunes of the southern kingdom vacillated, while the northern kingdom of Israel seemed destined from the first to decline—even though the prophets waged a magnificent effort to turn the course around.

With the surrender of Jerusalem, all the efforts for national survival seemed to have fallen short. The northern tribes had by then been subjected to the assimilation practices of their Assyrian captors for more than a century, with marked success. The first of a series of deportations from Judah occurred in 597 B.C. and bore away the elite of the population. Some estimate that the total number deported to Babylon would constitute no more than a third of the populace. However, one must also allow for a substantial migration to Egypt.

All of this would suggest a radical social upheaval in the land, followed by a time of unsettled social, political, and religious life. The loss of leadership must have been a critically significant factor, affecting all the rest. The captors used this means to destroy Israel's capability to resist, leaving themselves free to impose their will on the general public.

While it appears that Babylon was not excessively oppressive by ancient standards, the rise of Cyrus promised better things for those languishing in exile. Where Babylon had followed the practice of deporting their foreign subjects, Cyrus proclaimed that they might return to their homelands and worship their traditional gods in their proper sanctuaries. Harold Lamb reports that Cyrus pronounced: "All the gods of Sumer and Akkad which Nabu-naid—to the anger of the gods—had carried to Babylon, I, Cyrus, will bring back to their dwelling places to abide there forever that joy may be again in their hearts."[2]

The Hebrew people benefited from the policy of Cyrus, who made a decree that the temple be rebuilt in Jerusalem and that those who wished to return to their former land might do so (Ezra 1:2–4). About 538 B.C. a remnant of the people made the arduous trek to Jerusalem. They had sufficiently adjusted to their situation so that by the following year the erection of the temple could begin, although this was soon interrupted by the Samaritans and could not be continued until 520 B.C. The temple was completed in five years, and while its splendor could not rival that of Solomon's time, there was great rejoicing. The ark had been lost, presumably during the destruction of Jerusalem, and Flavius Josephus reports that on the Day of Atonement the high priest placed his censor on the slab of stone that marked the original position of the ark.[3]

Schultz elaborates: "The dedication of the Temple and the observance of the Passover in the spring of 515 B.C. marked an historic crisis in Jerusalem. The hopes of the exiles had been realized in re-establishing the Temple as their place of worship. At the same time they were reminded of the Passover of Israel's redemption from Egyptian bondage. In addition they enjoyed the reality of restoration from Babylonian exile."[4] It was a time for looking back over the difficult road they had traveled, reflecting on the grace of God which had brought them to this point, and setting a promising course for the future.

We might say that this was the first of a series of crises involving their effort to accommodate to the return. There were times, such as during the Maccabean revolt, when it seemed as if God's hand was upon the people of Israel, and their cause as a result would prove invincible. But then their fortune would be turned around because of internal strife, and their adversaries were quick to gather the spoils of the struggle.

The two incursions which were most difficult for the Hebrew people to deal with were the cultural imposition of Hellenism and the political oppression of Rome. We will look first at Hellenism. Alexander was born

---

2. Harold Lamb, *Cyrus the Great*, p. 240.
3. Flavius Josephus, *The Wars of the Jews*, V, v. 5.
4. Schultz, *The Old Testament Speaks*, p. 261.

in 356 B.C. and became king of Macedonia at the tender age of twenty. By the fall of 333, Alexander had decisively defeated the Persians at Issus and proceeded to secure control of Phoenicia and Egypt. A delegation of Jews, according to Josephus, met Alexander as he progressed down the Palestinian coast, and persuaded him to come to Jerusalem and there to offer sacrifice.[5] This was done so that the nation might be willingly subject to Alexander, and not troublesome as it had formerly proved to be for "the kings of Assyria." Alexander pressed his campaign as far as the Indus valley and died in June of 323 B.C.

As reported by Donald Gowan, "Alexander's contact with any given place in the East was fleeting, but its effects lasted a very long time. . . . In Syria and Palestine not only would the overlord be Greek, but more important, the Greek way of life would become a new standard rivaling the old, traditional, oriental ways."[6] Hellenism spread despite the brevity of Alexander's personal influence and the opposition of entrenched traditions.

Hellenism was promoted primarily through the founding of Greek cities. As far distant as Afghanistan, cities laid out after the Hellenistic model have been discovered—complete with gymnasium, theater, and hippodrome, as well as with accompanying Greek inscriptions. Werner Foerster notes that the Jewish people could not escape the profound impact of the Greek cities constructed in their midst: "If one takes into account the circle of Greek cities, centres of Greek culture which surrounded Palestine and even penetrated it, and if one goes on to ponder the number of Jews in the Decapolis and in the Palestinian coastal towns, it appears as if the Jewish terrain at that time, together with its economic development, was totally unable to escape the influence of Greek culture."[7]

All citizens of a Greek city (*polis*) had a voice in the general assembly, but the day-to-day decisions were rendered by an elected city council. Not all residents were considered citizens, which could and often did constitute only a minority of the total inhabitants. Gowan adds: "All of life tended to center around one's citizenship. The Greek participated in political decisions, in the cult of the gods of his city, and contributed to the gymnasiums and theater, so that for him politics, culture, and religion were a whole."[8] Those subjected people who were granted

---

5. Flavius Josephus, *The Antiquities of the Jews*, XIII, v. 9.
6. Donald Gowan, *Bridge Between the Testaments*, p. 669.
7. Werner Foerster, *From the Exile to Christ*, p. 137.
8. Gowan, *Bridge Between the Testaments*, p. 70.

permission by the general assembly to become citizens adopted a measure of the Hellenistic life, resulting in a cultural syncretism.

The rural population of Palestine was much less affected by the Hellenistic presence than their urban counterparts. The impact was least evident among the masses, who clung to their traditional ways and beliefs, and most felt by the upper classes, for whom the Hellenistic culture offered a means to retain their special privileges.

Some sort of cultural mix seemed inevitable in any case. The Jew searched for a means to change without surrendering his distinctive identity. Not all agreed as to how best to proceed. Tension and division followed on the heels of discord, and it was an exceedingly painful period for all those involved. This was complicated by the impatience of outsiders with the Jewish dispute, which solicited the intervention of Antiochus Ephiphanes, followed by the Maccabean revolt.

The specter of Rome was building in the west. Legend states that Romulus and Remus founded the city of Rome in 735 B.C., shortly before Samaria fell to Assyria. While a newcomer to the nations of antiquity, Rome rose quickly to a place of prominence. After three wars with the Carthaginians, Rome gained control of the western Mediterranean by 146 B.C., then turned to the east and added to its territories without serious opposition. Israel, weakened by internal strife, succumbed to Pompey in 63 B.C. Jerusalem held out for three months, the end coming with shocking suddenness. Josephus adds this: "Now all was full of slaughter; some of the Jews being slain by the Romans, and some by one another; nay, some there were who threw themselves down the precipices, or put fire to their houses, and burnt them, as not able to bear the miseries they were under. Of the Jews there fell twelve thousand; but of the Romans very few."[9]

The peace of Rome proved to be a mixed blessing. It delivered Israel from the painful struggle and uncertain future of independent rule, but returned it to foreign domination. The official Roman policy was one of toleration and even special privilege for the Jews. The integrity of the temple precincts was guaranteed, and special provision was made so that the Jews might observe the Sabbath. Coins minted in Palestine bore no images; normally the image-bearing standards of the Roman army were not displayed in Jerusalem. In general, the cult of the emperor was not required—the offering of sacrifices in Jerusalem being accepted as proof of loyalty.

9. Flavius Josephus, *The Antiquities of the Jews*, XIV, iv. 4.

Of course, there was a discrepancy between policy and practice. According to Gowan: "The problem the Jews faced under Roman rule is that their religion, as defined in the time of the Maccabean revolt, was so different from anything else in the world that things which were accepted as normal and commonplace by everyone else in the vast Roman empire were an abomination to the Jews: polytheism, images, marriage and eating customs, to name the major ones."[10] The pagans became increasingly impatient with the Jews, and impatience sometimes bred hatred. The Jews, on their part, developed mistrust and a growing conviction that Roman rule would inevitably lead to a compromise of cherished beliefs. While the influence of Hellenism at an earlier juncture might resemble the ebb and flow of the tide, under the patronage of Rome it appeared as a constant current that would eventually erode even the most fixed resolve.

19 Prophetic Legacy

We need not be reminded that one epoch builds upon what preceded it, which is, in this instance, to combine those of the Mosaic and monarchial periods. Robert and Feuillet explain: "Thus once the institutions of the Davidic monarchy are ruined, the people of God finds the means to survive in a form that is both very new and very old: after the royal period it reestablishes ties with social community born at Sinai."[11] There was a continuity throughout, which drew upon their understanding of how the Spirit had worked in the past, even though the monarchy had suffered demise.

Indeed, the result was "both very new and very old." The people of Israel were thrown into a situation unlike anything they had experienced previously, and yet there was something very familiar about it—not simply the experience as such but the predictable way in which the Spirit was available to them. The words of the psalmist would seem apropos: "Unless the Lord builds the house, they labor in vain who build it; unless the Lord guards the city, the watchman keeps awake in vain" (Ps. 127:1). Seeing that they had stifled the work of the Spirit, all that the nation had constructed now lay in ruins.

But life must go on. In the words of Robert and Feuillet, the "national hope which arose from the Sinaitic Covenant took on at this time an

---

10. Gowan, *Bridge Between the Testaments*, p. 139.

11. Andre Robert and A. Feuillet, *Introduction to the Old Testament*, pp. 588–589.

unequaled breadth thanks to the contribution of prophetic eschatology. The despised people draws from it a reason for living in the midst of difficult conditions imposed upon it."[12] Drawing upon the rich legacy of the past was a new development, in order to cope with the distressing circumstances of the present.

What the people of Israel knew at this point was *where* to turn; what they did not know was precisely *how* God would achieve His purpose through a repentant people. The apostle Paul refers to the latter as a messianic mystery (Eph. 3:3; Col. 1:26–27). In biblical terms, a mystery is something previously hidden, but now being revealed—if not in its entirety, then in some critical aspect. We have the advantage, shared with the apostle, of looking back on what God was bringing to pass. The people of Israel lacked the hindsight we enjoy. They could only turn from their perilous ways, seek His face, and trust in His benevolent purposes. As the earthly splendors of the Davidic monarchy faded away, the memories took on more splendid heavenly garb. The new Jerusalem would replace the old Jerusalem, given time and trying circumstances.

20 Fathers and Sons

We must not forget, even for the moment, the historic perspective of the Hebrew people. This vantage point embodies two elements, according to Oscar Cullmann: the explanation of history "as the creative action of God" and "its claim that the history of Israel constitutes a redemptive history."[13] History, when viewed from one direction, is God's way with wayward man, and from the other, man's response to divine challenge. In either case, it records a divine-human drama, wherein both elements are necessary ingredients.

But history is more than the interplay of God and His prodigal creature. It is redemptive in character. It reveals how God sets about to correct what has gone wrong, sometimes with man's cooperation, but all too often without.

The people fashioned a proverb, "The fathers eat the sour grapes, but the children's teeth are set on edge" (Ezek. 18:2). This was to say that the children were suffering for the sins of the fathers, but (as the context reveals) it was used as an excuse to continue in sin. History ought to be thought of as an ongoing process, whereby man can—by God's grace—

---

12. *Ibid.*, p. 589.
13. Oscar Cullmann, *Christ and Time*, p. 55.

cease being part of the problem, in order to become an agent of God's resolution. Man is never simply a pawn in life, controlled by some inexplicable destiny.

The "sins of the fathers" do not simply sit there as if they were inescapable burdens to be borne with resignation. They are to remind us of our own defection and cause us to turn into the paths of righteousness. Millar Burrows points out that we read in the Qumranic thanksgiving psalms the penitent refrain, "For I remember my guilty deeds, together with the faithlessness of my fathers, when the wicked rose against thy covenant, the hapless against thy word."[14] The emphasis is not upon *their* evil ways but *ours*. What is past, we must contend with; what is present, we may affect. History, from the Hebrew perspective, is always in the making.

We must not limit ourselves to the sins of the fathers and overlook their faith. They believed the promises of God, even when reluctant to walk in His ways. They left behind an inheritance unlike anything we can discover elsewhere. We may readily admit that it was a tarnished legacy, but one that could again be polished and adorn the household of faith.

There can be no doubt that the faith of the fathers was living still, in spite of all of the adversity which the people were experiencing. Perhaps it would have been easier for the time being if this were not the case. That faith created an almost unbearable tension between the high expectation of God's people and the low estate into which they had fallen. In those difficult days some would surrender their Jewish identity and the hope of their people. But others would, in a virtually miraculous way, somehow keep on affirming the faith of their fathers—if not always in a triumphant fashion.

All of this was a continuing reminder to the people of their historic role as an agent in God's redemptive design for the nations. Indeed, they had sinned, as had their fathers before them. But they dared to believe that through it all the Almighty would bring to pass all that He had promised and more than they could imagine. The past was little more than a prologue to the future, when viewed from an apocalyptic Hebrew perspective.

21 Travail

We do not have to search long before discovering a motif which describes the experience of Israel in those troublesome times. Burrows

---

14. Millar Burrows, *The Dead Sea Scrolls*, pp. 407–408.

observes that the *Manual of Discipline,* discovered as part of the Dead Sea library, reads, "I am in distress like a woman in travail with her firstborn."[15] It continues that "with pains of Sheol he bursts forth from the crucible of the pregnant one, a wonderful counselor with his power; yes, a man comes forth from the waves." Thus was their situation viewed as a messianic travail, now that all subsequent history had reached its climax.

The nation had entered into a time of deep anguish and introspection. What had brought them to this most recent catastrophe? *Judaism,* edited by Arthur Hertzberg, points out that there was an uncomplicated answer, which might account for their dilemma: "The Bible has a simple answer, that it was punishment for the sins of the people. Even less than the 'original' inhabitants of the land did the chosen people have a right to defile the soil that God had given it."[16] The sin of Israel was greater than that of the Canaanite before them because of Israel's privileged understanding of the ways of God. The more that is given, the more that is required of the recipient.

This explanation did not seem wholly adequate. Although it was accurate insofar as it went, it did not appear to go far enough. God seemed to have a larger purpose for which this time of suffering was meant to contribute. Somehow all this was meant to tie into the covenant which God had made with them to accomplish His purpose with the nation.

We note in *Judaism*: "The doctrine of the 'suffering servant' was invoked and expanded, that the people of Israel in the mysterious will of God was bearing not only its own sins but the sins of others. The Exile was a time of testing, a prolonged corporate trial, like God's trial of Abraham. The task of the people was to remain faithful and to remember Zion."[17] Israel had entered into a time of travail to purge away its sin, and, hopefully, introduce the messianic age.

Israel assumed this uninviting prospect as a corporate task. No individual or group could be singled out, since the people as a whole were involved. They resembled the suffering servant of Isaiah's prophecy, although the prophecy was not easy to accommodate to corporate Israel. The prophets had described the people of Israel as stubborn, sinful, haughty, and blind; the "suffering servant" as docile, humble,

---

15. *Ibid.*, p. 403.
16. Arthur Hertzberg, ed., *Judaism*, p. 154.
17. Ibid., pp. 154–55.

and guiltless. They had reprimanded Israel as a reproach among the nations, but eulogized the servant of the Lord as a light to the Gentiles. Given the gift of hindsight, William LaSor would write that "there is one Servant who stands apart from all others. He is the Servant who so perfectly fulfills the will of the Lord that he is able to take upon himself the sins of the rest of us who call ourselves servants."[18] Neither corporate Israel nor any select individual qualified at this point.

There was a sense of mystery in which the entire travail was immersed. Israel was caught up in the work of God, but just *how* appeared less than certain. The travail was real enough, and so was the anticipation that this would somehow eventuate in the messianic age.

It was left for Israel "to remain faithful and to remember Zion." In *Judaism* we read: "Just as the navel is found at the center of a human being, so the land of Israel is found at the center of the world. . . . Jerusalem is the center of the Land of Israel, the Temple is at the center of Jerusalem, the Holy of Holies is at the center of the Temple, the Ark is at the center of the Holy of Holies, and the Foundation Stone is in front of the Ark, which point is the foundation of the world."[19] So the reasoning went. Zion constituted the divine center from which all came into being and from which the messianic age would originate. The peace of God would flow from Jerusalem as if the Gihon Springs would expand to overflow into every dusty corner of the earth.

But Israel must persevere through the travail with faith undiminished. The travail was all part of the redemptive strategy of God. This was a strategy so shrouded in mystery that one could not make out the exact outline. One could not expect to walk by sight, only by faith.

22 The Spirit

Among the prophets of the exile, Ezekiel had the most to say about the Spirit. He repeats the comment that "the Spirit entered me" (Ezek. 2:2; 3:24). In what seems of synonymous intent, he states, "Then the Spirit of the Lord fell upon me" (11:5). Thus did the Spirit speak to the prophet and instruct him with the words to say to the people. This was to prepare them for the captivity to come, so that they might understand that the Almighty would not abandon them in their impending travail.

---

18. William LaSor, *Israel: A Biblical View*, p. 29.
19. Hertzberg, *Judaism*, p. 150.

"[Then said the Lord God,] I shall gather you from the peoples and assemble you out of the countries among which you have been scattered, and I will give you the land of Israel" (11:17). Not only that, but He promised to give them a new spirit, replacing their heart of stone with a heart of flesh (v. 19). They were thus consoled with the thought that God had not utterly rejected them and that they might expect better things in the future.

Seven times does Ezekiel speak of being transported by the Spirit, as though to show him what was transpiring and would come to pass—so that the prophet might speak the truth and not offer false hope to those who might like to escape the ordeal that awaited them. On eight occasions, the Spirit otherwise enabled the prophet in one manner or another. The prophetic task was not an easy one, especially when he had to bear such grim tidings. The Spirit empowered the prophet to stand against imposing obstacles to bring the Word of God to a wayward but not utterly forsaken people. The way ahead would not be easy, but it would be God's way, which was to imply that His grace would be sufficient.

The promise of the Spirit was thereupon extended to the people as a whole: "Behold, I will open your graves and cause you to come up out of your graves, My people; and I will bring you into the land of Israel. Then you will know that I am the Lord, when I have opened your graves and caused you to come up out of your graves, My people. And I will put My Spirit within you. . . . Then you will know that I, the Lord, have spoken and done it" (Ezek. 37:12–14). Israel awaits a fullness of the Spirit, of which His present ministry is but an earnest.

The remaining exilic and post-exilic prophets spoke along a similar line. Haggai spoke to those exiles returned from captivity: "My Spirit is abiding in your midst; do not fear!" (Hag. 2:5). God's word came to Zerubbabel: "'Not by might nor by power, but by My Spirit,' says the Lord of hosts" (Zech. 4:6). Thus was the Spirit present with the people to bring God's purpose to fruition and to comfort them in the process.

The documents of the wilderness community seem to exhibit a similar perspective, even though it saw its own role in a peculiar way. Viewing themselves as the sons of light set against the sons of darkness during the last times, the adherents prepared for the final conflict between the forces of good and evil and relied on the Spirit of God to intercede effectively on their behalf.

As reported by Millar Burrows, the *Manual of Discipline* declares, "These are the counsels of the Spirit for the sons of the truth of the world and the visitation of all who walk by it, for healing and abundance of peace in length of days, and bringing forth seed, with all eternal blessings and everlasting joy in the light of eternity, and a crown of glory with raiment of majesty in everlasting light."[20] In this manner was the Spirit thought to console the sons of righteousness and to provide for their every need in a situation threatening them from every side.

The community could not ignore the storm raging about them. They, too, sensed the travail of the times, the judgment of God, and the imminent character of the messianic age. They hoped to be vindicated by the Almighty for their ascetic retirement from the present evil age, a purification for the coming age. They described the Spirit as laying the foundation for the world to come, in consoling them for the present and instructing them in the ways of God—so that such travail as they were experiencing might result in a successful messianic birth.

The messianic age was viewed by canonical and extracanonical writers alike as the age of the Spirit. It seemed natural that as the messianic age was about to be born, the activity of the Spirit would somehow increase. This might be thought of as an earnest of the coming age, a source to turn to when things seemed most ominous. When the night is full come, the glimmer of dawn cannot be far off.

23 Consolation

The consolation of the Spirit may be viewed from two perspectives, although they are not so much two consolations as one. Keith Carley writes that we may describe "the post-exilic emphasis on the spirit as a unique representative or manifestation of Yahweh on earth, and the prophetic hope of a general out-pouring of the spirit on Israel (Joel 2:28)."[21] Thus the Spirit was viewed as the unique presence of God with the people in messianic travail. The emphasis was current, focusing on what God was accomplishing through His servant people, and from which the nations were thought to benefit.

The consolation was no less with regard to the future age, when there should be an "out-pouring of the Spirit" unlike anything previously. This was a consolation of hope, but one for which they already enjoyed an earnest. If sustained in the present trying situation, how much more might the people of Israel expect of the future? Certainly God would withhold no good thing from those who remain faithful to Him.

---

20. Burrows, *The Dead Sea Scrolls*, p. 375.
21. Keith Carley, *Ezekiel Among the Prophets*, p. 31.

However, Israel's prospect for the future sometimes seemed to bear little resemblance to its people's present lot in life. At such times the apocalyptic vision played an important role in enabling the prophet to escape the limitations of his earthly experience and gaze at the eternal verities of God. Carley adds: "Comparison of such accounts suggests that certain experiences of removal were felt so strongly that the subject felt he was actually taken bodily to the scene of the events. At other times, and more frequently, such feelings were less intense and were reported as visionary phenomena, in which the subject only imagined that he was present at the scene of the vision."[22] These were privileged experiences granted by the Spirit to the prophet for his ministry to the people. They replaced ambiguity—which of necessity plagues life here below—with the certainty of God's eternal promises.

So also was the prophet instructed as to what to say to the people, bringing a word from the Almighty for the difficult time through which they were living and a prospect of what the future age would hold for them. "Thus saith the Lord" was the popular refrain that so characterized the prophetic word. It was a message of certainty in the midst of a life of glaring uncertainties.

The Spirit resembled a midwife attending Israel in its messianic travail. He would sympathize with them in their pain, but remind them that it had a purpose with the anticipated birth of the new age. Then, as is the case in travail, the pain will be forgotten in the joy of birth (*cp.* John 16:21). One could expect to manage travail with such a knowing and compassionate attendant as the Spirit of God.

24 Transformation

It remains to be added that Israel's people would be transformed in the process. Peter Ackroyd suggests that their response to divine judgment "must be a response of acceptance, but this involves not merely a repentant attitude, appropriate and necessary though this is, because the disaster is not simply judgement, not simply a condemnation of the past but also a stage within the working out of a larger purpose."[23] It involves acceptance of their role and a willingness to comply with it.

This transformation is beautifully reflected in the thanksgiving psalms of the Dead Sea community, recorded by Burrows: "But though

22. *Ibid.*, p. 33.
23. Peter Ackroyd, *Exile and Restoration*, p. 234.

my heart melted like water, my soul took hold of Thy covenant."[24] The travail was thought to purify the resolve of the people. What better times had failed to accomplish, God's ministry to His people was thought to bring to fruition.

Jeremiah describes this transformation in terms of a new covenant (Jer. 31:33–34). According to Barton Payne, it would contrast with the old covenant at four points: "It would be internal—'In their heart will I write it'; it will be reconciling—'I will be their God, and they shall be my people'; it will be direct—'They shall all know me'; it will be explicit in forgiveness—'For I will forgive their iniquity.'"[25] It would also be peculiarly administered by the Spirit, as the divine agent of the messianic age—so that what the former covenant had anticipated would be brought to pass in the new covenant.

There was only a step or two from here to Paul's confident refrain: "For he is not a Jew who is one outwardly; neither is circumcision that which is outward in the flesh. But he is a Jew who is one inwardly; and circumcision is that which is of the heart, by the Spirit, not by the letter; and His praise is not from men, but from God" (Rom. 2:28–29). However, this is to rush ahead in the story and to see the beginning from the end, rather than the end from the beginning.

We return to the deliberation of the wilderness community. Burrows observes that they acknowledged the work of the Spirit in their midst: "I thank thee, O Lord, because thou hast sustained me with thy strength and hast shed abroad thy Holy Spirit in me; I shall not be moved."[26] They likewise testified: "With thy Holy Spirit thou dost delight me, and to this day dost lead me."[27] How else was the Hebrew to understand the change that God works in the heart of a rebellious people but by means of His sovereign Spirit? Indeed, they sensed the time had come for the Almighty to turn around the disposition of His people in order to serve His ends.

What the Qumran community sensed of the time in which they lived eventually escaped them, as it did so many others caught in the transition of the ages. There were those who placed their hopes in the high idealism with which the Maccabean period began, only to see them collapse in the bitter partisan politics that followed. Some supposed

---

24. Burrows, *The Dead Sea Scrolls*, p. 402.
25. Barton Payne, *The Theology of the Old Testament*, p. 115.
26. Burrows, *The Dead Sea Scrolls*, p. 409.
27. *Ibid.*, p. 412.

they had fallen victim to false labor. A peculiar silence seemed to grip the situation; the prophets ceased to speak.

What was to be done? Some beat their shields, as if to awaken God to get on with the messianic age. Others settled down in a remote spot to watch what might happen, there to perish, along with their hopes. For a time, the din of the temple ritual tended to fill the silence, but soon even this died away. There were false messiahs who gathered a small following for the moment, but none were able to fulfill what they promised to a desperate people.

The Spirit would be heard, breaking the silence, in the cry of a child. The age would dawn almost without notice. It would come on schedule, not with royal fanfare, but with a humble beginning. The angel would announce that "today in the city of David there has been born for you a Savior, who is Christ the Lord" (Luke 2:11). The Messiah would come to establish a new covenant and to transform ancient Israel. God was about to do a new thing through His Spirit in calling out a people not from any single fold, to serve Him faithfully in the task ahead. Thus would another episode in the saga of the Spirit come to an end and the final chapter get under way.

Summary

It was in some respects the worst of times and the best of times. Never had the covenant people been put in such dire straits, but here the Spirit of God seemed to pour out grace upon them and to heighten their anticipation for the messianic age. What Ackroyd says of the exile in particular could be as well extended to the whole era under consideration: It was "of paramount importance, a great divide between the earlier and later stages, but one which it was necessary to traverse if the new age was to be reached."[28] It was a time to try the souls of men. The people were subject to captivity, restored to an exceedingly tenuous situation, only to succumb once more to foreign invaders. They were submitted to cultural as well as political assimilation, which proved to be a grievous threat to the covenant people.

This most recent experience tended to confirm what Israel had come to anticipate regarding the Spirit, as One who would deliver the people of God and establish their ways before Him. But they were now

---

28. Ackroyd, *Exile and Restoration*, p 243.

caught in what resembled a downward spiral, where the sin of each succeeding generation seemed to weigh them down further. It was as if this left them only one way to look—upward to God's deliverance.

As the prospect of the Davidic kingdom diminished, the people cast both backward to the terms of the covenant and forward to an apocalyptic fulfillment of their expectations. All this was something of a mystery to them, in that what was—and remained—hidden was being—and would be—revealed. For now, they must repudiate the sins of their fathers while clinging to the faith of their fathers. God would assuredly honor His word spoken in times past.

The figure which best captures the experience, and points to the role of the Spirit in all this, is that of messianic travail. The wilderness community was not alone in grasping on to this motif to explain the times. Israel resembled a woman about to give birth to her first son. The Holy Spirit attended her as would a midwife as the moment of delivery approached.

Ezekiel's active concern with the Spirit, coupled with references from the other prophets, can be understood in this light. The Spirit does not leave the birthing mother for a moment, tending to her every need until the delivery has been accomplished. Israel had entered into travail, but was not forsaken by the Spirit of God.

This is understandably of great consolation to the suffering people. There are occasions when the comfort that others can give falls pitifully short. It is at such times that we desperately need divine consolation. This was such a time.

The experience of giving birth would leave its mark on reconstituted Israel. Jeremiah portrayed the transformation in terms of a new covenant that would, in contrast to the former experience of the people, be an internal covenant—so as to reconcile them to the Almighty, forgive their trespasses, and be dispersed throughout their company. Here, as in the past, the Spirit is present with the word of the covenant to bring about God's purpose.

We have added to the previous emphases on the Spirit that of "midwife." He provides divine consolation to those caught in the birth pains of messianic travail. He also ministers in such a way as to transform life in the process. There were intimations of this earlier, but now we can be certain: "Blessed are those who mourn, for they shall be comforted" (Matt. 5:4). In accepting their place in God's sovereign design, they will be comforted and transformed by His Spirit.

4

Calvary

No better vantage point exists for us to survey the saga of the Spirit than Calvary. Here Christ died to redeem man from his sin, and from here we gain perspective on all the rest. Calvary represents a dramatic shift of perspective, from the time of the prophets to the Son (Heb. 1:1–2), from anticipation to fulfillment.

25 Physical Site

The actual Calvary is debated, but earliest tradition suggests the precincts of the Church of the Holy Sepulchre, although there is little for the imagination to work with in reconstructing the original scene. Instead, we have an overlay of church tradition, complicated by the competing denominations which share its premises.

Some opt for Gordon's Calvary, northeast of the modern Damascus Gate. The scene is more appealing, as it preserves a tomb, skull-shaped knoll, and outdoor sanctuary. However, it is more a sentimental favorite than anything else.

Perhaps the actual site is of little consequence. However Calvary is remembered, it remains central to the gospel narrative. Here Christ died that man might live. The message radiated out from this point, borne by the disciples to every corner of the globe. All of this was understood in connection with Joel's earlier promise that God would pour out the Spirit on all mankind.

26 Historical Setting

The time was ripe for the appearance of the promised Messiah. The Hebrew people had been prepared throughout their unique experiences to bring into the world the One in whom all mankind would be blessed. They had at long last been weaned away from idolatry and acknowledged the living God. Their hopes had been directed away from the presumptive confidence in human resolutions, toward the intervention of the Almighty into the affairs of men. The Hebrews were strategically located around the Roman Empire, so that a word of messianic deliverance could travel with remarkable ease throughout the domain. "For Moses from ancient generations has in every city those who preach him, since he is read in the synagogues every Sabbath" (Acts 15:21). This ensured not only a strategic location but timely consideration of the gospel by a people peculiarly prepared for its reception.

The Gentile world also seemed poised for the promised advent of the Messiah. Hellenism, which had proved such a threat to the Hebrew faith, provided a conceptual and linguistic vehicle for the gospel to spread rapidly. Greek was spoken in virtually all the commercial centers, and especially in the eastern part of the Mediterranean, where Christianity first took roots. Kenneth Scott Latourette observes: "Yet those for whom Greek was a primary tongue were also present in Rome, in Sicily and the south of Italy, in some of the cities of the south of Gaul, and in several other centers of the western portion of the Mediterranean."[1] To these we must add the Greek cities scattered about and providing a base for Hellenic culture.

The *pax Romana* likewise contributed. A remarkable system of good roads traversed the Roman Empire, making travel and trade possible as never before. The pirates and robbers who had made ancient travel a nightmare were restrained by the Roman security system. The relative order provided an occasion for constructive enterprise, including the opportunity to reflect on such word as would come concerning the Messiah.

---

1. Kenneth Scott Latourette, *A History of Christianity*, p. 21.

There was also a religious and moral hunger that characterized much of the people of the time. The Roman Empire had uprooted its populace in the process of gaining a solid hold on them. Latourette elaborates: "The formation of an all-embracing empire promoted the decay of the local religious cults of the several states and cities which were brought within the inclusive political unity. To be sure, many were maintained as a matter of custom or civil pride, but the heart had largely gone out of them. Then, too, the advancing intelligence and moral sensitivity of the times cast doubt upon the stories about the gods."[2] It seemed difficult to believe the traditional accounts of the gods and their capricious ways with men. The age had more than its share of moral corruption to contribute to the rest, inviting a reconsideration of life in all its dimensions.

There were many competitors to fill the vacuum existing at the time: the empirical cult, the mystery religions, incipient Gnosticism, Stoicism—to identify a few. But, for one reason or another, none of these exhibited the tenacity of the messianic faith which came to be called "Christianity." This faith alone seemed to fit the times, as a hand might fit a glove.

The messianic faith culminated in Jesus, an itinerant teacher, who was raised in Nazareth of Galilee and moved to Capernaum, from which to carry on His ministry. He never traveled far, never went abroad, and was seldom in the vicinity of the Greek centers. His early life is relatively obscure. There were miraculous accounts associated with His birth, but the child Jesus seems to have developed quite normally (*cp.* Luke 2:40).

However the early years of His life were filled, this period of obscurity ended abruptly. John the Baptist, a kinsman of Jesus, had become the center of a significant religious awakening. He denounced the sins of the people, spoke of impending judgment, and urged repentance in preparation for the anticipated arrival of the kingdom of God. Jesus came to be baptized by John, who appeared reluctant to baptize Jesus, saying that Jesus ought rather to baptize him. Jesus persisted, apparently for the purpose of identifying with those whom He had come to redeem.

There followed about three years of active ministry, in which Jesus crisscrossed back and forth over the rugged Palestinian countryside. Jesus taught concerning the nature of the kingdom of God, often employing parables for this purpose. He demonstrated the power of the

---

2. *Ibid.*,p. 22.

present kingdom with healings and the exorcism of demons. His life and teachings reflected the perfect obedience which ought to characterize the subjects of the kingdom of God, even (and perhaps *most*) when confronting the hard realities of a fallen world. Jesus suggested that there would be a consummation of the kingdom, when He would return in power after His passion.

The populace often embraced Jesus for the wrong reasons. Some saw Him as a provider who would make little or no demands upon them; others hoped He would confirm their ethnic bias; still others promoted Him as a military leader. All these were disappointed, and in the end Jesus was crucified.

Jesus' disciples were scattered and went into hiding, but on the third day they were rallied with the word of His resurrection. From that point on, no one could stamp out their witness—not even the zealous persecutor of the church, Saul, who became Paul the apostle. His labors and that of others soon accounted for the rapid spread of the faith, radiating out from its center at Jerusalem.

This new movement at first appeared to be a sect within Judaism. It more resembled that of the Pharisees than the Sadducees, because of its emphasis on the resurrection and afterlife, and in its association with the common people. It also sided with the Pharisees rather than the Essenes, due to its involvement in the mainstream of Hebrew life. The faithful refused to join with the Zealots in attempting an overthrow of Rome by force. Their most insistent belief was in declaring Jesus to be the Messiah, pointing to His resurrection as attesting to the fact.

The faith seemed destined from the beginning to extend beyond its Jewish confines. God-fearing Gentiles were among the early converts, and their numbers began to swell the ranks of believers. Conflict with the Jewish authorities appeared inevitable, and persecution followed soon after.

The influx of Gentiles in increasing numbers also created tension with this messianic community. The issue seemed less whether Gentiles might join than whether they were obligated to observe the Jewish distinctives as a consequence. Since the dispute threatened to rend the community in two, a council was called in Jerusalem to hear the opposing points of view and reach a conclusion (Acts 15). It was decided that the Gentile converts would not have to keep the Jewish practices except at certain points where lack of observance seemed especially offensive to their Jewish brothers.

Paul had by now assumed the leading role in reaching the Gentiles with this messianic faith. He characteristically first proclaimed the gospel to the Jewish enclave upon arriving at his location and, when repulsed, turned to the Gentile inhabitants. The lines between the Jewish and Christian communities became increasingly fixed. Paul was by no means the only one to spread the faith. We read of Peter, Philip, Apollos, Barnabas, and others. Although the names of most have been lost to history, their results stand as a memorial to their faithful efforts.

The universal character of the faith was anticipated when on the day of Pentecost those people present heard the gospel in their own tongues. (This was a symbolic reversal of the dispersal of the nations at the Tower of Babel.) Some spoke Syriac, and others were Parthians, dwellers in Mesopotamia, Medes, and Elamites, as well as those more clearly associated with Hellenic culture (Acts 2:1–11).

From early times, the faith was predominantly urban. The evangelists settled down in commercial centers from which the word might be circulated into the countryside. The message characteristically moved along the trade routes, from city to city. Here and there it took root and a vigorous church came into being. Weaker and more struggling works looked to these centers for support and encouragement.

Rome seemed content to ignore Christianity as long as possible. Only when it began to appear as a threat to the *pax Romana* did the authorities strike back. By then Christianity had emerged from its protective security as a Jewish sect.

The new faith became a convenient scapegoat for the Emperor Nero. A great fire broke out in Rome in 64 A.D., destroying a large part of the city. Nero was suspected of having set the fire in order to make way for a splendid palace to be built on the Esquiline hill. However, he blamed the Christians for having caused the disaster, a charge that seemed fairly plausible because of their disdain for the heathen practices and talk of the ultimate destruction of the world by fire. Tacitus recalls the events: "Therefore, to overcome this rumor [that he was to blame], Nero put in his own place as culprits, and punished with most ingenious cruelty men whom the common people hated for their shameful crimes and called Christians. . . . Therefore, at the beginning, some were seized who made confessions; then, on their information, a vast multitude was convicted, not so much of arson as of hatred of the human race. And they were not only put to death, but subjected to insults, in that they were either dressed up in the skins of wild beasts and perished by the cruel mangling of dogs, or else put on crosses to be set on fire, and, as day declined, to be burned, being used as lights by night."[3] While their ranks were depleted by death and defection, there always appeared others to take their places.

The messianic fellowship found that it had to exercise discipline on its membership, so as to keep its faith pure and its morals uncorrupted. A Christian consensus on some matters took a painfully long time to be reached, and even longer to persuade others of its validity. The apostles played a prominent role in the beginning, but new leaders soon had to take over the growing work. For all of the growing pains, the church was coming of age.

We may wonder where all these converts came from. Some have thought Christianity to be a movement of the underprivileged. "Yet we know that even in the first century numbers of men and women of wealth, education, and social prominence became Christians, and that in the original Christian group in Jerusalem there were not only poor but also those who had the means to aid their less fortunate fellows. It is possible that members of some of the most prominent families in Rome were among the early converts, and that a near relative of the Emperor Domitian was a Christian, and, but for his death by execution, might himself have become Emperor. It may well have been that the proportion of the educated, the socially prominent, and the poor in the Christian communities was about that in the Empire as a whole."[4] While this reconstruction by Latourette might not fit our romantic notions, it may more realistically suggest the actual state of affairs.

The messianic community looked forward to the consummation promised by Jesus. They were genuinely "latter day saints"—looking forward to and living in the light of Christ's return. These early Christians faced death with a passion created out of the faith that Christ had conquered even death. Accordingly, they claimed victory from the arena and on their crosses.

The New Testament documents conclude at this point with the church still expanding in the face of obstacles. As the long shadow of Calvary extended from beginning to end, the Spirit was understood in the light of the advent of Christ. The age to come had dawned; the Spirit was being poured out as had been promised.

---

3. Tacitus, Annals, XV, 44.
4. Latourette, *A History of Christianity*, p. 80.

27 The Great Divide

Calvary is not simply the last among several episodes in the saga of the Spirit; it stands over all the rest. What we have covered up to this point amounts to preparation, and what follows is fulfillment. Calvary represents the great divide between the present age and the age to come.

Peter Ackroyd elaborates: "The reality of the embodiment of the rule of God in history which the New Testament proclaims is not a denial of that earlier sense of its reality, but a deepening and enlarging of its meaning. Nor does the fact that the new age has still not fully come alter the reality of Christian confidence that it is possible to live here and now in the context of that new age."[5] The Spirit has been active up to this moment—in delivering the people of God, building them up in the faith, and ministering to them during messianic travail. All of this continues to have significance for the people of God as they attempt to understand what has changed with the messianic advent.

The new emphasis, which is not altogether "new," may be described as the peace of God. This peace is understood in no narrow sense, but as a concept which embraces all that we signify as total well-being. The Spirit is portrayed in the messianic age as the harbinger of *shalom*.

There is a qualification we should make with regard to this dramatic transition from one age to another. Before the advent of Christ, there was already a rather subtle shift of disposition away from what had preceded it—and toward the age to come. Ackroyd adds: "The possibility of a right choice, of real repentance and turning to God is envisaged—though often in contexts which make it clear that the prophets and historians also recognized that such a repentance was in the event extremely unlikely, or even impossible. With the exile, this need for repentance and reform is set in the context of a new act of God."[6] This new initiative was in direct correlation with the messianic age and extended ministry of the Spirit.

We could say that this situation resembled the construction of a bridge over the great divide so as to help the people make the necessary transition. It closed off one alternative, in order to promote the other. The present age would soon come to an end, as the messianic age dawned.

---

5. Peter Ackroyd, *Exile and Restoration*, p. 254.
6. *Ibid.*,p. 235.

In any case, the time had come. The Spirit was being poured out, and the *shalom* of God was being realized in a deeper and broader way than ever before. Jesus needed only to point out to the inquiring disciples of John the Baptist what was transpiring as a result of His ministry (Luke 7:22).

28 An Overlap

The Jew differentiated between the present age and the age to come or the messianic age. While the former was not devoid of the Spirit, the latter was seen as the time when the Spirit would be lavished on all flesh. The forces of evil would be dispersed, and the righteous consoled for their toil and trials.

The Christian welcomed the messianic age with the advent of Jesus, but in its initial stage rather than full consummation. This resembled a time overlap, wherein the present age continued along with the age to come. The vestiges of the present age would finally dissolve with the second advent of Christ. Although, during the interim, the forces of evil would wage a last desperate struggle, righteousness would prevail in the end.

This is certainly different from the traditional Hebrew perspective. It seems to be saying "now" but "not yet" as relates to what might be anticipated concerning the messianic age. In other words, it was the beginning of the end, but not the end of the beginning.

Oscar Cullmann observes that, to further compound the situation, "the revelation consists precisely in the fact of the proclamation that the event on the cross, together with the resurrection which followed, was the already concluded decisive battle."[7] The period in which we now live resembles an overlap, where the decisive battle has been won. The work of the Spirit as viewed from Calvary appears as a triumphant course, obstacles notwithstanding, from start to finish. He has secured a messianic beachhead from which there can be no retreat, and in anticipation of final and total victory. Cullmann views the messianic age as the triumph of Christ, but it is no less the triumph of the Spirit.

What, then, becomes of the peace promised with the advent of the messianic age and the fullness of the Spirit? From his prison cell, Paul refers to "the peace of God, which surpasses all comprehension" (Phil. 4:7). It was for him a present possession, laid firm hold upon in the

7. Oscar Cullmann, *Christ and Time*, p. 84.

midst of privation. Although we do not yet see peace pervasive in the world at large, many persons have experienced through faith a deep and abiding peace, and they have become advocates of peace in turn.

It may at first seem that the Christian is laboring under an illusion, but nothing could be further from the truth. Cullmann points out that "Christ already rules over all things, but in a way visible only to faith."[8] Christ now sits on the right hand of the Father, and the Spirit has been sent forth to do His necessary work in bringing things to a consummation. The world may be said to be unconsciously under the rule of Christ, even though it fails both to recognize that fact and to lay down its arms.

It falls upon the church to reveal to the world what it does not know, and may not care to hear—that Christ is Lord. It testifies to this by word and deed, both *together*. The former taken alone appears hypocritical, and the latter alone as lacking concern. Here the Spirit picks up His task, to enable the church in its calling, and to persuade a reluctant world of the truth to which the church testifies.

29 Teaching of the Synoptics

We may now enlarge upon the ministry of the Spirit since the inauguration of the messianic age, turning first to the synoptic Gospels. Donald Guthrie identifies seven aspects of the Spirit's work as reflected in the first three Gospels.[9] We shall follow his line of thought with slight adjustments.

We begin with the announcement of John the Baptist: "As for me, I baptize you with water for repentance, but He who is coming after me is mightier than I, and I am not fit to remove His sandals; He will baptize you with the Holy Spirit and fire" (Matt. 3:11). The words are variously interpreted as pertinent to judgment, purging, or a combination of both. While it is difficult to be certain what the Baptist had in mind, the importance of the Holy Spirit in this connection is indisputable.

We may assume that this passage refers to Pentecost, when it was recorded that "there appeared to them tongues as of fire. . . . And they were all filled with the Holy Spirit" (Acts 2:3–4). John clearly stated that the Messiah would be instrumental in bringing about this subsequent

8. *Ibid.*,p. 184.

9. Donald Guthrie, *New Testament Theology*, pp. 514–21.

baptism of the Spirit. The results would be far greater than those witnessed as a consequence of John's activity.

Guthrie next picks up the Spirit's role with regard to the birth of Jesus. Both Matthew and Luke specifically attribute the conception of Jesus to the work of the Spirit (Matt. 1:18; Luke 1:35). Luke further draws a distinction between the activity of the Spirit as related to John the Baptist and Jesus. The former was said to "be filled with the Holy Spirit, while yet in his mother's womb" (Luke 1:15), but this is clearly meant to differ from Jesus' conception through the Holy Spirit.

There are echoes of the creation narrative in the inception of Jesus, especially as they relate to the delicate weave of divine intervention with the natural processes of reproduction. But the more striking reference, taken in its historical setting, is to set the whole life and mission of Jesus under the aegis of the Spirit.

Simeon's prediction next solicits our attention. Simeon appears to be one of a devout company who awaited "the consolation of Israel." We read that "the Holy Spirit was upon him. And it had been revealed to him by the Holy Spirit that he would not see death before he had seen the Lord's Christ" (Luke 2:25–26). Thus was Simeon brought "in the Spirit" to the temple, and when he had seen the child, he blessed God and declared that he was now ready to depart, "for my eyes have seen Thy salvation" (vv. 28–30). Simeon was moved to predict the universal scope of Jesus' ministry, its divisive character so far as the household of Israel was concerned, and the pain it would inflict on Mary. This would be a light to the Gentiles, and a glory to "Thy people Israel"—the opposition and suffering notwithstanding (vv. 32–35). It would also qualify as the distinctive work of the Spirit.

We turn in order to the Spirit at Jesus' baptism, as "the Holy Spirit descended upon Him in bodily form like a dove, and a voice came out of heaven, 'Thou art My beloved Son, in Thee I am well-pleased'" (Luke 3:22). This both constitutes the inauguration of Jesus' ministry and suggests that the Spirit put His special seal upon it. It was to bear witness that this mission was of God, to be accomplished in the power of the Spirit.

The reference to the Spirit's descending in the form of a dove is again reminiscent of the creation account, where the Spirit brooded over the chaos. Although it does not say that the Spirit *was* a dove, the writer obviously meant to describe an actual event. Whether we should speculate as to what the dove might symbolize, or merely restrict the mode to the idea of descent, is perhaps not of any great consequence. Guthrie reasons, "There is truth in the view that the main reason for the descent of the Spirit on Jesus was that he should baptize others with the Spirit as John the Baptist had predicted. In other words the mission of Jesus was not only Spirit-initiated, but also Spirit-oriented."[10] The declaration of the sonship of Jesus follows directly after the descent of the Spirit and must be closely associated with it.

We find the Spirit next with Jesus' temptation. Mark records that "immediately the Spirit compelled Him to go out into the wilderness" (Mark 1:12). Luke adds that "Jesus returned to Galilee in the power of the Spirit" (Luke 4:14), so that the temptation occurred between His being led into the wilderness by the urgency of the Spirit and His return in the Spirit's power. The testing was seen as a stage in the messianic mission designed and carried out by the Spirit.

Jesus would be tempted from time to time, but this instance was unique. It ties back into the voice from heaven suggesting that Jesus was the beloved Son. It demonstrates His obedience in the wilderness experience, as would be expected of a faithful Son who waxed strong in the Spirit.

We will reverse the final aspects concerning Jesus' mission in Guthrie's order, and first take up Jesus' announcement concerning His public ministry. Jesus stood up to read in the synagogue in Nazareth: "The Spirit of the Lord is upon Me," and when He had completed His text from Isaiah, He concluded, "Today this Scripture has been fulfilled in your hearing" (Luke 4:18, 21). The ministry described in Isaiah involved preaching, healing, and deliverance (*cp.* Isa. 61:1–2).

Jesus' opposition would argue that His power was derived from "Beelzebul the ruler of the demons," to which Jesus responded that "any sin and blasphemy shall be forgiven men, but blasphemy against the Spirit shall not be forgiven" (Matt. 12:24, 31). It was as if Jesus distinguished between the general opposition which had arisen to His teachings and that which deliberately distorted the Spirit's ministry through Him. What Jesus announced concerning His ministry at the outset, regarding it as being the work of the Spirit, He stoutly maintained under attack.

The Beelzebul controversy brings us to the final aspect of Jesus' mission, with regard to exorcism. Jesus declared: "But if I cast out demons by the Spirit of God, then the kingdom of God has come upon you" (Matt. 12:28). The many exorcisms in the Gospels remind us of the

10. *Ibid.*, p. 518.

spiritual nature of Jesus' conflict. But they do more than this: they are signs of His messianic ministry as performed by the Holy Spirit. In order to establish His kingdom, Jesus must overthrow the kingdom of evil. The exorcisms were dramatic evidence of the Spirit, demonstrating that a superior power had been brought to bear.

30 Fourth Gospel

Before going on to look at the passion account, we want to comment on the distinctive witness of the apostle John regarding the work of the Spirit. This Gospel adds to the synoptic accounts that John the Baptist recognized Jesus as He approached, and declared: "Behold, the Lamb of God who takes away the sin of the world!" (John 1:29). It was revealed to the Baptist that here was the One who would baptize with the Spirit.

A more substantial addition in John's Gospel has to do with Jesus' words to Nicodemus: "Truly, truly, I say to you, unless one is born of water and the Spirit, he cannot enter into the kingdom of God" (John 3:5). This was to emphasize the radically new character of life in Christ, in both its inception and continued existence.

John's further comment bears notice: "For He whom God has sent speaks the words of God; for He gives the Spirit without measure" (v. 34). This implies that the Word of God needs the Spirit of God to interpret it, and that the Spirit will be generously available. Through the Spirit, God will accomplish His messianic purpose.

Jesus observes to His disciples, "It is the Spirit who gives life; the flesh profits nothing; the words I have spoken to you are spirit and are life" (John 6:63). This pronouncement serves to tie together such truths as we have considered from the creation narrative, the subsequent messianic advent, and the intervening course of events. The Word of God and the life-generating role of the Spirit are coupled together once more, but now in a messianic setting.

Jesus declared: "If any man is thirsty, let him come to Me and drink. He who believes in Me, as the Scripture said, 'From his innermost being shall flow rivers of living water'" (John 7:37–38). John's account comments that this He spoke "of the Spirit, whom those who believed in Him were to receive; for the Spirit was not yet given, because Jesus was not yet glorified." We take this reference to be a general allusion to promises related to the coming of the Spirit, which were now to be fulfilled. Jesus would, through the outpouring of the Spirit, satisfy those who come to Him.

Enough has been said to illustrate how inexorably the Spirit was associated with Jesus in His mission and teaching. The Spirit would eventually be identified as "the Spirit of Christ" (Rom. 8:9; 2 Cor. 3:17; 1 Peter 1:11). We could likewise turn matters around and call Jesus "the Man of the Spirit."

31 Passion Narrative

Helmut Thielicke reflects on the cruel nature of life and imagines that the honest nihilist is closer to the Christian faith than the sentimental optimist. He adds: "The Father I believe in does not dwell above the starry sky. No, he was in a man who laughed and wept as you and I, who was tempted and who despaired as you and I, who was assaulted by meaninglessness as you and I . . . and who was shaken by the pangs of death as one day they will shake us."[11] We could readily conclude both from the events and such teaching as was incorporated in their account that such is also the concern of the Spirit. He cares little for what may be going on "in the eternal sabbath of heaven," but is consumed with thoughts about those caught up "in the sweat and drudgery" of our daily pilgrimage here below.

E. M. Blaiklock ponders the continuing significance of the passion account: "Christ certainly died because of sin. . . . But this is the seventh [now ninth] decade of a distant century. What standing and eternal value lay in the vast betrayal and ugly crime?"[12] As if to answer such a question, Guthrie elaborates on six functions of the Spirit which, taken together, suggest the complex role of the Spirit in probing the significance of the passion for the ongoing experience of the disciples.[13]

Guthrie proposes that *the* major function of the Spirit relates to glorifying Christ (John 16:14). The Spirit draws us to Christ and, if to Christ, then to the cross. The hymn writer was precisely on target with the refrain, "In the cross of Christ I'll glory."

How tempting it must have been to flee that ugly recollection of Calvary! To think of nicer things that warm one's religious sentimentality; to shut out the hard realities of life and the suffering that accompany them. But, in so doing, the disciples could shut out the Spirit as well.

---

11. Helmut Thielicke, *I Believe*, p. 23.
12. E. M. Blaiklock, *Layman's Answer*, p. 106.
13. Guthrie, *New Testament Theology*, pp. 531–533.

Yet, to glorify Christ was not only to dwell on the depth of His humiliation but on the height of His exaltation as well. Paul concludes, "Therefore also God highly exalted Him, and bestowed on Him the name which is above every name, that at the name of Jesus every knee should bow, of those who are in heaven, and on earth, and under the earth, and that every tongue should confess that Jesus Christ is Lord, to the glory of God the Father" (Phil. 2:9–11).

Closely allied to the foregoing function is the Spirit's enablement of believers to witness for Christ. Jesus said that when the Spirit comes, "He will bear witness of Me, and you will bear witness also . . ." (John 15:26–27). Thus the disciples were also instructed to tarry until they should "receive power when the Holy Spirit has come upon you; and you shall be My witnesses both in Jerusalem, and in Judea and Samaria, and even to the remotest part of the earth" (Acts 1:8).

The connection of witness *from* the Spirit and witness *by* the Spirit is an interesting one. The former seems to lend credibility to the latter. The disciple speaks what he has come to know from the testimony of the Spirit as to the truth concerning Christ. But confidence is further linked to courage, as once-intimidated men are enabled by the Spirit to speak boldly.

In order to bear an effective witness, it would be necessary that the Spirit likewise bring such things as are needed to the memory of the disciples. Jesus promised that "the Helper, the Holy Spirit, whom the Father will send in My name, He will teach you all things, and bring to your remembrance all that I said to you" (John 14:26). Guthrie observes, "The preservation of this priceless tradition was not to be left to chance. The Spirit would be the custodian of truth"[14]—not least of which were the passion accounts.

Of course, we do not want to take this promise out of context. Its specific reference is to the apostles and their distinctive role in the emerging church. There is only a derivative application for Christians in general, although some such significance may be implied elsewhere (*cp.* Matt. 28:20).

Another associated ministry of the Spirit is to "guide you into all the truth" (John 16:13). Guthrie adds: "'All the truth' embraces the developing understanding of the meaning of the mission of Jesus, the significance of his death and resurrection, and the application of the

---

14. *Ibid.*, p. 532.

newly established faith to life."[15] In other words, while this is akin to the former promise, "all the truth" extends beyond it.

We can only allow ourselves to sample what may be implied by bringing to mind "all the truth." We select the notion of reconciliation as it draws upon the passion narrative. Technically speaking, reconciliation is only one aspect of atonement, but will suffice for our present purpose.[16]

Paul reminds us that we have "access in one Spirit to the Father" (Eph. 2:18). There is no difference noted at this point, whether speaking of "the commonwealth of Israel" or "strangers to the covenants of promise" (v. 12). Once alienated, we are reconciled through the blood of Christ and have access by the Spirit.

We may say that the Spirit works out the process of reconciliation obtained through Christ in a way similar to His bringing order out of the creation. He implements reconciliation by making the fact a reality—both objectively as applied to an individual, and subjectively as the disciple experiences the work of the Spirit. Thus the prodigal is made to feel at home.

The disciples are likewise admonished to be reconciled to one another (Matt. 5:24). This was not to be as so many autonomous efforts, but as the Spirit would initiate and sustain their endeavor. He works through human resolve, but around it as well, and His ways are mysterious and wonderful to meditate upon.

The range of reconciliation stretches beyond mankind to creation at large. "For we know that the whole creation groans and suffers the pains of childbirth together until now" (Rom. 8:22), waiting for a time when all nature will be reconciled to the holy purposes of God. The material world will share in the power of the resurrection as it shared in the fall. Then, we can imagine the Spirit's surveying of all that He has brought to pass as a job well done.

Until such time, we may talk of a "ministry of reconciliation" (2 Cor. 5:18–19). "Whoever will call upon the name of the Lord will be saved. . . . And how shall they believe in Him whom they have not heard? And how shall they hear without a preacher?" (Rom. 10:13–14). Thus, persons must be enlisted in sharing the good news and empowered for their task by the indwelling Holy Spirit.

---

15. *Ibid.*

16. A. M. Hunter outlines "three picture phrases" concerning man's deliverance: redemption—a metaphor from the slave market; justification—taken from the law-court; and reconciliation—derived from the realm of interpersonal relations (*Introducing New Testament Theology*, p. 93).

The Spirit does not only recall the past and assist in developing its significance for the present but delves into the future. ". . . He will disclose to you what is to come" (John 16:13). The idea of things "to come" is sufficiently broad to cover whatever God intends to bring to pass. This would be especially as they relate to God's provision for His own. "Things which eye has not seen and ear has not heard, and which have not entered the heart of man, all that God has prepared for those who love Him" are the prerogative of the Spirit, who "searches all things, even the depths of God" (1 Cor. 2:9–10)—in order to make them known to such as are mature and diligently seek to understand the will of God.

While the previously mentioned functions of the Spirit deal with believers, the final one relates to those still in unbelief. It is said that the Spirit convicts the world of sin, righteousness, and judgment (John 16:8–11). Sin is defined here in terms of unbelief; righteousness in terms of Christ; judgment in that "the ruler of this world" has been overthrown.

The Spirit so elevates Christ as to demonstrate man's sinful disposition in failing to rally to the cross. Christ's passion demonstrates a new dimension of righteousness, the unqualified obedience of Christ to His Father's will. Judgment relates to Christ's victory *at* the cross and *from* the cross. All this combines to help the world understand its true situation, the extent to which it has fallen and the hope of recovery—providing it heeds the admonition of the Spirit to reconsider the implication of Calvary.

32 Acts of the Spirit

The church serves in Christ's stead and as the peculiar extension of the Holy Spirit's activity in the messianic age. As Karl Barth explains: "We cannot speak of the Holy Spirit—and that is why at this point the congregation immediately appears—without continuing *credo ecclesium*. I believe in the existence of the church."[17] To believe in the Holy Spirit is to believe in His work in reference to the church. (The reverse is not true.) Faith exists in the church where there is faith in the regenerating work of the Spirit.

Guthrie writes that "Jesus was the perfect example of a man of the Spirit, but not until Pentecost were others to become men of the Spirit in

17. Karl Barth, *Dogmatics in Outline*, pp. 141–142.

a dynamic way."[18] The church originated with Pentecost and the work of the Spirit in bringing into being a messianic fellowship. Guthrie adds that we might imagine that the Spirit would therefore be associated with Pentecost in some distinctive fashion.[19]

Pentecost was in fact the concluding act of the ascension. Jesus had told His disciples that the Spirit would not come until He (Jesus) went away: ". . . but if I go, I will send Him to you" (John 16:7). Pentecost was the fulfillment of that promise.

The outpouring of the Spirit extended to *all* believers, in contrast to the more selective application of the Spirit to certain persons in the former dispensation. The result was also viewed as more permanent, pervasive, and effective—so much so that nothing previous could be submitted as a genuine parallel.

There were extraordinary signs that accompanied the outpouring of the Spirit: the wind and fire, one unseen and the other seen. These do not seem to have been repeated elsewhere, as if to suggest an original breakthrough that would not have to be repeated even though the Spirit would continue to be outpoured.

One sign, the speaking in tongues, was repeated at least on two other occasions, according to Acts: the one with regard to the Gentiles (Acts 10:44–48) and the other with former disciples of John the Baptist (Acts 19:1–7). These were perhaps similar to the Pentecost experience in some particulars. Whether or not the tongues Paul refers to in his Corinthian correspondence should be associated with these instances has resulted in seemingly endless controversy.

The Spirit's activity on Pentecost was identified as that promised by the prophet Joel (Joel 2:28–32). These were declared to be "the last days" when God would "pour out My Spirit upon all mankind." While all those present on Pentecost were presumably Jews, many were of the Diaspora and spoke the languages of their exile, and when the Spirit was outpoured they heard one another in their own languages. It would only be a matter of time before the Spirit would be manifest with the Gentiles as well.

The Spirit was promised to all those who would likewise repent and be baptized. This meant that those who truly repented at the urging of the Spirit and believed—thereby identifying themselves with the com-

---

18. Guthrie, *New Testament Theology*, p. 537.
19. *Ibid.*, pp. 537–540.

munity of faith—would receive the promised baptism of the Holy Spirit. With that initial appeal, there was added some 3,000 persons.

There is no "theology of the Spirit" in the Book of Acts, were we to mean some detailed teaching. We have instead the actual acts of the apostles, or rather those of the Spirit through the apostles. There continued to be conversion as the church reached out to incorporate ever larger numbers of people, but the Spirit is also seen in other contexts, three of which we will touch on briefly.

On two occasions, Agabus is introduced as a prophet. He was apparently one of a number of prophets who came down from Jerusalem to Antioch, whereupon he announced "by the Spirit" that there would be "a great famine all over the world." At this, the disciples determined to send an offering to the brethren in Judea (Acts 11:27–28). Agabus appears again in Caesarea to warn Paul of his impending imprisonment (Acts 21:10–11). The first instance had social significance; the second was of more personal nature. Each implied the obligation to act on what had been revealed, although Paul put a different construction on the prediction than those who were attempting to persuade him not to go up to Jerusalem.

We also see the Spirit's involvement in settling the controversy concerning what obligations to place on the Gentile converts. The matter was concluded with the explanation: "For it seemed good to the Holy Spirit and to us to lay upon you no greater burden than these essentials" (Acts 15:28). This would seem to be an apt illustration of what was meant by guiding the disciples into "all the truth" (as previously considered). The Spirit helped forge an understanding of what it meant for the church to break out of its narrow Jewish confines and embrace persons everywhere.

The Spirit was likewise involved in the mission to the Gentiles. Thus, while the believers were ministering and fasting, the Holy Spirit said, "Set apart for Me Barnabas and Saul for the work to which I have called them" (Acts 13:2). The congregation obediently set aside those so designated, and "being sent out by the Holy Spirit" they went on their way (v. 4).

The disciples were subsequently guided by the Spirit as to where they might serve. They were "forbidden by the Holy Spirit to speak the word in Asia" (Acts 16:6) and so attempted to pass to Bithynia. But again "the Spirit of Jesus" disallowed their intention (v. 7). They pressed on to Troas, where they had a vision of a Macedonian man pleading that they come over to help him and—concluding this to be God's leading—they did so (vv. 8–10). This unique reference to the Spirit of Jesus is probably to accent the role of the Spirit as the representative of Jesus. In this instance, it was to direct the disciples to their field of labor.

33 Life in the Spirit

The precept that life in the Spirit is corporate in nature is reflected in the notion of "fellowship in the Spirit" (Phil. 2:1). Paul likewise reminds his readers that "there is one body and one Spirit" (Eph. 4:4). Believers are linked together through a common bond of the Spirit.

So, while Paul admonishes his readers to be of like mind with Christ (Phil. 2:2), it was the Spirit who bound them together and enabled them to be of one mind. Although Paul knew full well that there would be legitimate areas of disagreement, he advocated allegiance to the one Lord. He understood corporate life as a corrective on individual excess, personal bias, and parochial interest.

Paul urges his readers to be *filled* with the Spirit (Eph. 5:18). There is no comparable injunction to be *baptized* by the Spirit, which appears as an initial act of the Spirit by which the believer is regenerated (1 Cor. 12:13). Paul uses the present, continuous tense for being filled, so as to imply "keep on being filled." This would seem to exclude the notion of a once-and-for-all experience with the fullness of the Spirit.

It also suggests degrees of Christian experience in which the believer is either more or less yielded to the Spirit. Such differences ought not to result in pride or separation. Paul turns immediately to an expression of corporate praise and worship (Eph. 5:19–20) as a proper conclusion to his thoughts on the fullness of the Spirit. The Spirit-filled life is nothing if it is not life together.

The apostle has hardly concluded his emphasis on the unity in Christ than he launches into a discussion of the variety of gifts (Eph. 4:11–13). Paul had a great deal to say about gifts, sometimes resulting from their misuse but even then to describe their proper use. "But one and the same Spirit works all these things, distributing to each one individually just as He wills" (1 Cor. 12:11).

There ought to be no boasting as to which gift one has or how well he exercises it. The gifts are provided to edify the body. This is the way that the Spirit serves the corporate fellowship, by imparting desire to serve and the means to serve and rejoicing with those who serve.

There is also a personal dimension to the Spirit's work, all we have said about its corporate nature notwithstanding. Paul wrote to the brethren at Rome that they be as "a minister of Christ Jesus to the Gentiles, ministering as a priest the gospel of God, that my offering of the Gentiles might become acceptable, sanctified by the Holy Spirit" (Rom. 15:16). Likewise, the apostle urged "by the mercies of God . . . present your bodies a living and holy sacrifice, acceptable to God, which is your spiritual service of worship" (Rom. 12:1). Thereby, those who minister and those to whom they ministered might be sanctified by the Spirit.

We sense that the idea of sanctification is closely associated with being acceptable. According to Guthrie, "The standard of sanctification is a holiness acceptable to God, that is, a holiness in line with the Spirit's own character. The process of making holy is, therefore, peculiarly characteristic of the Spirit's activities."[20] This is a sanctifying process in which the Spirit more carefully tunes one's life to the perfect will of God.

Since we have already touched on the role of the Spirit in illuminating the disciple as to the things of God, we need only remind ourselves of it on this occasion. The Spirit recalls the past, elucidates the present, and reaches into the future, so that the person of God may be thoroughly furnished to perform the service of God.

We have also labored the idea of liberation as associated with the Spirit's work, although in an earlier connection. "It was for freedom that Christ set us free; therefore keep standing firm and do not be subject again to a yoke of slavery" (Gal. 5:1). Thus Paul warned those tempted by the Judaizers, adding the admonition to "walk by the Spirit, and you will not carry out the desire of the flesh" (v. 16). Walk between the snares of legalism on the one side and license on the other by recourse to the Spirit—for where the Spirit is, there is liberty.

It likewise comes as no surprise that the Spirit is prone to guide the ways of those who attend to His leading. We saw this with the mission to the Gentiles. We see it again with prayer life (Rom. 8:26–27). He helps the disciple in his weakness, not knowing how to pray effectively, by interceding on his behalf. Guthrie elaborates: "There is nothing mechanical about this, as if the Spirit's work in prayer proceeds wholly independently of the individual's own mind. It is rather that the Spirit in some way impresses his own mind on the believer so that what he asks is in accordance with the will of God."[21]

---

20. *Ibid.*, p. 554.
21. *Ibid.*, p. 558.

We naturally think of power in relationship to the Spirit's work, and the idea of spiritual power for personal advantage was alien to biblical teaching. When Simon thought to purchase the power to bestow the Holy Spirit, Peter declared: "You have no part or portion in this matter, for your heart is not right before God" (Acts 8:21). Such power as was allowed the disciple to preach the gospel was of greater significance, and such miracles as occurred were meant to attest to the truth of the preached word.

Corporate and individual life in the Spirit were one if not the same thing. One must learn what it means to experience life together and life alone as two aspects of the normal Christian life. The believer was meant to grow in the faith, leaving behind childish ways for the mature life of responsible service. To this end the Spirit bent every effort, so that all things might be said "to work together for good to those who love God, to those who are called according to His purpose" (Rom. 8:28).

The line between belief and disbelief is drawn by whether we confess Christ as Lord. ". . . no one speaking by the Spirit of God says, 'Jesus is accursed'; and no one can say, 'Jesus is Lord,' except by the Holy Spirit" (1 Cor. 12:3). Here the earliest Christians took their stand under the banner of Christ, enabled by the Spirit. From here they also understood their mission. Michael Green writes: "Empowered by that Spirit, and bearing witness to the crucified and risen Jesus, the early Christians and succeeding generations alike have found hard hearts softened, strong men brought to repentance, sceptics coming to faith, and people of all ages, backgrounds and classes coming to taste the salvation of the messianic community, and being born into the very family of God."[22]

Summary

We have selected four biblical vantage points from which to view the saga of the Spirit: Sinai, with the giving of the covenant; Zion, with the institution of the monarchy; the rivers of Babylon, with the captivity; and Calvary, with the dawn of the messianic age. As the saga unfolded, we saw the Spirit first in the role of liberator, then as the agent of the theocracy, followed by attendant to the messianic travail, and finally as superintendent of the messianic mission. Each episode may be said to contribute to the whole, so that we are left with a

---

22. Michael Green, *I Believe in the Holy Spirit*, p. 75.

general portrait of the Spirit as One who brings to successful conclusion the redemptive purposes of God.

There are also threads which can be traced backward to the beginning. We have in mind such obvious references to the Holy Spirit as the giver of life and liberator of the spirit. But we also consider the more subtle references, as when Paul requires that "things be done properly and in an orderly manner" (1 Cor. 14:40), as one would expect of the Spirit who brought order out of chaos.

The final episode in the saga of the Spirit was not simply another chapter of roughly equal importance with those which preceded, but the fulfillment of what the others taken together were the preparation. This was the eagerly awaited consolation of Israel and gathering of the Gentiles. This was the messianic age and the age of the Spirit.

However, this epoch differed from the traditional Hebrew perspective in that it inaugurated the messianic age without bringing it to a consummation. As such, it resembles an overlap of the present age and that to come. This results in a peculiar tension between what has already been introduced with the advent of Christ and the promise of His return.

To this notion of overlap, we add the confidence that Christ, in His death and resurrection, has won the decisive victory. This resembles, in Oscar Cullmann's thinking, D-Day during World War II, while the final conquest of evil awaits V-Day. It is true that Christ now sits at the right hand of the Father, and that the church is charged with making the world aware of this fact.

Cullmann concludes that: "The church is the place where the Spirit, this feature of the eschatological period, is already at work as 'earnest,' as 'firstfruits.'"[23] The Spirit is associated peculiarly with the church, in instilling it with life, strengthening its hand, and assailing the bastions of evil that stand against it. But the Spirit is also active in an uninhibited fashion characteristic of the anticipation for the messianic age.

We elaborated on the role of the Spirit in regard to the early days of the messianic era, first by turning to the synoptic Gospels. Here we dealt with the disclosure of John the Baptist, the birth of Jesus, Simeon's prediction, the baptism of Jesus, His temptation, the announcement

23. Cullmann, *Christ and Time*, p. 155.

of His public ministry, and the exorcism of demons. We saw how the Spirit urged Jesus into the wilderness and returned Him after the trial to Galilee—as did He oversee the entire messianic ministry from beginning to end.

We paused to look at some of the particular observations of the apostle John, before continuing with the significance of the passion account. We particularly noted John's comments concerning the need for a new birth, the giving of the Spirit without measure, the life-giving character of Jesus' words, and the soul-satisfying nature of His ministry. These observations were reminiscent of earlier accounts of the Spirit, but focused with regard to the messianic mission of Jesus.

The passion account next invited our attention, as we pondered the meaning of the passion for subsequent generations of believers. We also attempted a response in terms of the Spirit's work in glorifying Christ, in enabling the disciples to witness to Christ, in guiding into all truth, and in disclosing what was to come. To this we added a final ministry, associated not with the believer but the unbeliever, that of convicting the world of sin, righteousness, and judgment.

We then considered the acts of the apostles as the acts of the Spirit. We reviewed how Pentecost qualified as the concluding act of the ascension, involved the pouring out of the Spirit on all flesh, was accompanied by extraordinary signs, and promised the Spirit on condition of repentance and identification with the messianic community. This led us to review, in addition, the references to Agabus' prophecies, the controversy concerning what obligations to lay on the Gentile converts, and the mission to the Gentiles. We observed the peculiar role of the Spirit in each of these instances.

Thinking it not necessary to labor the subject much further, the concluding discussion consisted of the role of the Spirit with regard to life together and life alone, the corporate and personal dimensions of life in the Spirit. In the former case, we noted the common bond that believers enjoy in the Spirit, the admonition to be filled with the Spirit, and the variety of gifts. We considered, in the latter instance, the notion of sanctification, illumination, liberation, guidance, and empowering. These ideas were meant to be only suggestive and to lay some groundwork for the more systematic discussion to come later on.

Suffice it to say that the Spirit had instituted the new age promised in the prophets, now fulfilled in Christ. The Spirit oversaw the various developments from the inception of Jesus, throughout His mission, and with the construction of the messianic community. We conclude the biblical narrative with the church firmly entrenched on alien soil, waging conflict with the enemy, and sustained by the Spirit. The time of the end remained uncertain, but the outcome was already assured. The Spirit who had begun a good work would certainly see it to its successful conclusion.

PART 2

Systematic Theology

According to Gordon Kaufman, "A systematic theology is essentially an attempt to state as concisely and straightforwardly as possible a theological perspective."[1] It follows a logical order supplied by its author. Although it attempts to deal with the topic comprehensively, in so doing it leaves many of the details, "however important, for exposition and discussion elsewhere."

Systematic theology does not simply repeat what has already been said on a subject. Neither should it ignore what has been said. Each succeeding effort at systematic theology amounts to a prologue to what follows. What evolves is the product of the individual contributor, drawn from such sources as he has at hand, as seen through his particular perspective, and as it relates the issues he sees as being more pressing.

Systematic theology tends to reduce the ambiguity that goes with biblical theology and as relates to its historical setting. This approach also replaces the natural order associated with historical episodes with a reconstruction of its own making. It is likewise more comprehensive, even though it may not go into detailed exposition of the biblical text.

1. Gordon Kaufman, *Systematic Theology: A Historical Perspective*, p. x.

Method is an important feature of systematic theology. The method need not be stated, but it is there to be observed and critiqued. How has the writer generated and developed his doctrine? Has he carried through the theological method consistently? What are the strengths and weaknesses of his approach as compared with others? These and similar questions can be properly put to a systematic theology.

It may also be asked whether or not the system is faithful to the biblical revelation. Systematic theology obviously employs words and ideas not expressly found in Scripture, in order to state "as concisely and straightforwardly as possible a theological perspective." That is par for the course, but its author ought not to use this as an excuse for introducing thoughts extraneous to, much less deviant from, biblical teaching.

We begin our study with the preliminary question as to *who* the Spirit is before undertaking an investigation into what He does. We will pick up the operation of the Spirit with the world beloved of God, before moving on to the discussion of life together—the church; life alone—the disciple; and the powers—a consideration of the last things. This provides us with a generally comprehensive overview from which we may explore some of the more inviting aspects.[2]

---

2. Among the more recent doctrinal studies on the Holy Spirit are Frederick Brunner, *A Theology of the Holy Spirit;* Eric Fife, *The Holy Spirit;* W. Curry Maves, *The Holy Spirit;* Eduard Schweizer, *The Holy Spirit*. Jonathan Edwards' *The Distinguishing Marks of a Work of the Spirit* is a classic work in the field. Also worthy of note are Charles Ryrie, *The Holy Spirit;* and John Walvoord, *The Holy Spirit*.

5

Identity of the Spirit

Dietrich Bonhoeffer reminds us that the proper question we put to Christ is "Who are you?" rather than "How are you?"[1] We could press the same distinction with regard to the Holy Spirit. The question "Who?" probes the identity of the Holy Spirit; the question "How?" leads us prematurely into the operation of the Spirit.

34 Person

Many think of the Spirit in impersonal terms, as a power or influence. They pray that the Spirit be poured out, as if to fill a bucket with water. Or they call for the Spirit to turn back the forces of evil, one force to overwhelm the other. Even their choice of an impersonal pronoun to designate the Spirit (*It* rather than *He*) discloses the fallacy in their thinking.

"Who?" is the initial question to ask when we come to a person. "Who?" respects the integrity of the other, without which we cannot hope to establish his identity. It is, as Bonhoeffer correctly states, the recognition of transcendence in the other, our respect for all that is

1. Dietrich Bonhoeffer, *Christ the Center*, p. 31.

distinctive to him. This helps resist the temptation to reduce the other to some preconceived categories, to define him in our own terms and for our own purposes.

"How?" strips away the identity of the other. It starts with immanence, with what we perceive of another or can determine about him. It denies the distance that inevitably exists between persons. And, in the process, it makes the other an extension of one's self, without an identity of his own.

We may argue that the Spirit is not to be thought of as "person" in strictly the same sense as we refer to one another as persons. We allow that neither the Greek *hypostasis* nor the Latin *persona* were meant to mean a distinct person, as we would imply from the common English word. The latter, taken at face value, would result in tritheism, while the former intended to express the rich diversity of the *one* God. But, qualifications notwithstanding, the Holy Spirit must be thought of in personal rather than impersonal terms. Only the question "Who?" and not "How?" will suffice. We must take a resolute stand at this point or the whole enterprise will assuredly fail.

Our insistence on the personal nature of the Holy Spirit is part of a larger concern for the supernatural design of the Christian faith, rightly understood. Either the world is essentially impersonal in character, man being the exception—or personal, where man joins other personal beings. Within limits, we may learn to manipulate an impersonal universe to our own advantage, either through scientific design or magic (if we are disposed to think the latter can accomplish our purpose). But one cannot manipulate the Almighty or His righteous design. This suggests how much may be at stake in the issue set before us: whether we live in a personal or impersonal world, related to a personal agent or an impersonal force.

Having posed the proper question "Who?" we must wait in silence until the answer is given to us. We cannot supply the answer. It comes from the other, by way of revelation instead of intuition. The answer begins with "I am" rather than "You are."

This silence must not be confused with the silence that mystics delight in. One cannot dwell on his navel, as with Buddhism, but waits with respect for the response of another. It is not an inner search but a reach beyond oneself. This silent approach discovers self not in isolation but in relationship to the one whom we allow to speak.

Man fails to know himself because he does not know himself as created in the image of God or existing in the presence of God. The identity he assumes in isolation from God and alienation from others is not his true identity—so that to reach beyond himself is the only course to self-awareness, as well as understanding who is the Spirit.

35 Spirit

The answer to "Who?" comes to us in several forms, but we shall first accent what they have in common. Whenever we ask "Who are You?" the common element in the reply is "Spirit." He is the *Spirit* of God, the *Spirit* of the Lord, the *Spirit* of Christ, the Holy *Spirit*, and the *Spirit* of truth. Even the term *Paraclete* implies what it does not make explicit, that He is the *Spirit* of advocacy and consolation.

Spirit refers to "wind" and "breath," although the relation between the two is subject to conjecture. Did the Hebrew dwell first upon an invisible force as expressed in the wind and subsequently tie in the breath as evidence of life? The reverse? Or did the ideas develop alongside each other? We cannot say, but can only set aside the question and proceed with what can be known from the evidence at hand.

The associated ideas of Spirit as wind and breath are brought out in Jesus' comment to Nicodemus: "The wind blows where it wishes and you hear the sound of it, but do not know where it comes from and where it is going; so is everyone who is born of the Spirit" (John 3:8). To this we may add the words of Job: "The Spirit of God has made me,/And the breath of the Almighty gives me life" (Job 33:4).

We learn from such pointed references that the Spirit is sovereign. The Spirit, like the wind, operates as He wills. If the wind chooses to blow in one direction, we cannot change it to suit our purposes. At best, we can adjust to the prevailing wind or wait until it changes direction. Or we can struggle with the wind's impeding of our resolute progress. The Spirit similarly shapes our course of action, first gusting from one direction, only to shift to another; at one time a soft breeze and another reaching gale fury.

To put the matter differently, the Spirit is no man's slave but every man's servant. He serves best by denying each a monopoly on His time and energies. The Spirit exercises a sovereign will not selectively but impartially for the welfare of all those who recognize His prerogative and seek to benefit from His ministry.

The Spirit is likewise inscrutable, except for the results of His labor. We hear the sound of the wind, "but do not know where it comes from and where it is going." The way of the Spirit appears unpredictable and more than a little threatening, as if we were never quite sure what He has been up to or may be expected to do next.

This inscrutability is by design. God's ways transcend those of man's as the heaven is higher than the earth. Nor is man's finiteness the only problem with fathoming the purposes of God; his sin blinds him to the pattern of God's redemptive activity. Were man aggressively searching for God's will, the way of the Spirit would probably appear less inscrutable than otherwise.

Jesus further portrayed the Spirit as giving life to the recipient: ". . . so is everyone who is born of the Spirit." This reminds us of the passage concerning Ezekiel's valley of dry bones: "And I looked, and behold, sinews were on them, and flesh grew, and skin covered them; but there was no breath in them. Then He said to me, 'Prophesy to the breath, prophesy, son of man, and say to the breath, "Thus says the Lord God, 'Come from the four winds, O breath, and breathe on these slain, that they come to life'"'" (Ezek. 37:8–9). Once they had received the breath of life, they stood on their feet, a great army (v. 10).

In a similar vein, Edwin Hatch wrote as lyrics for a popular hymn,

> Breathe on me, Breath of God,
> Fill me with life anew,
> That I may love what Thou dost love,
> And do what Thou wouldst do.

The Spirit brings life in the first place, and renews it as necessary.

This already implies the indispensable nature of the Spirit. Jesus reinforced this fact by declaring, "Truly, truly, I say to you, unless one is born again, he cannot see the kingdom of God" (John 3:3). There are ever so many conditions we can do without, but the Spirit is not one of these. Life withers on the vine unless it draws from the bountiful resources of the Spirit.

There are few better places to meditate on the significance of the Spirit than in the Judean hill country during the heat of the summer months. The sun beats down relentlessly through the day, taking an almost imperceptible toll on those carrying on their daily routine. Then, at late afternoon, a breeze picks up, as a matter of course, to refresh the weary sojourner and prepare him for the night's rest and a new round of activities the next morning. Such has been our experience with the Holy Spirit, without whom we would never negotiate the demands of life.

We conclude the Spirit to be sovereign—operating as He wills; inscrutable—unpredictable and more than a little threatening; life-giving—the source of life and life abundant; and indispensable—there is no alternative. We might derive more from the notion of Spirit, but certainly not less. Whenever we see the branches sway or bend with the wind, or we draw a deep breath to relish its renewing qualities, these experiences remind us of such enduring qualities of the Spirit.

36 Spirit of God

We want to carry over what has been said about the Spirit in general to the "Spirit of God." Whatever else this extended designation is meant to imply, it at least means to distinguish the Spirit of God from any other use of the term *spirit*—thus to implicate all that we know of God's character and purposes.

Paul Jewett suggests that the Spirit of God, as employed in the Old Testament, never clearly sets forth a trinitarian distinction between Father and Son. He adds that "the Spirit of God is the divine nature viewed as vital energy."[2] One might debate the issue, but to little profit. Jewett's point is that the Spirit of God incorporates the nature of God, especially as it relates to the effective exercise of His sovereign power.

The sovereign character of the Almighty is most in evidence when we make reference to *God*. We are transported into a throne room, before the majesty of the King of Kings. Our heads are bowed, our eyes cast low, and we wait for His Word to come by way of some attendant.

Some have thought that Jesus' subsequent reference to the Almighty as *Father* would somehow reduce this accent on sovereignty, but this is not the case. Joachim Jeremias puts the record straight: "Whenever the word 'father' is used for a deity in this connection [of Near Eastern thought] it implies fatherhood in the sense of unconditional and inevocable authority."[3] His authority is unconditional—without imposed limitation, and irrevocable—without time of duration.

The psalmist captures the sovereignty of God for us: "O clap your hands, all peoples; shout to God with the voice of joy. For the Lord Most High is to be feared, a great King over all the earth" (Ps. 47:1–2). We ought therefore to acknowledge Him, and no other.

---

2. Paul Jewett, "Holy Spirit," *The Zondervan Pictorial Encyclopaedia of the Bible* (Merrill Tenney, ed.), III, p. 184.

3. Joachim Jeremias, *The Central Message*, p. 39.

The idea of divine transcendence is closely related to that of sovereignty. Karl Barth reminds us that God "stands *above* us and also above our highest and deepest feelings, strivings, intuitions, above the products, even the most sublime, of the human spirit."[4] He is the wholly Other or the fundamentally Other, of whom we could know nothing if He did not choose to reveal it.

Karl Barth wrote in protest against a century and more of characteristic neglect of the awesome "otherness" of God. The Almighty had become so associated with our feelings, strivings, intuitions, and products that He lost any identity of His own. Barth's commentary on Romans helped awaken a complacent church to the reality of a transcendent and sovereign God.

Only when we have assured ourselves of God's transcendence can we and must we turn to consider His immanence. Barth discovered the proper order during his early years of ministry, the necessity of proceeding from one concept to the other once the earlier debate had subsided. So, while the designation "Spirit of God" preserves the "otherness" of God, it has in proportion to references of God in general a greater emphasis on His nearness and availability. (This is the best context in which to appreciate Jewett's characterization of the Spirit of God as "the divine nature viewed as vital energy.")

This accent on divine immanence is not peculiar to any single designation for the Spirit, but common to them all. We are reminded that God is active in our midst and on our behalf. We are also called upon to assume our proper responsibilities, seeing that God invites us to join with Him in a ministry of reconciliation.

There are reported to be nearly ninety direct references to the Spirit of God in the Old Testament alone. They point to the work of a transcendent and sovereign deity who not only created the world but sustains it by His power. This is our Father's world, qualifications not to the contrary, as the presence of the Spirit of God testifies.

37 Spirit of the Lord

There comes a subtle shift of emphasis when one moves from the "Spirit of God" to the "Spirit of the Lord." This is best illustrated first, and discussed thereafter.[5] "God" announced to Noah that He had

---

4. Karl Barth, *Dogmatics in Outline*, p. 37.

5. I am indebted to Rabbi Yechiel Eckstein for his suggestion as to the basic differentiation between the "Spirit of God" and the "Spirit of the Lord."

weighed the wickedness of man and was prepared to bring a great flood as judgment (Gen. 6:12–13, 17). However, "the Lord" directed Noah and his household to enter into the ark and safety (Gen. 7:1). The former accents the justice of God, and the latter emphasizes His mercy.

We have a similar instance with Abraham's taking Isaac to be offered as a sacrifice. It is said that "God" tested Abraham, but the angel of "the Lord" stayed his hand from the sacrifice (Gen. 22:1, 11). The accent again shifts from justice to mercy.

Frederick Faber's lyrics seem especially apropos:

> There's a wideness in God's mercy,
> Like the wideness of the sea;
> There's a kindness in His justice,
> Which is more than liberty.

How extensive *is* God's mercy? It resembles the sea, which stretches away beyond the horizon, and it permeates His justice through and through.

Mercy is the outstanding quality of God reflected in the "Spirit of the Lord," and it is associated with forgiveness. God does not wish that any perish, but that all come to repentance. He gazes toward the far country, anticipating that the prodigal may see the errors of his ways and return to a compassionate and forgiving Father.

Mercy is also related to the forbearance of God. The psalmist observes that "The Lord is gracious and merciful; Slow to anger and great in lovingkindness" (Ps. 145:8). Accordingly, the prophets warn us not to presume on His forbearance and let our evil course run its distance.

The mercy of God is especially revealed in His covenants with man and the sweep of concern associated with those covenants. Thus God promised to bless Abraham and make him a blessing to all mankind. The covenant is the compassionate offer of God to those who deserve only reproach. Mercy eventuates in help, as when the Almighty declared Himself ready to liberate those in bondage to Egypt (Exod. 3:7–8). Mercy is never sentiment alone but action on behalf of another, so that we can say that those who are merciful assist their fellowmen, and those who assist are (allowing for lesser motivations) the merciful.

The psalmist concludes that "Thou, Lord, art good, and ready to forgive, And abundant in lovingkindness to all who call upon Thee" (Ps. 86:5). This suggests the great resources of divine mercy. We ought not to imagine our needs are ever too great for His provision.

As we recall that Jesus washed the feet of His disciples, we view this as a paradigm of mercy. He came not to be ministered to, but to minister to others; not to demand His right, but to serve the needs of others. Thus He taught, "Blessed are the merciful, for they shall receive mercy" (Matt. 5:7).

"Who are You?" we asked. The answer came not at once, nor is it yet complete. But what we have heard has begun to fill in the identity of the Spirit. The reply, "Spirit of God," reminded us to associate with the Spirit the character and purposes of God, especially such as relate to His sovereign and transcendent character. But this is not to exclude His availability—which is a common feature in reference to "the Spirit."

The further response, "Spirit of the Lord," shifted our attention to His bountiful mercy. He wants to share the bounty of His storehouses with all, so that He hastens to forgive, bears with man's disobedience, offers His grace by way of covenants, and extends His grace in merciful assistance—all from resources that boggle the mind. His hand is stretched out to man continually.

"Who are You?" The sovereign Spirit of God. "Who are You?" The servant Spirit of the Lord—not two, but one expression of divine justice and mercy at work in the world. While preserving the transcendence of God, the Spirit especially reveals the presence and availability of the Almighty to those who seek His will and desire to serve Him.

38 Holy Spirit

Scripture takes the greatest of care in accurately identifying the Spirit. Some years ago, my Chinese students decided to bestow on me a proper Chinese name. The process took several days, while they attempted to determine what would correspond with my English name, fit well the Chinese format, and (perhaps most important) express my character as they perceived it. The name attributed to the Holy Spirit should be viewed with a similar serious attempt to convey His nature and work.

The New Testament has virtually a monopoly on the use of the designation "Holy Spirit." Only three references, two in the same context, occur elsewhere in the canonical writings. The first reference is found in Psalm 51, attributed to David upon confession of his sin with Bathsheba. The author pleads: "Create in me a clean heart, O God; and renew a right spirit within me. Cast me not away from thy presence; and take not thy holy spirit from me" (vv. 10–11, KJV). He concludes with the importance of a grateful and contrite heart as opposed to the intrinsic value of burnt offerings. Hence the psalm creates a paradigm for the penitent person or people, as they turn from sin to experience God's restoration.

The remaining references are found in Isaiah 63:10–11. Here the covenant people are portrayed as having rebelled and grieved God's Holy Spirit. The passage recalls to mind that they were called to be a holy people and asks that God will forgive and redeem them from their plight.

The New Testament, less than a quarter the length of the Old Testament, contains more than three times as many references to the Spirit. More important for our present consideration, it abounds with references to the *Holy* Spirit—so much so that we would be aware of making the transition from one testament to the other on this ground alone.

The question of continuity and discontinuity between the testaments is critical to any theological endeavor. Some have stressed the continuity of the biblical text, others the discontinuity. All have to face the task of how best to relate the two.

Michael Ramsey observes: "The words 'Holy Spirit' describe a large part of Christianity. It has always been the belief of Christians that God revealed himself in a unique way in the story of Jesus, and this belief has given to Christianity its character as an historical religion. But Christians also believe that this revelation is corroborated in experience through a divine power in saintly lives in the subsequent centuries."[6] This is to say that the term has come to have a distinctively trinitarian cast. What might have earlier been described as little more than a personification of God has developed into a distinct identity (hypostasis, substance).

The significance of Ramsey's comment is not to be taken lightly. Were it not for the trinitarian cast of the New Testament, the designation *Holy Spirit* could at least be subsumed under some more major consideration, if not delegated to an appendage. It is with the Christian's conviction concerning Jesus Christ and the subsequent ministry of the Spirit to the church that the Holy Spirit takes on such distinctive importance.

It seems evident, even at this early point in our discussion, that we have uncovered both a continuity and discontinuity with the Holy Spirit as relates to a transition between the testaments. There is a continuity in the context of a call to holiness, and the agency of God is bringing that

6. Michael Ramsey, *Holy Spirit*, p. 9.

about. There is also a discontinuity that results from the messianic advent and subsequent provision for these last days. Only a blend of the two can fit the mosaic pieces together.

39 Call to Holiness

We are concerned here not with holiness *per se*, but the *call* to holiness. Donald Bloesch expounds on the subject: "According to the Bible only God is holy in the full sense of this word. His holiness is his power, majesty, righteousness, and love. Such holiness has the character of depth and mystery and elicits reverence, awe, and fascination. While God's holiness is realized in its fullness on the plane of humanity only in Jesus Christ, all believers participate to some degree in it."[7] God instructed Moses to declare to the people, "You shall be holy, for I the Lord your God am holy" (Lev. 19:2). The refrain was picked up time and again throughout the biblical text (Lev. 20:7, 26; Eph. 1:4; 1 Peter 1:16).

Only God is holy "in the full sense of the word," and for that reason there can be only one *Holy* Spirit. The Holy Spirit may be distinguished by His purpose. He purposes what is right and good, without qualification or exception. We say "without qualification" because (unlike man) His motives are not mixed; we say "without exception" because it is not this way at one time and another way some other time.

Jesus' disciples were troubled with the thought of His leaving them (John 14). He confronted them with the thought that this would provide Him with the opportunity to intercede on their behalf and send the Holy Spirit to them. All of this reflected the good purposes of God, that the servant of God be thoroughly equipped for his ministry.

The Holy Spirit may also be differentiated by His power. Paul lamented: "For the good that I wish, I do not do; but I practice the very evil that I do not wish" (Rom. 7:19). So could say we all. We aspire and fail; we resist but fall prey, in contrast to the resolute power of the Holy Spirit who triumphs over every obstacle.

Jesus promised His disciples that they would "receive power when the Holy Spirit has come upon you" (Acts 1:8). They had previously been intimidated by the course of events and had retreated in fear, but the Holy Spirit would make them bold to testify of the Lord, as illustrated by the apostle Peter when he stood to give an account of what had transpired at Pentecost.

---

7. Donald Bloesch, *Essentials of Evangelical Theology*, II, p. 31.

This suggests that we may likewise distinguish the Holy Spirit by His ready availability to those who call upon Him. Some can help but will not be bothered; others would like to be of help but lack the ability. The Holy Spirit both can and will assist us, regardless of our station in life or what we have to offer in return. We err in thinking that it is necessary to beg the Holy Spirit to help us. He is not the least bit reluctant, whether in regard to what we consider things of great import or in the trivial matters of life. In fact, He is quicker to respond than we are to call upon Him or allow His help.

The Holy Spirit differs from the human spirit in all these connections: with regard to purpose, power, and availability. This underscores the meaning of mankind's "total depravity," which does not mean that man is as bad as he possibly could be or that each person behaves as badly as the next, but that the human spirit falls short *at every point* of the holiness of God.

The people of God are no exception to the rule. They, too, play the prodigal. They rebel against the Almighty, preferring the far country to their Father's home. But the Holy Spirit is not content to leave them in this state. He calls them home, and He calls them to holiness.

40 The Holy One

Peter charged his audience with disowning "the Holy and Righteous One" (Acts 3:14). Ramsey reminded us that it has been the belief that God revealed Himself "in a unique way in the story of Jesus" that "has given to Christianity its character as an historical religion." Other faiths share with Christianity the belief in a personal God; other faiths will even allow that God revealed Himself in Jesus in a way similar to other religious figures—but only the Christian faith attributes a genuinely unique revelation of God in Christ. Here the ways part, and here we pick up the ongoing course of the Holy Spirit.

Karl Barth rightly asserts that "the second article ['I believe in Jesus Christ'] does not just follow the first ['I believe in God, the Father'], nor does it just precede the third ['I believe in the Holy Spirit']; but it is the fountain of light by which the other two are lit."[8] Our particular concern is with how the second article *lights* the third: how belief in Jesus Christ effects belief in the Holy Spirit. In the simplest of terms, the Holy Spirit gives us Jesus, and Jesus gives us the Holy Spirit.

8. Karl Barth, *Dogmatics in Outline*, p. 65.

The Holy Spirit gives us Jesus. We read of an angel announcing to Mary: "The Holy Spirit will come upon you, and the power of the Most High will overshadow you; and for that reason the holy offspring shall be called the Son of God" (Luke 1:35). We read further that at Jesus' baptism the Spirit of God descended upon Him as a dove, while a voice from heaven affirmed, "Thou art My beloved Son, in Thee I am well-pleased" (Luke 3:22). Jesus, being "full of the Holy Spirit, returned from the Jordan and was led about by the Spirit in the wilderness," there "being tempted by the devil" (Luke 4:1–2). Jesus announced His ministry with the text from Isaiah, "The Spirit of the Lord is upon Me, Because He anointed Me to preach the gospel to the poor. He has sent Me to proclaim release to the captives, and recovery of sight to the blind, to set free those who are downtrodden, to proclaim the favorable year of the Lord" (Luke 4:18–19). Luke adds that Jesus had "returned to Galilee in the power of the Spirit" (Luke 4:14), as if to suggest that His entire subsequent ministry was with the direction of and under the power of the Holy Spirit. Jesus undertook a ministry which would take Him to the cross and beyond the cross—with the resurrection, ascension, and session, and anticipation of His return in triumph. All of this was by the good graces of the Holy Spirit.

Jesus gives us the Holy Spirit. The Master promised, "When the Helper comes, whom I will send to you from the Father, that is the Spirit of truth, who proceeds from the Father, He will bear witness of Me" (John 15:26). He asserted again, ". . . I will send Him to you" (John 16:7). The coming of the Holy Spirit will, in a manner of speaking, transfer the work of the kingdom from Jesus' shoulders to those of His disciples (of this we shall say more once we have been able to tie together the present subject).

Both Paul (Rom. 8:9) and Peter (1 Peter 1:11) refer to the "Spirit of Christ." Each instance has to do with the indwelling presence of the Holy Spirit, and both alike remind us of the rich association of the Holy Spirit with Christ. Neither would have been possible were it not for the fact that the Holy Spirit gave us Jesus, and Jesus gave us the Holy Spirit. Jesus expressly promised that the Spirit would bring to mind His own teaching (John 14:26), while guiding the disciples "into all the truth" (John 16:13).

41 The Saints

We recall Ramsey's final word that "Christians also believe that this revelation is corroborated in experience through a divine power in saintly lives in the subsequent centuries." The believers experienced the Holy Spirit as being present in their midst, as Jesus promised He would be. They believed in the church as an extension of their faith in the Holy Spirit. That does not imply that this knowledge of the Holy Spirit was something strictly new. The Holy Spirit was, as we have observed, the Spirit of Christ. What genuinely counted was belonging to Christ. The Holy Spirit would then minister the things of Christ to them as a matter of course.

Neither do we mean to suggest that one believes in the church in the same way one believes in the Holy Spirit. One believes in the church *because* he believes in the Holy Spirit. In one sense, the church is not the object of our faith but the result. We believe in the Holy Spirit for bringing into being and sustaining the church.

This is an involved subject, and each qualification seems to require another. Hans Küng reminds us that—although God calls individuals to faith—"without the community which believes, the individual would not attain faith. . . . They have their faith through the community, which as a believing community proclaims the message to them and provokes the response of faith in them."[9] Therefore, the church is not simply the result of faith, but the agency God employs in soliciting faith.

We are only scratching the surface of the subject at this time, but can allow it to drop for the time being. Suffice it to say that the Holy Spirit in Christian thought is associated not only with the Holy One but with those called to be saints. The designation draws upon an earlier association with the call of God's people to holiness, and extends this with reference to Christ—as the One who seeks out and saves the lost—and the church—which embraces them in pastoral care.

The early church likely found it quite natural to employ the designation "Holy Spirit." They had precedent from the Old Testament. That precedent had to do with the falling away and restoration of the people of God. The message of John the Baptist and Jesus after him seemed to fit the theological framework. There was a continuity from the times of preparation to those of fulfillment.

But this was not a continuity accepted by the Hebrew people in general. John stated it for the record: "He came to His own, and those who were His own did not receive Him. But as many as received Him, to them He gave the right to become children of God, even to those who

9. Hans Küng, *The Church*, p. 33.

believe in His name" (John 1:11–12). Many of those we might have expected to be receptive were not, but other less likely candidates (the irreligious and immoral among the Jews, along with the Gentiles) responded appreciatively. Thus there was forged a new messianic community out of bits and pieces of all sorts.

This was an amazing thing to witness, no less for the Jew than the Gentile. The Holy Spirit was blending together an odd mixture of people to render praise to the Almighty and serve His purposes. There were growing pains of the severest kind. Some turned back, rather than face the problems building on every hand. But some also pressed on, encouraged by the Holy Spirit to believe that God was at work, and that the powers and principalities could not prevail against so apparently fragile a community of faith.

We would be hard pressed to find a more appropriate name than the *Holy Spirit*. Why? Because it puts us immediately into the context of falling away and the call to holiness before the Almighty. Is there any further reason? Yes, because it calls our attention to the Holy One. It also directs us to the community of saints, those called out of every people to serve the Almighty. Who are You? The Holy Spirit, guardian of the holiness of God, troubler of the prodigal, consoler of the repentant. Who are You? Giver of Jesus and gift of Jesus. Distinct from all else, as to His holy zeal, mighty power, and ready availability—the Holy Spirit.

42 Paraclete

We take one final exploration into the identity of the Holy Spirit—with reference to the Paraclete and Spirit of truth. This takes us to five groups of sayings concerning the promise of the Holy Spirit in John's Gospel: 14:16–17, 25–26; 15:26–27; 16:5–11, 12–15. These passages have especially to do with the experience of the disciples after the departure of the Lord and before His return. They will allow us both to develop some ideas previously introduced and tie together some loose ends from prior discussion.

The term *Paraclete* is usually associated with the notion of an advocate in a court of law. However, the note of consolation appears unmistakable in this instance, as Ramsey observes: "It is, then, both as Advocate and as Comforter that the Spirit will aid the disciples."[10]

---

10. Ramsey, *Holy Spirit*, p. 104.

John reveals the purpose for his writing: "Many other signs therefore Jesus also performed in the presence of the disciples, which are not written in this book; but these have been written that you may believe that Jesus is the Christ, the Son of God; and that believing you may have life in His name" (John 20:30–31). The apostle approaches his task as if he were a trial lawyer, bent on establishing the case for his client.

Although John records the trial of Jesus before the High Priest and before Pilate, on reading the account one wonders whether it is not rather Caiaphas and the Roman governor who were actually on trial. Jesus taught that "in the way you judge, you will be judged; and by your standard of measure, it will be measured to you" (Matt. 7:2), and so it seems in the instances John recalls for us.

Moreover, the court atmosphere is not reserved for these occasions alone. It seems to permeate the text as John calls a long series of witnesses: John the Baptist, the Scripture, the words of Jesus, the works of Jesus, and the Father. John allows that there was much more that could have been said, were it needed and deemed advisable.

Was Christ on trial? So it would seem at first glance, but in a larger sense, the world was on trial. Jesus brought light, and people preferred darkness; Jesus brought truth, and the world opted for falsehood. In the judgment, all will be required to give account for what they have received. The greater the gift, the greater the accountability. Judgment hangs heavy throughout John's discourse.

There is another sense in which the disciples were on trial for their faith in Christ. John speaks to and for the suffering community, telling them of the consolation of the Holy Spirit. He reports the words of Jesus to the disciples: "In the world you have tribulation, but take courage; I have overcome the world" (John 16:33). He adds that the Holy Spirit is *another* Paraclete, to further encourage the disciples in their demanding encounter with the world.

To translate Paraclete as "Comforter" is to lose much in the process. The Holy Spirit would not only console but also strengthen the disciples with inner resolve and for aggressive witness. While the demands would be greater, the provision was more than adequate.

The distinction between the disciples and the world is made painfully evident. It is also evident, as writes George Johnston, "that this spirit is meant only for the disciples of Jesus and not for the *cosmos*. In the Gospel of John the *cosmos* is the object of divine love and saving grace; at the same time it is the realm of darkness and untruth."[11] It is

11. George Johnston, *The Spirit-Paraclete in the Gospel of John*, p. 31.

the world loved by God, and the object of Jesus' saving mission (John 3:16). But it is also the world which rejects the gracious offer of God through unbelief: "And this is the judgment, that the light is come into the world, and men loved the darkness rather than the light; for their deeds were evil" (John 3:19).

The disciples are not *of* this world, but they are *in* it. They abide in a tension between the world to come and the world that persists to this moment. They sustain the tension through the ministry of the Paraclete, given for such an age as this.

But the Holy Spirit ought not to be thought of as simply abiding in the community. He, too, is in the world, and this is what we meant earlier by saying that the Holy Spirit speaks *for* the suffering fellowship. He convicts the world of sin, righteousness, and judgment (John 16:8). The Holy Spirit as Advocate presses the case as if in a vigorous cross-examination of the witness. He "convicts the world" with regard to (or of) sin, because it had refused Christ. He lays bare the sin and awakens a consciousness of guilt.

The world's rejection of Christ resembles a divine probe of the conscience. We can always reason that our attitude or behavior toward another was somehow solicited by his or her attitude or behavior toward us. Or, to press the point further, to excuse our inability to act in loving constraint. Neither of these ploys work with regard to Christ. He was, as some have put it, "the man for others." Since He asked only to serve, there was no cause for us to have so despitefully used Him.

But more than this, He offered us God's aid in overcoming our hateful disposition and in strengthening our good intentions. Our rejection meant that we were content to let things go on the way they were, without regard for their effect on others. It was a refusal of God's grace to overcome our sin.

The Paraclete also convicts the world of righteousness because Jesus returned to His Father. The resurrection was God's stamp of approval on Jesus' life and work (Acts 2:22–24; Rom. 1:4); the ascension was His return in triumph. Some said of Jesus, "He ought to die" (John 19:7), but God decreed that He live. They charged Him as an evildoer (John 18:30), but God declared Him righteous.

It seemed to certain observers that Christians were turning the world upside down (Acts 17:6), while in reality they were putting it right side up. This seems ever so clear from the reversal of thought concerning the righteousness of Jesus. The Paraclete turns the world on its feet, so it can think clearly.

The Holy Spirit likewise convicts the world of judgment, because the ruler of this world is judged. ". . . he who does not believe has been judged *already* . . ." (John 3:18, italics added). Men are already lost, along with "the ruler of this world." If the matter was ever in doubt, Calvary settled it once and for all. The forces of evil are in retreat, and their end is certain.

The cosmos seems reassuring, at least from time to time. The sun rises and sets, and the order of events runs its course. It is easy to settle down to what others expect of us, and not to be concerned with what God has in mind. But it is easy only so long as we do not stop to consider that the world lies under the present, cosmic judgment of God. The power which rules—"the ruler of this world"—has been put on notice, as well as all of those who trust in him.

We conclude that the Paraclete serves to comfort the afflicted. He stands beside those who waver in the cause of Christ—to reassure, encourage, and enable—urging them to stand tall before their accusers, and shake off their uncertainties. He intercedes when they cannot seem to find the appropriate words to pray, and He undertakes when they seem to have come to the end of their possibilities.

But we observe that the Paraclete also afflicts the comfortable and disturbs the complacent with thoughts of sin, righteousness, and judgment. Recalling to them their disobedience to God's will and rejection of God's grace, He reminds them of the passing nature of the present world and the inevitability of the One who will come to judge. He likewise points out the great chasm between the disciples and the world, the hope of the one group and the utter hopelessness of the other.

43 Spirit of Truth

John recalls Jesus referring to the Holy Spirit as the "Spirit of truth," as if to bring out something missing in Jesus' discussion of the Paraclete or perhaps to emphasize some aspect of what He had already considered. In any case, this adds to our understanding of the character of the Holy Spirit.

To be explicit: "But when He, the Spirit of truth, comes, He will guide you into all the truth . . ." (John 16:13)—bringing to remembrance those things concerning Christ; bearing witness of Him; and disclosing "what is to come" (John 14:26; 15:27; 16:13). The Spirit of truth makes available all the riches of the past and all the possibilities of the future for those who are in Christ. It is so bold a claim as to stagger the imagination.

How can this be? Dietrich Bonhoeffer details this project with reference to human existence, history, and nature. Christ is the center of our existence, which is not to claim that He is central to our personality, our thinking, or our feeling. "In the fallen world the centre is also the boundary. . . . So he [Christ] is in turn the boundary and judgment of man, but also the beginning of his new existence, its centre. Christ as the centre of human existence means that he is the judgement and justification of man."[12] This is what John has been saying throughout. Men create their own existence so as to leave out the Almighty and force Him to the boundary, where Jesus stands in judgment and the Spirit of truth bears witness to Him. Here also lies man's hope for recovery: with Christ, enabled by the Holy Spirit.

Bonhoeffer's discussion of Christ as the center of history follows a similar pattern. History lies, according to Bonhoeffer, between promise and fulfillment: "The promise of a Messiah is everywhere alive in history. . . . But history relates itself to this promise much as the individual man relates to the law; it cannot fulfil it. The promise is corrupted by sin"[13]—and compounded by man's efforts to create his own messiahs. Therefore, Christ alone proves to be the answer to man's quest, the fulfillment of the promise he senses.

Christ similarly stands at the center of creation. Nature stands for the moment under the curse laid on Adam's ground, but that will pass. For now, creation waits expectantly for a new freedom, an earnest of which it received in the nature miracles of Christ. The Spirit of truth bears witness to this fact as well.

The passage saying that He "will guide you into all the truth" does not mean that the Holy Spirit will stand at a distance to direct the disciples, or even come along after they have made progress. It means that He leads the way, as if anxious to reveal some new aspect of the truth as related to Christ. And, the text continues, He discloses what is to come, as if He from His perspective could see better than the rest.

The Spirit of truth appears in this setting as something of a trailblazer. He makes His way through virgin territory, over difficult terrain, in order to lead the pilgrim travelers safely through. If He pauses from

---

12. Dietrich Bonhoeffer, *Christ the Center*, p. 61.
13. *Ibid.*, p. 62.

time to time to give encouragement, it all fits together with His purpose and ministry.

There is something virtually tangible about the Holy Spirit as represented by the Paraclete and Spirit of truth. They seem to convey the conviction that the presence of the Spirit is a guarantee of the ultimate consummation of God's purposes in the end.[14] This emphasis was less pronounced with regard to the designation "Holy Spirit," merely faintly suggested in the "Spirit of the Lord," and indistinct in the "Spirit of God." But all these must be taken together in order to focus effectively on the identity of the Spirit. He has, as promised by Jesus, come to abide with the disciples.

Summary

It comes time to cast back over the course we have taken. We determined at the outset that the proper direction was to entertain the question "Who?". Only in this way could we counter the common temptation to think of the Spirit in impersonal terms—as a force or ideal. "Who?" rather than "How?" set us on the proper course toward an uncertain destination.

The answer did not come at once or in one fashion; it tied together a variety of designations for the Spirit into a single mosaic. It started with the idea of "spirit," which we found associated with wind and breath. We discovered the Spirit to be sovereign, inscrutable, life-giving, and indispensable. This provided an initial understanding from which we might move on to investigate more precise designations.

The first of these was the "Spirit of God." This assured that the Spirit must be distinguished as God's Spirit, and differentiated from any and all other uses of the term *spirit*. Its emphasis lay upon the sovereign and transcendent character of God, lest we confuse the Spirit of God with the human spirit. Having established a proper distance between the Spirit and ourselves, we could allow that any reference to the Spirit (the present included) accents God's immanence. The Spirit conveys the idea of God as being active in our midst and on our behalf.

---

14. C.F.D. Moule comments on certain Pauline metaphors and the Acts narrative, but John's treatment seems even more striking than these (*The Holy Spirit*, pp. 35–36).

The "Spirit of the Lord" shifted our attention from the attribute of justice to mercy, from God's exalted place as ruler of the universe to His redemptive involvement in it. We discovered that mercy was associated with forgiveness, forbearance, grace—as expressed by the covenants—and grace—as extended through His compassionate assistance. Thus, we ought to identify the Spirit neither with justice alone, nor with mercy alone, but both together, realizing that one is not genuinely possible without the other.

We came to the heart of the issue with the designation "Holy Spirit." The Old Testament references, few though they are, locate this usage with the call to holiness. The situation was that the people of God had rebelled against the will of God. They discovered in their state of rebellion that it was, in the words spoken to Saul, hard "to kick against the goads" (Acts 26:14). The Holy Spirit contested their defection each step of the way. We especially considered the purpose, power, and availability of the Holy Spirit in His ministry to the prodigal.

Having created the setting, we took up the relationship of the Holy Spirit to Christ. We decided that the Holy Spirit gave us Jesus—and Jesus gave us the Holy Spirit. These ideas, when put together, supplied us with the related term "Spirit of Christ"—as a composite for the indwelling presence of the Spirit.

We concluded our discussion of the Holy Spirit with reference to the church, acknowledging that to believe in the Holy Spirit was to believe in the church as His handiwork—to see the church not simply as the product of faith but an agent in inculcating faith. Thereby, the designation "Holy Spirit" drew upon the call to holiness, as applied to the person and work of Christ, and in association with the community of faith.

The related terms "Paraclete" and "Spirit of truth" enabled us to look more closely at the distinctive place of the Spirit with reference to the disciples of Christ. They drove a solid wedge between the world and the people of the Way. The notion of Paraclete includes that of Advocate and Comforter, the latter not simply to ease the burden but to enable the disciple to stand resolute against the onslaughts of the enemy. We found that the Paraclete provided a twofold ministry: to comfort the afflicted and to afflict the comfortable. While He ministers to the disciples, He actively engages the world in regard to sin, righteousness, and judgment.

We located the "Spirit of truth" in connection with His testimony for Christ as the center of personal existence, history, and nature. Thus, even when Jesus appears to exist at the border of any of these, He stands at God's center, in judgment and with the offer of salvation—as witnessed by the Spirit of truth. The Spirit brings to remembrance the things of Christ and guides (leads) the disciples into all truth—as might a trailblazer who takes an enthusiastic interest in his vocation.

Who are You? A careful blend of all that we have noted and more. You are One of whom we still have much more to learn, but not so as to alter even the slightest thing we know as of now. Who is He? The Spirit of God, Witness to Christ, Life of the Church, Scourge of the World—and so the titles might be multiplied to accommodate the biblical teaching. But we need not press the matter further. We have identified the Spirit well enough to forge ahead with a more systematic and detailed account of the Holy Spirit's operation in our midst.

6

Beloved World

Dietrich Bonhoeffer decided that it is necessary, once we have settled on *who* Christ is, to ask *where* He is at work.[1] The same could be said of the Holy Spirit. Once we have solved His identity, we should inquire into His activity. The point at which we find ourselves is that we have left the question "Who?" in order to take up the question "Where?".

44 Where?

There have been two answers commonly proposed to the question of "Where?" as relates to the Holy Spirit. Some begin with the church, which makes the relationship of the Spirit to the world tenuous, at best. Others begin with the world, which—while it may minimize the special relationship of the Spirit with the church—seems the wiser course of action. The Spirit and the world coincided long before there was a church.

Were we to press the question in order to get a more exact answer, we might inquire "Where in the world are You?" The reply would seem

1. Dietrich Bonhoeffer, *Christ the Center*, pp. 60–61.

contradictory: "Everywhere and nowhere." The Spirit is everywhere, as the psalmist reminds us: "Where can I go from Thy Spirit? Or where can I flee from Thy presence? If I ascend to heaven, Thou art there; if I make my bed in Sheol, behold, Thou art there. If I take the wings of the dawn, if I dwell in the remotest part of the sea, even there Thy hand will lead me, and Thy right hand will lay hold of me" (Ps. 139:7–10). We cannot climb so high or dig so low, nor can we travel so far east or west, but that we confront the Spirit.

But He is also "nowhere," in the sense that He is distinct from creation, history, and self. The Spirit transcends all these while being present with them all. He was before all these and exists *apart* from them. We ought not to entertain for a moment anything that approaches pantheism!

This distinction between Spirit and cosmos was fixed at the creation account. Emil Brunner reminds us that "God is the One who absolutely determines all things, and is determined by none."[2] Not until God spoke did creation come into existence. There was, as Brunner suggests, not *a* nothing (waiting to become something), but nothing at all—so that God created at His pleasure the world and all that dwells therein.

We might have imagined that God would retire after creation and let the creation manage as best it could, but this was not the case. The creation was not and is not an entity unto itself. It owes its existence and continuation to the active involvement of the Almighty. Were God dead, as it was popular to suggest some years ago, we would not be around to talk about it—for we would have experienced an early demise as well.

When Bonhoeffer attempted to find one idea that would express where Christ was, he came up with the thought that He was "pro me." We can say the same thing in regard to the Holy Spirit. He is for me, even when I am not for myself. He sustains life, even when I behave in such a way as to threaten it.

We mean no exclusive claim on the Holy Spirit by saying He is "pro me." He is for others as well as for myself, and for corporate life as well as for individuals. His concern embraces all and in every regard. Although we may draw circles to restrict our own concern, the circumference of His circle includes all.

However, we must add that the Spirit exists for me in a fallen world. He exists "pro me" in a world of sin, suffering, and death. This is a world where death may seem more desirable than continuing to live under

---

2. Emil Brunner, *The Christian Doctrine of Creation and Redemption*, p. 10.

some circumstance or another, if only for the hope of some relief and without any sure conviction of a glory beyond. Here, in a fallen world, the Spirit acts on our behalf, and it is with this realization that we can begin to talk about common grace.

45 Grace

Of whatever variety, "grace" is nonetheless grace, the unmerited expression of God's favor toward some aspect of His creation or creation as a whole. Man generally becomes the focus of God's grace.

J. M. Myers elaborates: "Deliverance and covenant belong together. Both are acts of divine grace. What developed later in line with 'these words' and which is known as the torah was nothing more or less than an application of these principles to situational exigencies. . . . It (the torah) is the repertoire of God's gracious will for a people who had accepted his prior gift and in appreciation therefor placed themselves under his tutelage."[3] Our efforts to contrast grace and law ought not to confuse the fact that *all* is through grace. Life in whatever circumstance we experience it is an undeserved gift, an opportunity for which we have a responsibility. Were there no grace, there could be no biblical concept of obligation.

We experience grace so regularly as to take it for granted, as if warranted under the circumstances. But when we give thanks for our food or the dawn of an inviting day, we are recognizing life for what it is—the grace of God. Herein we discover the Spirit at work, if happily we can break through the obstacles we erect to shield us from recognizing that this is our Father's world, and sense a providential concern with the bounty we enjoy.

46 Common Grace

The term *common grace* refers to what we experience of God's grace in common, as man and not in particular as the people of God. This is grace as experienced in the world created by God and the subject of His concern. It is grace as ministered by the Spirit of an impartial deity toward those for whom He offers more than they care to receive.

In what particulars can we discover common grace? Certainly with regard to the restraint of evil. We read that men's rebellion not only

3. J. M. Myers, *Grace and Torah*, p. 17.

grieves the Holy Spirit, but causes the Spirit "to become their enemy" (Isa. 63:10). The fallen world is not a forsaken world, but rather a world of conflict between the forces of evil and the mediator of common grace.

It is tempting to think how much better the world might be under different circumstances, but it appears that it could even be much worse, were it not for the restraining influence of the Holy Spirit. For the most part, the Spirit seems to parry evil at some point or another. Here He gains some high ground, and there appears driven before the onrush of hostile forces. Now and then He unleashes a major offensive, as with the deliverance of Israel from bondage or with the dawn of the messianic age.

Closely related to the foregoing, the Spirit stays the sentence of judgment. This leads Paul to inquire: "Or do you think lightly of the riches of His kindness and forbearance and patience, not knowing that the kindness of God leads you to repentance?" (Rom. 2:4). The stay of judgment was to give every opportunity for the people to repent of their evil and turn back into the paths of righteousness.

Thus, too, were the martyrs led to cry out: "How long, O Lord, holy and true, wilt Thou refrain from judging and avenging our blood on those who dwell on the earth?" (Rev. 6:10)—for God does not normally shield the righteous from the fallout of sin that consumes all indiscriminately. How long will the Spirit allow such terrible things to go on as an expression of common grace? "This long" is all we can say, for we do not know how much longer. The cup of God's wrath seems filled to overflowing.

The role of the Spirit with common grace should not be thought of as only negative; it has a positive side. Paul pointed out to those of Lystra that God "did not leave Himself without witness, in that He did good and gave you rains from heaven and fruitful seasons, satisfying your hearts with food and gladness" (Acts 14:17)—not as a single favor to them, but as part of His common grace expressed to mankind everywhere. These gifts are expressions of God's benevolent concern for human need. He renders them not for some ulterior motive, as if to solicit a more favorable response than might otherwise be the case. They are simply the expression of a loving God for His beloved world.

But the gifts do act as incentives as well. They remind man of God's gracious provision, his own lack of proper gratitude, and his need for contrition. So, while guilt may drive man to reconsider his ways, grace incites him to do the same.

The positive side to common grace also involves the preservation of truth, morality, and a religious awareness. When we hear someone admit, "There is truth to what you say," he may not agree with the application the other has in mind or even the perspective from which it is represented. But there is an element of truth preserved for both to observe and agree upon, and this is part of the domain of common grace.

The preservation of morality is likewise an aspect of common grace. We sometimes miss the impact of this truth because our views of morality differ so extensively from one person to another. But two things can be said in response: all people have some idea of morality, and our views are not as dissimilar as we might at first suspect. However we explain the presence of morality, man seems incurably concerned with what he and others ought and ought not to do. There are also significant similarities. So, for example, while people may differ on their views of modesty, each has some opinion as to what is modest and what is not.

Our religious awareness is no less a factor of common grace than are truth and morality. Paul observed that his Athenian audience was "very religious in all respects" (Acts 17:22). Having noted an inscription to an unknown god, he announced: "What therefore you worship in ignorance, I declare to you" (v. 23). Their religious bent, no matter how distorted, offered Paul a point of departure for proclaiming the gospel.

The world has not fallen so far but that the Spirit preserves something of the truth, morality, and religious character with which it was endowed. Accordingly, while man distorts all these to serve his own ends, the Holy Spirit employs them for a contrary purpose, as a witness to a benevolent Creator. This is no insignificant feature of common grace.

We may also consider the skills with which the Spirit endows people as a further instance of common grace. As G. W. H. Lampe explains: "Here the divine and the human interact with one another in such a way that it is impossible to distinguish the artist's natural ability, that which belongs inherently to his temperament, capacity and training, from what he experiences as 'given' from beyond himself: the freshness of inspiration that comes to him from beyond the normal limits of his consciousness, and which he recognizes as that which 'finds' him rather than as that which he himself creates and produces."[4] The distinction, if such exists, often occurs with reference to the object which is served

4. G.W.H. Lampe, *God as Spirit*, p. 46.

rather than with regard to some natural or special endowment by the Spirit. Nor should such endowment be thought of in strictly individual terms. Since the Spirit ministers through each individual to those with whom He is associated, we may conceive of the larger perspective as within the realm of common grace.

This leads quite naturally to a consideration of civil affairs as an example of common grace. Paul admonishes his readers: "Let every person be in subjection to the governing authorities. For there is no authority except from God, and those which exist are established by God" (Rom. 13:1). The apostle goes on to state that those who resist authority oppose the ordinance of God. He views civil authority as a gift of God meant to restrain evil and further the good, which ties together both the negative and positive aspects of common grace.

We reaffirm that God has not forsaken the fallen world. He exercises common grace with respect to persons, so that the Holy Spirit can be said to be *for me*, in my situation and for my benefit. He extends God's grace toward me, not simply in creation but through preservation and providence.

This is so sweeping a statement as to require greater specificity. Where is the Spirit operative in people's lives regardless of their lot in life or position before the Almighty? The Spirit operates in certain negative roles: the restraint of evil and the stay of sentence. This creates difficulties for those who suffer from the behavior of others, but creates a middle way between a precipitous termination of things and letting them go totally out of control. It also accents the corporate nature of life, for both good and evil.

The Spirit likewise exercises common grace in various positive connections: with natural blessings; the preservation of truth, morality, and religious awareness; the award of skills to serve the aggregate need; the agencies of government. These are means by which life may be nurtured, truth exonerated, good behavior rewarded, religious sensitivities awakened, skills employed, and order preserved.

While such considerations are by no means exhaustive, they sketch out the domain of common grace as the effusion of the Spirit. He seems to pour out more of God's blessing than our feeble vessels can contain, so that we are constantly replacing the one with something large enough to hold what would otherwise overflow—only to discover that our replacement is still much too small.

God plays no favorites with regard to common grace. We learn that "He causes His sun to rise on the evil and the good, and sends rain on the righteous and the unrighteous" (Matt. 5:45). In the light of this, Jesus admonished His disciples to love their enemies and pray for those who persecuted them. In so doing, they would reflect the operation of the Holy Spirit's common grace and be true servants of Christ to the beloved world.

47 Revelation

We allowed that "grace" is grace, whether delineated as common or in some other manner. "Revelation" is similarly revelation, although we are concerned for the moment with general revelation. Are we doing injustice to the unitary character of revelation by distinguishing general from special revelation? It is a danger we run in order to sharpen our focus on what the Holy Spirit accomplishes in regard to the world at large.

Leon Morris observes: "Revelation is not concerned with knowledge we once had but have forgotten for the time being. Nor does it refer to the kind of knowledge that we might attain by diligent research. It is knowledge that comes to us from outside ourselves and beyond our own ability to discover."[5] Man has a notoriously short memory when it comes to the things of God, but revelation does not concern itself with bringing to mind what was forgotten or uncovered as a matter of laborious search. Revelation takes the hidden truths of God and makes them available to man.

Man appears able to derive an incredible amount of knowledge through "diligent research." He surveys the heavens, probes the infinitesimal building blocks of life, analyzes his finds, and adds to a growing storehouse of knowledge. But revelation yields what man cannot discover through such means, no matter how long he labors or whatever determination he brings to his undertaking. As Emil Brunner adds, "Thus revelation issues from a region which, as such, is not accessible to man. The absolutely Mysterious is not only partially hidden from the natural knowledge of man; it is wholly inaccessible to man's natural faculties for research and discovery."[6]

To speak of "the absolutely Mysterious," as Brunner chooses to do, is not to deny that truth may be revealed and, once revealed, be understood by man. The revelation contains, along with whatever else it may

5. Leon Morris, *I Believe in Revelation*, p. 10.
6. Emil Brunner, *Revelation and Reason*, p. 23.

involve, the testimony to God's transcendence. God is revealed to us as having thoughts higher than our thoughts, as the heaven surpasses the earth.

Nor could we otherwise know, as affirmed earlier, that God has our best interests at heart. Our experience is ambiguous at this point. Sometimes it appears as if there were a benevolent agent interceding on our behalf, and at other times we seem left alone, if not in the grips of some sadistic monster. Were it not for revelation, we would generate little confidence in a loving God who delights in rewarding His people.

That is not to suggest that our experience contradicts what revelation asserts to be true. Rather, revelation provides a framework in which we can better understand our experience. It gives us a broader scope and throws light on many specific areas as a result. Revelation not only provides us with what would otherwise be lacking, but illumines much of what we know from other sources. Revelation creates a sort of gestalt, a configuration which is greater than we could derive from its parts. It is as if fragments were somehow pulled together by introducing what was previously missing, so that we awaken to being in God's world.

We do not want to overstate the case, because there inevitably seem to be loose ends and tension that result. Things do not come comfortably together, even though they appear in place, as if to remind us that it is not the configuration itself but the Almighty who is the true object of revelation. Without Him, revelation resembles a house of cards that collapses the moment we stir.

While this is true, revelation consists of God-as-He-reveals-Himself, and not, strictly speaking, as God-in-Himself. We encounter the Almighty in concrete situations to which revelation is characteristically addressed. Thus, the revelation of God is more direct, more pointed, more relevant than some suppose.

The Spirit may be said to initiate revelation. Having privileged recourse to the counsels of God, He delights in making them known to man. The result is that man may discover how better to live in God's world, where the conditions are not of private preference but by divine decree. Here, as with common grace, the Holy Spirit provides the otherwise missing dynamic.

48 General Revelation

A more particular aspect of the Spirit's activity is general revelation—what is said to be indiscriminately available to mankind. It also lacks the redemptive focus of special revelation. This does not imply that revelation is so immersed in the universe as to be perceived at all times, by all men, in all places. That is not our understanding of general revelation. As Leon Morris explains: "The thought is that in nature and in man there is always the possibility of some revelation of God but that revelation becomes actual only as God brings it home to some individual. The thought of the divine initiative is to be preserved."[7]

General revelation is not embedded in the universe as if man could discover it on his own. It rather testifies to the fact that God continues to reveal Himself in the course of events, as man wrestles with his circumstances. He does not limit Himself in this regard to biblical (redemptive, special) revelation, but addresses men everywhere with regard to life in general.

This does not mean that the recipient of revelation is unimportant. God reveals Himself characteristically to the humble, searching, and circumspect. Since He does not normally cast His truth at someone's feet to be trampled on, His ways become known to those who want His will above their own.

Paul affirms: "For since the creation of the world His invisible attributes, His eternal power and divine nature, have been clearly seen, being understood through what has been made, so that they are without excuse" (Rom. 1:20). In other words, those who suppress the revealed truth suppress it in unrighteousness. Having a preliminary knowledge of God, they do not want to honor Him as God. They prefer instead to struggle on blindly, seeking their pleasures through whatever base means are available to them.

Such general revelation is confined (according to Paul) to manifestations of His power—as reflected in His creation and His sovereign place—as residing over His creation. The heavens declare the sovereign glory of God, and the earth tells of His handiwork. "Their line has gone out through all the earth,/And their utterances to the end of the world" (Ps. 19:4). This is as if the cosmos were testifying to the truth of God but, in fact, God is bearing witness to His truth through the cosmos.

In contrast to the works of God, man's labors seem as nothing. Before His majesty, man feels his own insignificance. "When I consider Thy heaven, the work of Thy fingers, the moon and the stars, which Thou hast ordained; what is man, that Thou dost take thought of him? And the son of man, that Thou dost care for him?" (Ps. 8:3–4). Man has been

---

7. Morris, *I Believe in Revelation*, p. 35.

created lower than the angels and yet given great responsibility over the creation. How heavy an obligation, were it not for the grace of God as revealed to sons of men!

We conclude that general revelation involves the created order—and so it does—but it also incorporates the providence of God with regard to nature and history. The sage wrote, "Go to the ant, O sluggard, observe her ways and be wise" (Prov. 6:6). Learn from the responsible ways of His creatures what He expects from you.

Learn also from the course of history: "Righteousness exalts a nation, but sin is a disgrace to any people" (Prov. 14:34). The rise and fall of nations testify to the ravages of sin and the wisdom of righteousness. Such knowledge is not tucked away in some secluded corner of the universe, but is on open display, that all may observe and take counsel from it. God's providence is all-embracing: for all persons, events, and actions. It suggests that events have moved and continue to move according to God's purposes toward the goal He envisages, not as though man were crushed by the rush of events, but so as to encourage his cooperation—and to remind man that he is no match for the Almighty.

This implies that general revelation is somehow related to the moral life and capacities of man. General revelation is not simply out there—with the natural life and circumstances beyond our control—but in here—among the interplay of feelings, thought, and purposed action. Man, being created in the image of God, reveals his origins.

The psalmist decided: "I will give thanks to Thee, for I am fearfully and wonderfully made" (Ps. 139:14). He needed no special revelation to conclude this; general revelation would suffice. The "noble beast" provides, along with the creation and providence of God, the avenue for general revelation to take. Therefore, as Paul keeps reminding us, we are without excuse. There are none excepted, but all of us have been confronted from time to time with the reality of God, suppress it though we may.

49 Natural Theology

From time to time, there has been debate as to whether one can produce a theology based on general revelation alone. Some "hold that unless the Christian can draw attention to grounds for his faith [i.e., some evidence of God in the universe or in man] there is strictly speaking no *reason* for his being a Christian. To profess the Christian faith without such grounds they would hold is to make a choice for God on arbitrary, perhaps even on trivial grounds."[8] Others accent the need of faith to make visible the revelation now concealed by sin. The latter may go so far as to deny the relevance of general revelation.

But even if one holds on to the idea of general revelation, he must set limits on natural theology. For instance, we ought not to press natural theology so as to undercut the importance of special revelation. We must also set proper constraints on what can be known and consider how such limited knowledge may distort the rest.

Such a persisting question is not easily laid to rest, but we can attempt to point a direction through it. We admit that sin has affected man in every regard, although not exhaustively. This is to suggest that while man is a sinner through and through, he has not lost his ability to think and talk about God, however limited and defective the results might be.

We must also allow the Spirit His prerogative in the world, whether with common grace or general revelation. We must not unduly restrict Him to some select instances or to too narrow a scope of concern. The entire world is His parish.

50 Extraordinary Means

Emil Brunner comments on the many-faceted character of revelation: "God reveals Himself through theophanies, through angels, through dreams, through oracles [such as Urim and Thummim], through visions and locations, through natural phenomena and through historical events, through wonderful guidance given to human beings, and through the words and deeds of the prophets."[9] Most of these apply to general revelation, but have much to do with extraordinary means: such as theophanies, angels, dreams, oracles, and visions.

We must back up in order to put these extraordinary means in context. Norman Pittenger alleges that "the economy of the Spirit is the conforming of the whole creation to the divine intention."[10] This would, we assume, be true whether we thought in corporate or in individual terms. The Holy Spirit seeks to bring man into conformity to the will of God, which would apply to whatever means He chose to employ.

---

8. *Ibid.*,p. 34.
9. Brunner, *Revelation and Reason*, p. 21.
10. Norman Pittenger, *The Holy Spirit*, p. 73.

But why select such extraordinary means as detailed previously? They may be thought of as concessions to man in his need, given his limited perspective. They capture his attention in a way that other means would not, and they contribute, along with whatever other means the Spirit chooses, to directing persons into the way of the Almighty. And these extraordinary means, as many will testify, are widely disseminated throughout human experience.

The term *concession* is a good one for our purpose, if we do not read some derogatory connotation into it. The critical concern is not the means, but the purpose it serves. Such extraordinary experiences can be introduced neither as evidence for advanced spirituality nor for spiritual immaturity. One should welcome any means the Spirit selects and not covet the experience of another. Our experiences, varied as they are, fit into a grand mosaic when it comes to seeing God's purpose with our lives.

The Holy Spirit does work with individuals, but not with individuals in isolation from one another. There is a social cast to the ministry of the Spirit through common grace and general revelation to the world. He touches someone, someplace, somehow, for a purpose that transcends his individual life. The Spirit is ever thinking beyond that first step, as if He were a polished chess player, bent on subsequent moves.

It is possible to sense something of this long-range point of view as we reflect back on how the Spirit has led us through others, and others through us. It is a partial perspective, to be sure, but at least a glimpse of what so often seems to make no sense at all at the time.

In any case, we must hold fast to the idea of divine initiative, without which revelation would appear meaningless. Revelation consists not in what we might otherwise discover, but in what the Holy Spirit will uncover for us. In short, revelation testifies to the divine initiative, whenever and wherever it takes place.

We have argued for general revelation as a facet of the Holy Spirit's ministry to the beloved world. This, contrary to popular understanding, does not mean that it is perceived at all times, by all men, in all places. But we believe that the Spirit delights in revealing the truth of God to man in any setting and under whatever circumstances may prevail. He resembles an itinerant preacher, who rests neither day nor night in carrying out His demanding calling.

General revelation seems confined to the manifestation of God's power in creation and His rule over it. We saw this expressed through the natural creation, the providence of God as related to nature and history, and with the moral life and capacities of man. These three generally blend together in our actual experience, as an awareness of being in God's world and ultimately subject to His will.

Whether we can build a theology with such limited resources remains a matter of controversy. It seems obvious that man thinks about God and makes statements about Him, even without what we usually consider special revelation. So, while we may struggle over the semantics involved, we ought not to restrict the universal sphere of the Spirit's ministry—whether in connection with common grace or with general revelation.

The extraordinary means employed from time to time by the Holy Spirit ought neither to embarrass us nor cause us to covet them. They are rather like concessions to particular persons, at peculiar times, and neutral in and of themselves. They serve only as they serve the purposes of God, not simply with individuals as such but in their larger social context. God's concern for His beloved world can be seen in the way He works through some to achieve His purpose in the lives of others.

Those who herald the gospel enter into a field already broken up by the Spirit of God to receive their seed. When Paul first confronted the Lystrans, he was able to say with full confidence that God "did not leave Himself without witness" (Acts 14:17). The rains from heaven and the seasons of fruitbearing had satisfied their hearts with food and gladness—until such time, in the providence of God, that the apostle might bring to them the word of life.

This suggests the progressive character of revelation, as it reaches out to man where he is and seeks to lead him through a maze of obstacles to the perfect will of God for his life. The Holy Spirit shows no evidence of tiring in such activity, or in encouraging those who have the will to contribute to the effort, so that all may learn the way of the Almighty that leads to life abundant and eternal.

51 Redemptive History

We come to what is likely the most controversial aspect of our discussion of the role of the Holy Spirit in the world at large: redemptive history. The incarnation lies at the center of redemptive history, and it incorporates the peculiar history of Israel as preparation for, and the church as extension of, the saving event. The author of Hebrews observes the scope of redemptive history when he declares that "God, after He spoke long ago to the fathers in the prophets in many portions and in many ways, in these last days has spoken to us in His Son . . ." (Heb. 1:1–2). Therein he makes reference to the preparatory revelation, its fulfillment in Christ, and its declaration by the community of faith. This is not to exclude the hand of God in *all* of history, but to suggest the particular aspect of history which records the redemptive drama.

Redemptive history could be considered in connection with the world—in that it is history—or the church—in that it deals with salvation. We choose to accent the former and blend in the latter at a later point. Thus we emphasize redemptive history as history that can be observed by *all*, even though experienced only by some.

Eric Rust brings us to the heart of the matter: "So the process of revelation is consummated in the incarnation. God in the person of his Son enters history as man, and does for man what man cannot do for himself. . . . God enters history and becomes a part of his own created order, a part in whom the whole meaning of that order is gathered up and actualized."[11] Accordingly, we may say that redemptive history lies at the center of universal history, and the advent of Christ at the core of redemptive history.

Rust describes this event as "the scandal of particularity." The scandal would at first seem to do with the selection of a rustic teacher from a minor people of antiquity to be God's means of redemption, which seems to challenge the world's idea of greatness.

But the scandal has a more pronounced characteristic. Jesus came, as the biblical text likes to remind us, from above. His "particularity" was more particular still. He lived among us, but as one not of us. He was never *our* man.

The passage of time has a way of obscuring the extraordinary nature of Jesus. His acts become familiar, His words commonplace, and His claims somehow accommodated. We have to struggle to sense how unique this life was, how threatening for the opposition and compelling for the disciples. But struggle we must, if we are to appreciate the impact of redemptive history. Michael Green observes: "Each in his own way, the four evangelists make it abundantly plain that a new era has dawned with the coming of Jesus of Nazareth. It is the long-awaited era of the messianic kingdom, the age characterized by the availability of the Spirit of God. And Jesus is the Messiah, by virtue of his unprecedented endowment with the Spirit of God. He is both the unique bearer of the Spirit, and the unique dispenser of that Spirit to the disciples;

11. Eric Rust, *Salvation History*, pp. 20–21.

moreover, forever afterwards the Spirit remains stamped with his character."[12] All this preserves the unique character of the advent, while turning it in the direction of the Holy Spirit and thus serving our present purpose.

The mark of this advent was "the availability of the Spirit of God." Whereas the Holy Spirit was active previously, He now became readily available, at first with Christ and then the church. There was no actual precedent for the manner in which the Holy Spirit attended to Jesus as the Messiah. John the Baptist said of Jesus, "For He whom God has sent speaks the words of God; for He gives the Spirit without measure" (John 3:34).

"The Spirit without measure" aptly characterizes Jesus as the Messiah. To suggest that He is the Messiah is to acknowledge the fullness of the Holy Spirit, and to speak of the fullness of the Holy Spirit in such unbridled manner is to relate Him as the Messiah. While the two may be distinguished, they may not be separated.

Green encourages us to think of Jesus as not only the recipient but the dispenser of the Holy Spirit. This would, in a more qualified sense, be true during the earthly life and ministry of Jesus. It would be true in a larger sense once He had dispatched the Spirit to serve in His stead (John 16:7). Thus, "for ever afterwards the Spirit remains stamped with his character."

This is to say that the Holy Spirit loses something of His anonymity due to His association with Christ. Wind and breath have no face such as Jesus presents to us. We now know the Spirit as being Christ-like in service and redemptive in design. The two are one so far as their essential disposition and priorities are concerned.

Oscar Cullman observes: "It is already the time of the end, and yet is not *the end*. The tension finds expression in the entire theology of Primitive Christianity. The present period of the church is the time between the decisive battle, which has already occurred, and the 'Victory Day.'"[13] The Jewish division of time is twofold: the present age and the age to come. But Christianity modifies the perspective, allowing a time between the first and second advents of Christ. The present age has continued in the sense that this "is not *the end*," but the age to come has dawned as "the time of the end."

---

12. Michael Green, *I Believe in the Holy Spirit*, p. 32.
13. Oscar Cullmann, *Christ and Time*, p. 145.

The decisive point in redemptive history is, for Cullmann, the death and resurrection of Christ. This was the crucial conflict, which assures us of ultimate victory. Everything this side of the resurrection is anticlimactic. Neither sin nor death has any final claim on those who have experienced deliverance in and through Christ.

Although the world cannot easily ignore what has transpired, it has difficulty understanding. "This has not been done in a corner" (Acts 26:26), Paul reminded Agrippa. All this had apparently not escaped the king's notice, but he stopped short somewhere between observation and conviction—as does the world at large.

Some have attempted to write Jesus out of history, but these efforts have for the most part met with little success. Others attempt to cast Him in some minor role, as one of the prophets or a sage instructor, and this view has sometimes proved to be more convincing to those who search for an alternative more to their liking. Less often, the full impact of the advent message breaks through the defenses we carefully raise to protect out personal domains, and we are driven to some more decisive response: to either opposition or faith.

This, then, is the thrust of redemptive history: "But when the fullness of the time came, God sent forth His Son . . . in order that . . . we might receive the adoption as sons" (Gal. 4:4–5). When all was in order, at the auspicious moment, God sent His Son *that we might receive adoption as sons*. The design had run its course to the climax.

52 Former Times

Redemptive history begins, as noted earlier, with God's selection of a people through whom to work His purpose and bring forth the Messiah. We repeat Eichrodt's observation that "God's activity in history, aimed at the creation of a consecrated people of God, was discerned not only in isolated marvellous events, but also in the emergence of specially equipped men and women whose leadership in word and deed, by wars of liberation without and by the establishment of the will of God in the social and moral order within, dragged the dull mass of the people with them, again and again smashing and sweeping away all the obstacles which the incursion of healthy morals and ways of thought raised against them."[14] Thus did the Spirit work, through some to affect all, and to prepare the way for what would follow.

14. Walther Eichrodt, *Theology of the Old Testament*, II, p. 50.

The key idea about redemptive history, as described by Eichrodt and promoted by Wolfart Pannenberg, is *election*, and the subsidiary concept *judgment*.[15] God chose a people through whom to fulfill His larger purposes. It is not evident whether He chose them because of some advantage over other peoples, or in order to demonstrate His strength through feeble means, or some combination of the two. What is evident is the matter of God's sovereign will in the matter.

Israel was God's means, even when it complained and rebelled. But this is the point where judgment entered in: to express God's wrath over wrongdoing, His uncompromising demand for a holy people, and His willingness to forgive those who genuinely repent. The two taken together—election and judgment—effectively portray the course of redemptive history.

The idea of "covenant" entered with the former two in place. It expressed God's concern and provision for His people, and it also established the conditions under which they could receive His blessing and do His service. The covenant tied a sometimes reluctant people to the persisting resolve of God.

However, the covenant would have been worth little more than the paper it was recorded on, were it not for the Holy Spirit as the instrument of redemptive history in general and the covenantal process in particular. The Spirit mediated its provisions to the people through the prophetic office, and interceded on their behalf through the priestly office. Thereby, the relationship between the Almighty and Israel was permeated by the Spirit.

These ideas fall out into countless concrete incidents as the people of God picked their way along, encouraged by the Spirit of God. At times their progress seemed painfully slow, but at other times they appeared to rise magnificently to the occasion. Seldom were they long without some reminder of their covenant obligation and the resources available to them for keeping its provisions.

Even at such moments as sorely try the souls of men, there remained before them the anticipation of the messianic age. Their experience with the Spirit, limited though it was, offered a rich future for the people of God. Thus far it might seem a mere trickle, but then it would gush forth to overflow the cup of Israel and bless all the nations gathered around her. In this manner, the people were not so much

15. Wolfart Pannenberg, *Human Nature, Election, and History*, pp. 89–95.

pushed along by some previous condition, or swayed by their present circumstances, as drawn by the vision of a glorious age to come.

53 Subsequent Times

With the coming of Christ, the course of redemptive history reaches its climax, but not its consummation. Everything prior to Christ may be called preparation; anything related to and subsequent to Him must be viewed as fulfillment. Thereby, the *promise* of Joel concerning the outpouring of the Spirit was preparation (Joel 2:28–32), and Peter's *announcement* of the outpouring was fulfillment (Acts 2:17–21).

But redemptive history continues, with Christ ascended to the right hand of God, and the church acting as His surrogate. Oscar Cullmann comments: "The Church was conscious that every day it was carrying forward the divine redemptive activity; it was taking part in a process that is as much a redemptive process as was that which took place before the incarnation. . . ."[16] The church resembles a beachhead of the messianic age, sustained by the Holy Spirit against the sometimes desperate assault of the enemy.

There is a sort of ebb and flow to the church, as it retires to recapture its identity as the messianic people of God and extends itself in service. Both movements are necessary for it to realize its purpose as a servant people, and both are encouraged by the Holy Spirit. In this fashion, the church builds an awareness of being in the world but not of the world.

To state matters differently, the church is caught between the overlap of the present age and the age to come, and it resides at the point of tension between the two. Thus it senses acutely the discrepancy between what is and what God would have it to be. This tension relates first to the church and, thereafter, to the world at large. This is why Scripture inquires, "And if it is with difficulty that the righteous is saved, what will become of the godless man and the sinner?" (1 Peter 4:18).

Strictly speaking, there is no such thing as the invisible church. The church requires visibility, even though it may not be what it appears to be. It is given visibility through the call of Christ, assuming the role of a servant community, with whatever features designated by Christ or assumed in response.

The most obvious aspects of the church's visibility to the world are the Scriptures and the sacraments (or "ordinances," if one prefers the latter

---

16. Cullmann, *Christ and Time*, p. 167.

designation). The Scriptures are also central to the continuing character of redemptive history. We have in mind Scripture *per se*, the reading of Scripture and its faithful exposition. The church, rightfully understood, stands under the authority of the Scripture.

The sacraments of baptism and the Lord's Supper are likewise required of the community of faith. These must be faithfully administered and appropriated, providing further visibility to the church.

The offices of the church and the respect with which they are accorded also increase the church's visibility, as does the lifestyle of the adherents and such accommodation as is made for public meeting. Therefore, even if we think there is more to the church than is visible to the world, the latter is not insignificant.

The world pays more attention to what can be seen of the church than to its more subtle aspects. It is where redemptive history touches general history that secular man pauses to watch, wonder, and sometimes act. This was true in regard to Israel, Christ, and now the church.

Redemptive history looks different from the outside. Some supposed that the early Christians were cannibalistic, because they had overheard references to their "eating the flesh of the Lord." Others were willing to accept that they were involved in arson, for they talked of the world's being destroyed by fire. Christians were even charged with being atheists, the reason being that they refused to worship the pagan gods. Such misunderstanding could be tragic, and it often resulted in persecution of the church.

But redemptive history, in spite of the ambiguity associated with it, witnesses to God's faithfulness with a wayward people. Sometimes it seems that this was less the result of an effective effort on man's part than the mysterious working of the Spirit. Therefore, the task of the church is to point men to Christ, trusting the Holy Spirit to contend with their hardness of heart.

We conclude that redemptive history is no less history for being redemptive. However, it has as a peculiar concern the progress of God in redeeming man. It focuses in on such matters as culminate with the advent of Christ and expressly extend from it—understood, we may add, as a work of the Spirit.

Summary

We turned from considering the person of the Spirit to looking at the nature of His work, from the question of "Who?" to "Where?". We learned that He works on our behalf, and for our advantage. This is true even when it relates to the chastening of the Lord. He means to correct what keeps us from experiencing the fullness of His blessing.

We first investigated the character of common grace, the unmerited favor which God extends toward His creation. It is indiscriminate in that it applies to all, and not to the people of God in particular. Such grace can be seen in negative terms: with the restraint of evil and the stay of sentence; and in positive terms: with natural blessings; the preservation of truth, morality, and religious awareness; the award of skills and the opportunity for their use; and the agencies of government. These may be seen as the genuine expressions of God's goodwill toward man, but they also act as restraints on the forces of evil and as incentives to good. For such purposes, the Holy Spirit exercises His presence in the world.

General revelation constitutes a second aspect of the Holy Spirit's activity within the cosmos. General revelation is no less "revelation" for being distributed to man in general. It applies not to what we have forgotten for the time being or could derive if we diligently attempted to do so, but to what we could not otherwise know. Neither does it suggest that what can be known in this fashion can be perceived at all times, by all men, in all places. It is rather that there is always the possibility of some revelation of God, which can become actual as the Holy Spirit brings it to someone's attention. General revelation is expressed by means of the natural creation, the providence of God as related to nature and history, and through the moral life and capacity of men.

We ought not to allow the controversy over natural theology to either restrict unduly the notion of special revelation or extend the scope of general revelation. Futhermore, we can discover a constructive role for the extraordinary leading of God within the context of general revelation, not as the rule (which would make the concept of "extraordinary" meaningless), but as further evidence of the Spirit's delight with revealing the things of God to those who would be otherwise the poorer.

Redemptive history, along with common grace and general revelation, rounds out the ways in which the Spirit is viewed as operative in the world at large. The incarnation lies at the heart of redemptive history—everything before may be said to prepare for the incarnation and everything thereafter to extend from it. The characteristic feature of the advent of Christ was "the availability of the Spirit of God," which can be seen in the fact that Jesus is both the unique bearer of the Spirit and the unique dispenser of the Spirit to His disciples.

Redemptive history began earlier than the incarnation, with the selection and guidance of a particular people to fulfill the purposes of God. The idea of election stands out as the most prominent aspect of early redemptive history, but was coupled with judgment and eventuated with the covenant—so that God might witness to the world of His faithfulness with an often rebellious people. This was in anticipation of the messianic age, during which the Spirit would be poured out without measure.

The advent of Christ initiated the time of the end, but was not yet the consummation. Redemptive history continued, with the church becoming the focus for redemptive activity. The church appears to ebb and flow, caught between the overlap of the former age and its messianic substitute. It is visible to the world (in terms of the Scripture, sacraments, its offices, the lifestyle of its adherents, and accommodation to worship), although often misunderstood. It also serves to draw men's attention to the work of the Spirit in their midst.

Taken together, common grace, general revelation, and redemptive history provide ample evidence of God's concern for His beloved world. We see the Holy Spirit active in each regard, so as to sustain man until such time as he has had every reasonable opportunity to turn from his evil ways into the paths of righteousness. And thereafter, the Spirit will sustain him in his pilgrim journey.

7

Life Together

The Holy Spirit is distinctively, although not exclusively, at work with the church. It was with this fact in mind that a veteran missionary pondered: "Had the Holy Spirit been at work? Yes. What was the manifestation of the Spirit? That messianic community which had been called to serve the living God and minister in his name."[1]

He might have considered the work of the Spirit more generally, but turned to the more specific ministry, where the Spirit of God serves the people of God.

54 Ekklesia

The term *ekklesia* was used of the summons for an army to assemble, and also with regard to the political gathering of the citizenry of a Greek city. However, these have questionable importance for its use as a designation for the church. The latter is more closely associated with the Old Testament phrase "of the Lord." Hans Küng observes that while "the process of congregating has not been forgotten . . . in this case it is not a congregation of anybody for any purpose: God gathers together

1. Morris Inch, "Manifestation of the Spirit," p. 152.

and the ekklesia therefore becomes a community of God."[2] The ekklesia of God is not an arbitrary people gathered for just any purpose. Rather, it is assembled at God's bidding and for such purposes as He cares to designate.

Here we must correct a one-sided emphasis on the conversion of individuals. It is not the intent of the Spirit to fragment, but rather to create a fellowship. By virtue of coming to Christ, one enters into a community of faith—and, from that moment on, is entrusted to the community and assumes responsibility for others bound together with him in Christ.

This community of which the believer becomes a part should not be understood as a natural one. That is to say, one does not become a member by birth or status. There are no second-generation Christians in the strict sense of the word. A godly heritage offers much, but cannot guarantee that faith will pass from one generation to the next. Nor can self-determination, in and of itself, provide the means for entering the community. One enters at the invitation of God and by means of the enablement of the Spirit. It is a miracle of grace, not the result of human endeavor.

The common ingredient that binds the fellowship together is Christ. There are no common ethnic, political, social, or racial characteristics. The fellowship not only allows, but encourages, a seemingly endless variety in the service of Christ.

This community bears witness to the advent of Christ. Since it is a messianic community, its very existence testifies to the fact that the latter days have dawned. This is what Paul has in mind when he declares that "now is 'the acceptable time,'" *now* is the day of salvation (2 Cor. 6:2)—what the prophets had foretold and the devout patiently awaited had come to pass.

But the community also cautions us that we must still await the final consummation, resisting such utopian dreams as would disguise the hard realities of life. It calls us to live and labor in anticipation of the future. The present experience is but an earnest of what may be anticipated. Whether present or future, the common element running throughout is Christ. He is Lord, as the Spirit testifies, and the church joins in the refrain.

We have correctly inferred that the community is not *of* this world. It came into being in response to the call of Christ and through the

2. Hans Küng, *The Church*, p. 82.

endowment of the Spirit. It persists as well by divine prerogative. What the world has not given, it cannot take away. No wonder Jesus announced that "the gates of Hades shall not overpower it [the church]" (Matt. 16:18).

But the community is no less *in* the world for not being *of* the world. It is keenly aware of the multitude, standing at a distance, often indifferent, sometimes curious, and ever capable of overt hostility. This is the beloved enemy, those for whom Christ died and with whom the Spirit pleads.

The ekklesia exists as a servant community. Just as its Lord came not to be ministered to but to minister, so the church is sent to minister to those in need. This implies more than waiting for some pressing need to surface for all to see, for by that time it is generally too late to render an effective service. The church ought rather to be so alert and so involved with people at every level of life that it will respond virtually before the need is realized, so as to minimize the trauma related to unmet needs.

In summary, the ekklesia is the people of God. It is not *of* the world, but for that very reason is more *in* the world. The Spirit fosters a holy discontent with things as they are and empowers a ministry to the downtrodden, infirm, and forsaken, which acts as evidence that the messianic age has indeed begun.

55 Variations

Hans Küng suggests that ekklesia can best be translated in three ways, so as to capture its rich and many-faceted character: congregation, community, and church. "'Congregation' expresses the fact that the ekklesia is never merely a static institution, but one that exists through the repeated event of a concrete coming together."[3] The ekklesia is not something formed and—having been formed—remains unchanged; it is ekklesia by virtue of its repeated gathering.

Ekklesia is a much more dynamic reality than our institutional way of thinking allows us to imagine. We are called "to church," not to a building but to God's building. This is what Küng means by *congregation*: the repeated gathering of the people of God in response to the urging of the Spirit of God.

Küng uses the term *community* to emphasize that the ekklesia is a fellowship of people who meet regularly at a given time and place for a

3. *Ibid.*,p. 84.

given purpose. The ekklesia functions along the lines of concretely organized communities. It has a predictable character that lends structure and direction to the fellowship of believers. *Community* is what we likely have in mind when we allude to a local church. We can visualize a location, times of services, stated liturgy, and the like. Fleshing out what would otherwise seem abstract and theoretical when we discuss the nature of the church, all this provides handles for the concerned churchman.

Küng reserves the term *church* for the all-embracing fellowship of believers. The church consists of all the redeemed, spread throughout the world, living, dead, and yet to be born. This reminds us that the ekklesia is never a disconnected "jumble of isolated and self-sufficient religious groups," but part of one overarching fellowship.

Paul has in view the ekklesia as *church* when he describes "the building up of the body of Christ" (Eph. 4:12). He sweeps together all those in Christ, urging them no longer to be as children, tossed about as the waves of the sea, but to become grounded in the faith. Thus, while this Epistle was directed to a particular destination, its truth applies to all.

Although we have represented Küng's threefold translation of ekklesia, we ought not lose sight of the more basic division between ekklesia as event and continuity. The ekklesia is act *and* being. It is not act alone, as if there were no continuing identity. Neither is it being alone, as if both summons and response were simply matters of the past. The people of God are called to refresh themselves in the presence of God, in continuity with succeeding generations of the faithful.

56 Hard Realities

The fact is that the church often presents a disappointing resemblance to what we have described in ideal terms. That ought not surprise us, since the church is a pilgrim people, on its way but not yet arrived. The Spirit has not yet completed His sanctifying work with the people of God.

What does this suggest to the earnest Christian? That he live by faith in the promises of God, that having begun a good work in him, the Almighty will bring it to fruition. His righteousness is that of hope and not sight. Of course, Christian hope has a purifying effect on one's life. We do not mean to question that fact, but rather the unrealistic expectations that people impose on biblical teaching. When faced with the frustrations of discipleship, the Christian ought not to despair—as if he were faced with some uncommon lot—but to recall the nature of his faith and rejoice in the sustaining grace of God.

What of one's attitude to the unresponsiveness of others in the fellowship? Dietrich Bonhoeffer writes: "There is probably no Christian to whom God has not given the uplifting *experience* of genuine Christian community at least once in his life. But in this world such experiences can be no more than a gracious extra beyond the daily bread of Christian community life. We have no claim upon such experiences, and we do not live with other Christians for the sake of acquiring them."[4] One ought not to expect expressions of Christian concern from others, as if guaranteed or as if the fellowship existed to serve that end. He ought rather to treat them as welcomed bonuses to what he already enjoys in Christ.

Two related things could be added. The first is that the Christian should not feel guilty for desiring the encouragement of others. This does not signify that our faith is lacking. Bonhoeffer reminds us that we were created a body—a body that relishes a morsel of food offered by another and the friendship expressed by the act. The test of devotion comes when the offer is conditioned on the compromise of our faith, and then a choice between the two is required. Until such time, we can rejoice in Christ's concern through others for our welfare.

Our second observation may at first appear to deny the previous one, but this is not the case. Bonhoeffer observes: "The more genuine and the deeper our community becomes, the more will everything else between us recede, the more clearly and purely will Jesus Christ and his work become the one and only thing that is vital between us. We have one another only through Christ, but through Christ we do have one another, wholly, and for all eternity."[5] Thus, time seems to blend into eternity, and the passing features of life together take on eternal significance.

As a result, we no longer require as much from the situation itself, but can rest confidently in the unfolding design of God. We discover that there is nothing to preserve that is not already in Christ, and nothing to lose that has not been entrusted to Him. There is no need to perpetuate a compulsive and self-defeating drive for fellowship.

The exigencies of life, all that has been said not to the contrary, can weigh heavily on the church. Some waver in the face of obstacles, while

---

4. Dietrich Bonhoeffer, *Life Together*, p. 39.
5. *Ibid.*, p. 26.

others thoroughly succumb. The true believer seems characterized not by how well he begins the race but whether he pushes on to its conclusion. He cannot afford pride in his own case or presume upon another.

Those who hear the preaching and take the elements are a mixed company of believers, hypocrites, and apostates. We must allow it to be such for the present, once we have exercised our responsibility to discipline. God will straighten matters out in the end, but for now we take confidence in the Spirit who gives and sustains life in the church.

57 Life in the Spirit

This seems a proper place to elaborate more fully on the baptism of the Spirit. Billy Graham confesses, "The Biblical truth, it seems to me, is that we are baptized into the body of Christ by the Spirit at conversion. This is the only Spirit Baptism."[6] This seems consistent with Paul's observation that "by one Spirit we were all baptized into one body" (1 Cor. 12:13).

Why should people think otherwise? Primarily because of the association of speaking in tongues in connection with three incidents in Acts, and taking these as normative for baptism with the Spirit. These instances are the coming of the Spirit at Pentecost (Acts 2:4), the outpouring of the Spirit in the home of Cornelius (Acts 10:44–46), and again upon certain disciples of John the Baptist (Acts 19:6).

What is the significance of these events? They appear to be a reversal of the confusion of tongues associated with the Tower of Babel (Gen. 11:1–9). They constitute at least a token restoration of what man had lost on the previous occasion and were as such an earnest of the messianic age.

The first of these involved the devout Jews of the Diaspora (Acts 2:5); the second, the God-fearing Gentiles; and the last, those followers of John—caught as they were between the turn of the ages (from the preparation with the Baptist to the fulfillment in Jesus). Thus were included in the scope of the latter-day advent of the Spirit both Jews and Gentiles, and moreover the disciples of John. There were no exceptions made.

Baptism with the Spirit is not explicitly mentioned in any of these instances. Those assembled on Pentecost were *filled with* the Spirit, the

6. Billy Graham, *The Holy Spirit*, p. 64.

Spirit was *poured out* upon Cornelius' associates and *came upon* the disciples of John. Nor were tongues mentioned in connection with the 3,000 subsequently converted at Pentecost, or in any of the other occasions where we might have expected it to occur. Graham suggests that the norm for today ought to be the 3,000 rather than the 120. But it is difficult to establish norms on historical precedent alone, whether in favor of the 3,000 or the 120, lacking more explicit teaching.

Such explicit teaching as we have seems to connect baptism with the Spirit to conversion. Paul introduces the subject in order to discourage the divisions arising in the church. He points out they were all baptized into one body by the one Spirit. Thus, baptism with the Spirit reminds us of our common heritage and unitary character as the people of God.

So it would seem that Paul has returned us to the place where we began: with regard to that unique work of the Spirit in calling out a messianic people of God. But in calling out a people, He has not called them away from their place of ministry. They are more involved in the world for being baptized together with the Spirit. Life in the Spirit is a dynamic experience of event and continuity. Each day in the fellowship is refreshingly new and yet builds upon what has passed. It resembles what some have described as "the people of God moving through history."

We have had to admit that the realities of life in the church differ substantially from the ideals we express. There are the weak and faltering, as well as the hypocrites and apostates. We often look in vain for some word of encouragement or evidence of a triumphant Christian life. Yet the church struggles on, even when the night seems its darkest, in anticipation of the first glimmer of light.

The fellowship of the Spirit is a fellowship born of hope and sustained by hope. It holds fast to the confidence that the Spirit, having begun His task, will follow it through to successful conclusion. The world and the devil are no match for the people of God as they are sustained by the Spirit of God.

This is likewise a fellowship of the committed. In the words of a gospel chorus, it has "decided to follow Jesus." There is no turning back. As the resolve of one kindles resolve in the other, they press on together. Baptized with the one Spirit, they are borne on by the same Spirit.

58 Variety of Gifts

Paul put the matter succinctly when he exclaimed that "He [Jesus] led captive a host of captives, and He gave gifts to men" (Eph. 4:8). This was accomplished through the Spirit who "works all these things, distributing to each one individually just as He wills" (1 Cor. 12:11). Thereby the church might be equipped to carry on the ministry assigned to it.

The discussion of gifts of the Spirit often flounders with regard to the institutional structure of the church. Seeing that we have both designated officials and charismatic leadership present in the one fellowship, who is responsible for what? The tension between the two has contributed to the divisions within the church and (depending on which is accented) the variant ecclesiologies developed to support one partisan position or another.

The problem persists so long as we treat it as a contest over who exercises authority. We make headway only when partisan interests are subordinated to selfless service. This is not an easy goal to achieve, as history well documents. So, while we have mentioned the issue only in passing, it often influences in one way or another the perspective we take on the gifts.

"Now there are varieties of gifts . . ." (1 Cor. 12:4). Paul lists the gifts in three passages: Romans 12:6–8, 1 Corinthians 12:8–10, and Ephesians 4:11. These lists are not identical, nor should we think of them as necessarily exhaustive. Yet the apostle repeats himself sufficiently so as to suggest that certain prominent examples are included.

The gifts are a mixed lot, which has led to various classifications. For instance, Leslie Flynn suggests three categories: speaking, ministering, and signifying gifts.[7] He includes as "speaking" gifts: apostleship, prophecy, evangelism, pastoring, teaching, exhorting, word of wisdom, word of knowledge, tongues, and interpretation. He classifies as "ministering" gifts: helps (including hospitality), giving, ruling, showing mercy, faith, discernment, miracles, and healing. Flynn selects the last two gifts from each category to make up the "signifying" gifts: miracles, healing, tongues, and interpretation. The gifts overlap, not merely from category to category but from gift to gift. Prophecy incorporates elements of teaching, and the gifts of helps and mercy are closely related—to mention but two instances where gifts blend together.

The diversity of gifts is further accented by the fact that the Holy Spirit dispenses gifts as He wills (1 Cor. 12:11). Each person is responsible both for the gifts he has received and to respect the complementary

---

7. Leslie Flynn, *19 Gifts of the Spirit*, p. 32.

value of those given to others. This implies a peculiar blend of gifts through any given fellowship of believers.

Paul warns his readers against restricting the range of gifts to those thought most desirable—that is to say, to those gifts which give their recipients a high visibility in the congregation. The more critical gifts are accorded less visibility, so that what seems less necessary is actually more necessary for the well-being of the Church.

What is the relationship between gifts and natural talents? The apostle seems less interested in this question than we may be. Both ultimately come from God and may be designed by the Spirit for service within the fellowship. This is, so to speak, the bottom line, and Scripture often fails to answer our idle curiosity on more speculative matters.

We shall limit our discussion of specific gifts to the list set forth in 1 Corinthians 12:8–11. (This will serve to illustrate what line of thought would run through the rest.) Paul begins with *wisdom*, having earlier distinguished between the wisdom of the world and the wisdom of God (1 Cor. 1:20–25). Men crucified Christ according to their worldly wisdom, but God has demonstrated that the "foolishness [wisdom] of God . . . is stronger than men." The cross has triumphed over the evil strategy of this world.

Wisdom has to do more with the practical application of knowledge than with knowledge itself. It relates to skill, whether in connection with a craft or life in general. The gift of wisdom assists in discerning how best to live in God's world and in keeping with His design.

The subsequent reference to *knowledge* probably includes both the ability to gain understanding and to retain what has been learned. More particularly, it relates to bringing out the implications of faith—to see all truth as God's truth. As the more theoretical counterpart of wisdom, knowledge provides a needed balance within the fellowship of believers.

Faith as a gift must be distinguished from faith as applied to the community as a whole. While all believers have faith, only select individuals have the gift of faith. The latter are given the confidence to believe that God will accomplish what would normally seem impossible. They walk where others waver, and as a result lift the general expectation of the congregation.

We normally think of *miracles* and *healing* in contrast to natural order, but they stand rather in opposition to the disruption of God's creation by evil forces. Miracles demonstrate the sovereign authority of God over the powers of this world. This is true whether they are in the form of healing, exorcism, or stilling a violent storm. Those who exercise this gift remind us that "our struggle is not against flesh and blood, but against the rulers, against the powers, against the world forces of this darkness, against the spiritual forces of wickedness in the heavenly places" (Eph. 6:12). This is not simply a reminder about the nature of our struggle, but also a notice that God keeps such evil principalities on a short leash until such time as He shall put an end to their power.

We may consider the gifts of *prophecy* and *discernment* together. The prophetic gift enables its recipient to stand within a company of those who have gone before him and declare God's truth. As Helmut Thielicke explains: "There is thus a chain of prophets whose members are interrelated. They cannot fail to be connected to one another. They will be ready to seek the manifestation of God's Spirit, and open to hear him, not only in themselves but others, too."[8] Yet, there are false as well as true prophets. The unchallenged claim of the prophet would leave us helpless to differentiate between truth and falsehood. Here the gift of discernment ("distinguishing the spirits") comes to our aid. When human reason fails, the ability to make distinctions at the deepest level is a gift of the Spirit.

This leaves us to consider the gifts of *tongues* and their *interpretation*. The gift of tongues enables one to express something in a "language" he has not learned. Whether it refers to a known or an unknown human language as ecstatic utterance, or a combination of the two, continues to be debated. There are also such striking differences between the gift of tongues described in 1 Corinthians and the speaking in tongues recorded in Acts as to bridge the gap between them with caution.[9]

Perhaps of more critical concern is how the gift of tongues serves the community. Likely this comes in an indirect fashion except where interpretation accompanies it, as Paul requires for public use (1 Cor. 14:28). Otherwise, one "edifies himself" (1 Cor. 14:4), and being so edified may contribute the more to the fellowship of which he is a part.

Paul further describes tongues as a sign "to unbelievers" (1 Cor. 14:22), which might be understood in the earlier context of discussing the nature of miracles. In any case, the apostle urges that tongues be used with care, and "if there is no interpreter, let him keep silent in the church; and let him speak to himself and to God" (v. 28). Thereby all gifts may complement one another in order to edify the people of God.

---

8. Helmut Thielicke, *The Evangelical Faith*, III, p. 79.
9. For a listing of the differences, see Oswald Sanders' *The Holy Spirit and His Gifts*, p. 125.

There ought to be no lack of creativity in a church so richly endowed by the Spirit. The possibilities would seem virtually endless, and the prospect thoroughly exciting—on the condition that believers do not quench the Holy Spirit or ignore their gifts.

59 Singular Purpose of Gifts

Paul reports the purpose of the gifts "for the equipping of the saints for the work of service, to the building up of the body of Christ" (Eph. 4:12). One is neither to depreciate the gift nor promote it so as to bring recognition to himself. He is rather to use it "for the common good" (1 Cor. 12:7).

The apostle Paul sets the proper attitude for exercising the gifts when he urges: "Do nothing from selfishness or empty conceit, but with humility of mind let each of you regard one another as more important than himself; do not merely look out for your own personal interests, but also for the interests of others" (Phil. 2:3–4). Remember how Jesus did not grasp on to His prerogatives, but humbled Himself even to the point of death on a cruel cross for the welfare of others? Let this be your paradigm; let this be your passion.

The gifts were meant to accent the unity of the fellowship (1 Cor. 12:20, 22–25). They ought never to support divisions, let alone give rise to them, since they remind us of the responsibility we have for others. Of course, this obligation is not limited to the fellowship alone. The church, as we observed earlier, exists to serve others in Christ's name. It is a servant community, equipped by the Spirit for that task. But its members must work together as the people of God if they are to succeed in the ministry set before them. This was designed as a corporate service that calls for a team effort.

So, while the purpose of the gifts is to edify the church, the church is not only an end in itself but a means to an end. It is gifted in order to be able to give, and there is no surer way to dry up its own spiritual vitality than to shrink back from its ministry. Gifts left unused soon atrophy.

This suggests that we must recognize and employ the gifts to their best advantage. Billy Graham suggests the following guidelines: recognize that God has given us at least one gift and means that we use it to His glory, seek to discover our spiritual gifts through deliberate and sustained prayer, understand what Scripture teaches concerning gifts, discover how our spiritual gifts involve a knowledge of ourselves and our abilities, and humbly and gratefully accept the apparent gifts in order to use them as fully as possible.[10] He adds the conviction: "I believe a person who is Spirit-filled—constantly submitting to the Lordship of Christ—will come to discover his gifts with some degree of ease." This will occur perhaps not at the time or under the circumstances he would have chosen, but when and how it fits into God's perfect will for his ministry to others—which is, after all else has been said, the purpose for which the gifts were intended in the first place.

60 Filled with the Spirit

Graham perceptively links the filling with the Spirit to discernment and use of our gifts. We ought not to pass over his suggestion thoughtlessly, because it provides an otherwise missing link in a discussion of the gifts of the Spirit. Without this, the remainder would not be simply lacking but hopelessly distorted as well.

Note that Scripture instructs believers to be filled with the Spirit (Eph. 5:18). Believers *have* the Spirit indwelling them, but are not necessarily *filled* with the Spirit. To be filled with the Spirit is to be in submission to the Spirit. It requires that we yield to God's will without reservation.

It must be obvious even to the casual reader that such commitment does not come readily or persist without interruption. The believer must hear the admonition time and again, repent of his failure, and yield himself afresh to the Almighty. This is not as though there were merit in the act of submission itself, but that it provides the necessary occasion for the Spirit to fill one's life to overflowing.

But we err in thinking of being filled with the Spirit in strictly passive terms. It resembles less the analogy of filling a bucket of water than the resolve of a runner at the beginning of a race. The latter fixes his full attention on the task before him, drawing upon every known resource to get away quickly at the sound of the gun and hold a steady pace to the end.

One cannot hope to exercise his gifts effectively while neglecting to be filled with the Spirit. The believer's spiritual task requires that he draw on spiritual resources. He cannot hope to succeed on his own, since the gifts are not his to use without recourse to the Giver.

---

10. Graham, *The Holy Spirit*, pp. 136–137.

61 Walking by the Spirit

Paul likewise charges believers to "walk by the Spirit, and you will not carry out the desire of the flesh" (Gal. 5:16). The context suggests that walking by the Spirit will involve loving one's neighbor, a love that requires not sentiment alone but appropriate action.

The former and present injunctions create an interesting paradox. How is one to wait on the Spirit and walk by the Spirit, all at the same time? There is a profound underlying wisdom to these seemingly contradictory commands. Does one find it difficult to wait? Then let him *walk* in loving constraint until the propitious moment for wholehearted submission comes. And if one has a problem with compassionate service, let him *wait* upon the Spirit. Both admonitions serve us well, judging from the differences in our experiences and recognizing that the mandates complement one another.

When taken together, these mandates locate the gifts in their source and for their purpose. They remind us that the gift without the Giver is nothing, and without the purpose is meaningless. The gifts provide a link between the Spirit as source and those served as the purpose for which the gifts are meant.

Graham reflects on a negative consideration: "Unfortunately, many Christians are disobedient and, having prayed for power, have no intention of using it, or else neglect to follow through in active obedience. I think it is a waste of time for us Christians to look for power we do not intend to use: for might in prayer, unless we pray; for strength to testify, without witnessing; for power unto holiness, without attempting to live a holy life; for grace to suffer, unless we take up the cross; for power in service, unless we serve."[11] In other words, it is a waste to covet the gifts of the Spirit unless we intend to serve as empowered by the indwelling Paraclete.

62 Fruit of the Spirit

We have deliberately chosen to treat the fruit of the Spirit within a corporate setting. As the gifts of the Spirit are held in sacred trust for others, so the fruit of the Spirit evidences itself in relationship to others. Fruit is not simply borne in isolation, as a matter of personal piety, but in the process of social interaction.

11. *Ibid.*, p. 107.

It seems curious that Scripture speaks of the fruit of the Spirit rather than fruits, especially where it goes on to enumerate nine particulars (Gal. 5:22–23). Various explanations have been advanced, but two of them seem more likely: the unifying nature of the fruit of the Spirit as opposed to the deeds of the flesh, and the preeminence of love among those traits listed. James inquires, "What is the source of quarrels and conflicts among you? Is not the source your pleasures that wage war in your members?" (James 4:1). It is as though the deeds of the flesh were pulling first one way and then another, or in different directions at the same time. This also seems to be the context of Paul's thinking: the deeds of the flesh resemble many masters striving with one another and tearing the individual apart in the process, while the fruit of the Spirit heals, restores, and unifies (Gal. 5:16–21).

We also observe that love stands at the head of "such things" (Gal. 5:23) as Paul mentions. It appears likely that the extended list develops more fully what the apostle associates with love. For instance, joy is impossible without love and inseparable from it. Joy, like the rest, finds its source and significance with regard to love, thus to accent the singular notion of the fruit of the Spirit.

"Fruit" provides one of the most forceful images in an agrarian society. Long hours are spent in restoring the terraces, tending the vines, and watching against intruders. One anticipates a good harvest as a time of joyful celebration and, hopefully, diligent labor will be rewarded by a bumper crop. The more we are removed from such an agrarian setting, the less the impact of the imagery on our thinking, and the greater the need to reflect on its critical significance.

63 Such Things

Love is the key concept; the remainder hinges on our understanding of love. The etymology of *agapao* is less clear than other Greek verbs we translate as "love," as it may be used in some very general sense or as a synonym. *The New International Dictionary of New Testament Theology* says: "When, on rare occasions, it refers to someone favored by a god, it is clear that, unlike *erao*, it is not the man's own longing for possessions or worth that is meant, but a generous move by one for the sake of the other."[12] This seems to be the point of departure for the biblical writers

12. Colin Brown (ed.), *The New International Dictionary of New Testament Theology*, II, p. 539.

in investing a relatively colorless word with an exceedingly rich meaning.

Such love as Paul has in mind is not solicited by filial relationship, the attractiveness of someone of the opposite sex, or some enviable trait in another. It is not solicited at all, but extended. It comes about not because the object is lovable, but because the subject is loving.

God commands such love, as a legitimate response to Himself and to our neighbor. But it is a mandate which man finds impossible to observe in and of himself. Paul complains, "For the good that I wish, I do not do; but I practice the very evil that I do not wish" (Rom. 7:19). The resolution to the apostle's dilemma resides with the fruit of the Spirit as love. It is faith in a loving God reflected inward toward oneself and outward toward others. But to appreciate what this means, we must analyze the character of this love more carefully.[13]

Love involves esteem. One who loves places a value on the object of his love. When God "so loved the world," He indicated that it had inestimable value for Him, regardless of the disregard that others might have. The object of God's love ought not to depreciate himself or others, and the fact that he is enjoined to love others *as* himself suggests the pervasive nature of such esteem.

Love also incorporates the effort to be of help. It cannot be content to sit back and relish some advantage when others are in need. It recognizes no political, social, or racial barriers in its obsession to serve. Nor does it limit service to spiritual needs alone. Love reaches out to serve the whole man in his total situation, and it does so without thought of remuneration or recognition.

Finally, love embraces the idea of mutuality, allowing the other to be there for you. It does not demand, but welcomes and expresses appreciation—not in a legalistic fashion, as if exchanging services of equal worth, but in a natural, unassuming manner when the occasion for ministry may occur.

Such love obviously involves personal risk. To love is to become vulnerable. This flies in the face of man's natural defenses and causes him to draw back into a protective position, unless he is so motivated by the indwelling Spirit as to risk all for the sake of the One who gave all. Then, at such a moment, we sense that love is being activated as the fruit of the Spirit.

---

13. Compare with Rayman Stamm's exposition in *The Interpreter's Bible*, X, pp. 557–559, 565–566.

Love resembles a well from which joy, peace, and the rest may be drawn. *Joy* attends the one who has learned that it is more blessed to give than receive. He is generous, enthusiastic, and forgiving. Joy is love in celebration.

The Semitic root for *peace* predominates in Paul's writing. It is total well-being rather than harmony that forges to the front. This peace is more than absence from strife, in that it implies accord with God and justice among men. Peace is love at rest in the providence of God.

Patience is calm endurance in the face of resolute opposition or apparent delay. It does not imply a passive acceptance of things as they are, but the willingness to let God have time to work out His purposes in and for us. It is also going the second mile, in giving more than may be expected of us. Patience is love as it endures all that would deny it.

We are reminded of Paul's earlier comment, "Love is patient, love is kind . . ." (1 Cor. 13:4). *Kindness* is showing sympathy, concern, and understanding. It reflects that quality of reaching beyond selfish interests or partisan causes to touch the lives of others. Kindness is love as it seeks one's neighbor.

Goodness relates to personal rectitude, and it results from a life generously spent on behalf of others. (One does not become "good" by sitting idly by while the world goes to ruin.) It is the ebb that accompanies the flow of kindness. Goodness is love returned in full measure and overflowing.

Paul witnessed before the Ephesian elders: "Therefore I testify to you this day, that I am innocent of the blood of all men. For I did not shrink from declaring to you the whole purpose of God" (Acts 20:26–27). Paul had been *faithful* to the charge given to him. He had exonerated his mission as the apostle to the Gentiles. Faithfulness is love as it assumes obligation.

Gentleness suggests a sober estimate of oneself, counting others better than oneself and treating them graciously. It does not depreciate self, but allows others to commend, rather than boasting or promoting oneself. Jesus taught that it would be people of such character who would, contrary to popular opinion, inherit the world (Matt. 5:5), and He described Himself in such a fashion (Matt. 11:29). Gentleness is love without pretense.

It has been said that although man was meant to rule the world, he cannot even control himself. *Self-control* implies that man does not give free rein to his impulses and desires, but this does not suggest taking a dispassionate attitude toward life. It resembles the discipline of an athlete who trains for the contest so that he can give his best. Self-control is love expressed in discipline.

Paul concludes with the observation that "against such things there is no law" (Gal. 5:23). Thus, by way of contrast to the deeds of the flesh, the apostle encourages the believer to bear the fruit of the Spirit in all dimensions of life. This would be appropriate to the people of God, for—unlike the gifts of the Spirit—the fruit of the Spirit pertains to all.

64 The Means

We turn from the subject of "What?" to "How?"—how does the Holy Spirit work in the lives of God's people so as to produce the fruit of the Spirit? Jesus taught: "Abide in Me, and I in you. As the branch cannot bear fruit of itself, unless it abides in the vine, so neither can you, unless you abide in Me" (John 15:4). Abiding in Christ is the key to bearing the fruit of the Spirit.

William Barclay reflects on the meaning of abiding in Christ: "For some few of us abiding in Christ will be a mystical experience which is beyond words to express. For most of us, it will mean a constant contest with Jesus Christ. It will mean arranging life, arranging prayer, arranging silence in such a way that there is never a day when we give ourselves a chance to forget Him."[14] The mystical alternative Barclay alludes to may have more to do with the individual's disposition than his state of spirituality. The important thing is to cultivate one's relationship with Christ on a regular basis. It means not only leaving some space for Christ, but weaving our lives around Him.

We must always struggle with the temptation to make the Christian life somehow more complex than it is, wasting our time and energy on searching for some obscure path into a deeper life. We complicate matters by extended introspection and endless discussions with others. Abiding in Christ is a relatively simple, uncomplicated lifestyle.

Dietrich Bonhoeffer instructs us that "Christ stands where man has failed before the law. Christ as the centre means that he is the fulfilment of the law. So he is in turn the boundary and judgement of man, but also the beginning of his new existence, its centre."[15] Christ stands at the center in judgment and reconciliation. To abide in Christ is to be reminded of both.

---

14. William Barclay, *The Gospel of John*, II, p. 205.
15. Dietrich Bonhoeffer, *Christ the Center*, p. 61.

We turn to a related consideration. The psalmist describes the blessed man as one whose "delight is in the law of the Lord, and in His law he meditates day and night. And he will be like a tree firmly planted by streams of water, which yields its fruit in its season . . ." (Ps. 1:2–3). Here the bearing of fruit is more specifically tied to the medium of Scripture.

Scripture was uniquely prepared by the Holy Spirit as a special resource for the people of God. We read: "All Scripture is inspired by God and profitable for teaching, for reproof, for correction, for training in righteousness; that the man of God may be adequate, equipped for every good work" (2 Tim. 3:16–17). This special revelation deals with the advent of Christ, such events which lead up to it (primarily as relates to Israel), and what resulted subsequently (in reference to the church).

We may conclude that Scripture points us to Christ. He is the central character, on whom all else turns and without which there would be no unifying figure. Wherever we begin with Scripture, the path leads us quickly to consider the Christ.

Christ also points us to the Scripture, and this fact is more pertinent for our present consideration. Those who hope to bear fruit must become people of the Book: reading its content, reflecting on its teaching, meditating on its truth, and putting its precepts to practice. Only in this way can they hope to resemble "a tree firmly planted by streams of water."

The Christian ought to read many books, but there is for him only one Book written under the inspiration of the Spirit in order to produce the fruit of the Spirit. His life flourishes or withers depending on how he manages to draw upon the resources of Scripture. He has no alternative text to turn to or any mystical presence that can substitute for the solid teaching of Holy Writ.

Helmut Thielicke recalls Luther's confidence that "we can be sure that it is impossible that there should be no Christians when the gospel goes forth, no matter how few or sinful or frail they may be, just as it is impossible that there should be Christians and not pagans where the gospel does not go forth."[16] Luther has reference to the preached word, keeping in mind the promise from Isaiah: "So shall My word be which goes forth from My mouth; it shall not return to Me empty, without

---

16. Thielicke, *The Evangelical Faith*, III, p. 215.

accomplishing what I desire, and without succeeding in the matter for which I sent it" (Isa. 55:11).

We are told not to forsake "our own assembling together, as is the habit of some, but encouraging one another; and all the more, as you see the day drawing near" (Heb. 10:25). This squarely places Scripture within the fellowship of God's people, where it may be faithfully expounded and mutually ministered. The notion of a solitary Christian sitting under a tree reading his Bible is a partial truth at best. He needs the experience of the community of faith as it waits the ministry of the Word in its midst and for its task.

How does the fruit of the Spirit come to take place? Through the Word: the living Word, the written Word, and the preached Word. These should be thought of in conjunction with each other, rather than as three distinct sources. Abiding in Christ is *the* key to bearing fruit, while Scripture provides our context for understanding, and proclamation interprets its application to the assembled congregation.

Paul concludes: "But earnestly desire the greater gifts. And I show you a still more excellent way" (1 Cor. 12:31). His readers had coveted what they supposed were the greater gifts, while lacking love—the fruit of the Spirit. Paul meant to help them to a better sense of priorities, based upon self-sacrificing love, so that his discussion of gifts and fruit of the Spirit blend together in a very natural way as he instructs the church.

Summary

We have turned from the general activity of the Spirit to His more specific work in these last days—with the church. What particular evidence do we have of His activity with the dawn of the messianic age? The coming into being of a messianic community of believers derived out of all nations.

We considered the ekklesia as "congregation" (the repeated gathering of God's people in response to a divine summons), as "community" (the stated meeting of the fellowship), and as "church" (the all-embracing fellowship of believers). But the realities fall far short of the ideals thus expressed, which should not surprise us—seeing that the church is a pilgrim people who press on in faith that He who has begun a good work will complete it in due time.

This suggests that we ought to treat evidences of Christian community as "a gracious extra" beyond the stable of Christian life. The fellowship experiences Christ, and this alone is enough to incite it to devotion and service. There is no cause to turn back from some failure on our part or that of others.

Our exploration into the topic of baptism with the Spirit merely serves to reenforce what has already been stated with regard to the Spirit's bringing into being a messianic people of God. Baptism with the Spirit reminds us not only of our origin as a people but of our source. Thus, life in the Spirit takes on a dynamic quality made up of the event of Pentecost and our continuity of experience with that event. It is also a fellowship born of and sustained by hope, from which there can be no turning back, the problems associated with discipleship notwithstanding.

But it would be presumptive to press so uncompromisingly were it not that the Spirit fortified the people of God for the task ahead. We limited our discussion of gifts of the Spirit to those recorded in 1 Corinthians 12: wisdom—skill with living in God's world; knowledge—how to see all truth as God's truth; faith—the confidence to see God work in exceptional ways; miracles and healing—to demonstrate God's authority over the powers of this world; prophecy and discernment—declaring of and discerning God's word; and tongues and their interpretation—expression and understanding of an unlearned "language." This led us to conclude that the church ought not to lack for creativity, being so richly endowed by the Spirit.

The gifts of the Spirit were meant to edify the fellowship. And seeing that the church was called as a servant community, the gifts indirectly support that purpose. All of this suggests that Christians individually and collectively ought to discover such gifts as are present in the fellowship and employ them responsibly.

Gifts of the Spirit were linked with the admonitions to be filled with the Spirit and to walk by the Spirit. One may be repeatedly filled upon repentance and yielding anew to the lordship of Christ. Walking by the Spirit involves loving constraint for others. The two, taken together, provide a complementary balance for the gifts of the Spirit, locating them on the one hand with the divine source for our labor and on the other in its purpose to serve.

We turned, as did the apostle Paul in Galatians 5, from the admonition to walk in the Spirit to a consideration of the fruit of the Spirit. We gathered that love was the central feature of the fruit of the Spirit, involving esteem, the effort to be of help, and the idea of mutuality. Joy might be described as love in celebration; peace as love at rest in the providence of God; patience as love's enduring all that would deny it; kindness as love's seeking one's neighbor; goodness as love returned in full measure; faithfulness as love's assuming obligation; gentleness as love without pretense; and self-control as love expressed in discipline.

Turning from the character of the fruit of the Spirit, we considered how it came about—first with regard to abiding in Christ, and thereafter in connection with the Scriptures and the preached word. Abiding in Christ provides the basic condition, the Scripture our proper understanding, and proclamation an application to the congregation. Through these means we may appreciate Paul's comment that he would show us a more excellent way whereby our priorities with the gifts of the Spirit may be set in order as we experience the fruit of the Spirit. Thus the community comes to understand what it means to live together as the people of God.

8

Life Alone

Dietrich Bonhoeffer observes: "The person who comes into a fellowship because he is running away from himself is misusing it for the sake of diversion, no matter how spiritual this diversion may appear. He is really not seeking community at all, but only distraction which will allow him to forget his loneliness for a brief time, the very alienation that creates the deadly isolation of man."[1] He needs instead to learn to cope with life alone.

65 Warning Explored

Bonhoeffer cautions that if one feels he cannot be alone, beware of community. Man can only do harm to himself and to the community if he ignores the place of solitude before God: "Alone you stood before God when he called you; alone you had to answer that call; alone you had to struggle and pray; and alone you will die and give an account to God. You cannot escape from yourself; for God has singled you out."[2] To refuse solitude is to reject the conditions of life and the circumstance under which we were called.

---

1. Dietrich Bonhoeffer, *Life Together*, p. 76.
2. *Ibid.*, p. 77.

The reverse is also true. One is ill-equipped for solitude without community. We are called to pursue the Christian life together, as we have seen in the previous chapter. Without fellowship one stumbles into the grasp of egoism, vain imagination, and unrelenting despair.

We have already discussed the communal dimension of life. It remains to consider life alone, as a necessary balance to life together. Any discussion of life in the Spirit would otherwise be not only incomplete but also badly distorted. It is in the tension between life together and life alone that we come to appreciate the wide range of the Holy Spirit's ministry.

66 Confession

The first place we confront solitude is with confession. In contrast to common prayer, whereby we pray to *our* Father about *our* needs, the creed begins with the words "I believe." At that moment the confessor stands quite alone, since he cannot assume that others stand with him, and he knows that no proxy can stand for him. He realizes that he cannot necessarily demonstrate to the satisfaction of others what he believes, but he believes nonetheless. Here he takes his solitary stand, with God helping him.

What one knows in the empirical sense is relatively small and inconsequential when left to itself. It is what one *believes* that ties these bits of information together into a meaningful mosaic. This realm of faith must be negotiated alone.

Helmut Thielicke shares an unforgettable story about a mother who had been estranged from the church for decades. He recounts how she sensitively ministered to her son, who was dying in excruciating pain. She betrayed not the slightest sign of how she herself was consumed by concern and anxiety. One day Thielicke blurted forth quite spontaneously, "I admire your attitude." Her equally candid reply was, "Yes, attitude perhaps, but don't look underneath. I haven't a thing to hold on to."[3] She carried on by rote, learned in her childhood, but without personal conviction or hope.

One can sort of ride on the faith of another, as did this pathetic woman, but lack any genuine foundation of faith. Confronted with her solitude, she had nothing to hold on to, and were it not for solitude, she

3. Helmut Thielicke, *I Believe*, pp. 7–8.

would have no way of knowing. She could have told us about the faith articulated by her parents, but nothing about her own faith or lack of it.

The precise way in which the Holy Spirit is associated with our decision to believe has long been debated. It is sufficient for our purposes to observe that in this solitary moment, when we have entered into the recesses of our innermost being, there the Spirit helps translate our wishes and hopes into firm conviction and trust. We are born again or born from above by the Holy Spirit who stirs up faith.

While the Holy Spirit is further away than we can imagine, He is also nearer than we think—so that it becomes difficult to define exactly how the divine and human elements in activating faith are associated. But both are somehow there, related in the miracle of the new birth.

67 Prayer

Prayer constitutes another aspect of life alone. We differentiate between personal and public prayer. The former relates things which apply particularly to the individual, even when these involve concerns for others. Public prayer deals with corporate concerns. One may be mistaken for the other, as when a person gets carried away with personal matters and forgets that he was meant to bring the petitions of the congregation before the throne of grace. But we mean to observe the distinction in treating prayer in the context of life together.

The solitary character of prayer becomes evident once we begin to consider the subjects for which we legitimately pray. We pray for God's guidance for the day before us, and even when we pray that His guidance be extended to others, it still is we who intercede for them. We pray alone, whether for ourselves or others.

We also pray to be preserved from sin, asking to be delivered from such things as we ought not to do and to be enabled to do the things we should. This is an intensely personal thing, which recognizes both our tragic failures in the past and such tokens of victory as God has allowed us to experience.

Likewise, we pray for growth in grace, for higher ground than we have experienced in the past. We pray that God will lift us from where we are to where we can better serve Him. This concerns our place before God and our progress in the Christian life.

As we become still more pointed with our prayers, we touch on countless specifics especially related to our perspective on life and the contribution we hope to render by God's grace. No two prayer lists are the same. Every individual assumes a peculiar prayer responsibility, reflecting his place alone before God in prayer.

68 Intercession

It is appropriate to single out intercession for special consideration. Every Christian has his or her own circle of friends who have asked to be remembered in prayer, sometimes in a general way and other times with certain particulars in view. The Christian assumes a peculiar obligation with regard to those whom God has brought his way, especially those who somehow get on the same track with him. There are certain kindred spirits who seem to understand each other, their way of doing things and their individual needs. Such people provide the best candidates for prayer partners.

But these kindred spirits are not the only ones for whom we intercede. We are often called upon to pray for those we instinctively dislike, have serious disagreement with, and would prefer for the sake of our peace of mind to forget about. Neither should we intercede as though the bulk of the problem were their own responsibility to set straight. We may even discover that *we* are at the heart of the problem as we bear up the other person before the throne of grace. In any case, one cannot readily condemn or callously depreciate those for whom one earnestly prays. Bonhoeffer observes in passing, "A Christian fellowship lives and exists by the intercession of its members for one another, or it collapses."[4]

We do not limit our intercession to those who ask it of us, but add such people for whom we feel burdened. (Otherwise, the more forward would receive all our attention and the more reticent little or none at all.) Although these are more often our associates—because we are constantly reminded of their needs—they can be other little-known persons or obscure situations which come to our attention. We need not restrict the range of our prayer concern in any way.

Believers ought especially to intercede for those who assume responsibility for them: parents, public officials, and church officers. Their ministries have special bearing on us, and it is not enough that they assume the task prayerfully. Whether or not they pray, we are obligated to intercede on their behalf—that they might act wisely, compassionately, and justly.

4. Bonhoeffer, *Life Together*, p. 86.

Scripture affirms that the Spirit assists us in "our weakness; for we do not know how to pray as we should, but the Spirit Himself intercedes for us with groanings too deep for words; and He who searches the hearts knows what the mind of the Spirit is, because He intercedes for the saints according to the will of God" (Rom. 8:26–27). Accordingly, we have a partnership with the Spirit in prayer, as the Lord intercedes for those who intercede for others.

69 Meditation

Another aspect of "life alone" is meditation, at least as much a private matter as prayer. Here we reflect on such matters as are of interest and concern to us. We consider what assumes a place of priority and pass over the rest quickly—as if of little or no personal consequence.

Christian meditation revolves around the Word of God. It dwells on His promises and our appropriate response. Here we find the alternative of introspection no substitute for the revelation of God. For the Word is drink for the thirsty and food for the famished disciple.

This is strikingly evident when it comes to biblical symbolism. A. Berkeley Mickelsen comments: "The reason Paul could glory or boast in the cross of Christ (Gal. 6:14) is that he knew what this symbol stood for. Meditation always precedes such a response."[5] Otherwise, we slip through the reference with little or no appreciation.

Meditation slows Bible reading to a walk. It resists both marathon and sprint mentalities: the temptations to cover too much ground or do it too quickly. It advocates looking first from one vantage point and then another, so that we will miss no feature or fail to give it a proper consideration.

Those who meditate on Scripture find that it lifts their horizons to see the world around them, thus to sense what needs exist and what means God has made available to meet such needs. Then also we identify where we fit into the scope of things, as God's instruments in serving others. This is to uncover one's personal responsibility, individually and in league with others.

The Spirit delights in instructing the people of God with the Word of God. We call this "illumination," in order to distinguish it from the

---

5. A. Berkeley Mickelsen, *Interpreting the Bible*, p. 279.

inspiration of Scripture. Strictly speaking, illumination provides nothing new, although it may throw new light on abiding truth.

How may we test the effectiveness of meditation? Bonhoeffer reminds us that we spend many hours each day alone in an un-Christian environment. These are the times of testing. "This is the place where we find out whether the Christian's meditation has led him into the unreal, from which he awakens in terror when he returns to the workaday world, or whether it has led him into a real contact with God, from which he emerges strengthened and purified. Has it transported him for a moment into a spiritual ecstasy that vanishes when everyday life returns, or has it lodged the Word of God so securely and deeply in his heart that it holds and fortifies him, impelling him to active love, to obedience, to good works?"[6] Such times demonstrate whether meditation has served its purpose, and whether the disciple has learned to negotiate life alone successfully.

70 Alone with God

We encounter God in solitude. Saint Teresa describes her experience as "the manifestation of the Lord's mighty power: as we are unable to resist His Majesty's will, either in soul or in body, and are not our own masters, we realize that, however irksome this truth may be, there is One stronger than ourselves, and that these favours are bestowed by Him, and that we, ourselves, can do absolutely nothing."[7] This may account at least in part for our reluctance to be alone, for there, at some unguarded moment, we may encounter God.

Thus are we brought to realize how little we are masters of our own destiny, and how thoroughly we depend on God for even the most elementary needs of life—coupled with the fact that we have neglected our responsibilities and have invited His chastisement. It is as though a bright light were shone into eyes accustomed to pitch darkness. So we build complex defenses against experiencing God in our solitude. Some are of an intellectual nature, others of an ethical character, and still others of religious import. But when their superficial distinctives have been removed, they rise from a common dread of facing God alone.

The Holy Spirit allows us no escape from solitude or the possibility of confronting the Almighty. He probes our defenses for some vulnerable

6. Bonhoeffer, *Life Together*, p. 88.
7. Frederick Streng, et al. (eds.), *Ways of Being Religious*, p. 41.

spot, pressing any advantage relentlessly. This is done not out of a sense of vindictiveness, but so that a gracious God may pour out His blessings on a reluctant creature.

We conclude, as we began, with the emphasis that the summonses to life together and life alone are complementary. Let him who cannot bear to be alone beware of community, and the one who stands apart from community beware of being alone. For now, we have stressed the significance of being alone. It is as we are alone that we reap a valid confession, probe the rich regions of prayer, cultivate the practice of intercession, explore the dynamics of meditation, and in and through it all, encounter the living God—as orchestrated by the Spirit.

71 Indwelling

We have encountered the idea of the Spirit's indwelling of the believer on other occasions, but now want to treat it in a more systematic fashion. Having indicated that those in the flesh cannot please God, Paul adds: "However, you are not in the flesh but in the Spirit, if indeed the Spirit of God dwells in you . . ." (Rom. 8:9). Paul concludes that we cannot presume to belong to Christ unless the Spirit indwells us. The whole Christian life pivots on this central truth.

Paul had struggled long and hard with the bondage of sin, so that the good he would do was left undone, and he fell prey to the evil he would refrain from. This situation seemed intolerable but without solution. This is what the apostle recalls as being "in the flesh," which contrasts with being "in the Spirit"—or indwelt by the Spirit. He has in mind everything that estranges man from God, everything that reflects man's vulnerability to temptation and sin. These are the chains rusted in place, which refuse to let their prisoner go. Paul knew of what he spoke.

He could boast of a godly heritage, a dedication to the Law, and a zeal for orthodoxy (Phil. 3:4–6), but all these served him poorly. Paul himself knew what others may have failed to see, that his good deeds and religious acts were plagued by baser motives, and that he invoked the name of God in order to frustrate the will of God and steer an alternate course. For all of his being "found blameless," he lived according to the flesh.

Lesser men would have accepted the imitation for the real thing. They would have basked in the acclaim of others, taking satisfaction in not being as other men who flaunt their evil practices. But Paul's noble spirit would allow him no such respite. The words of the Law lay heavily upon him, judging his behavior but offering no relief.

Then, when the last vestige of hope seemed crushed, all heaven broke loose in the apostle's life. The Spirit came to indwell, and he was free at last. What the Law could not do, God did in sending His Son and releasing His Spirit to dwell within man.

The vivid contrast that Paul portrays between life in the flesh and life in the Spirit is not simply a literary device. He had passed from night to day, from death to life, from defeat to victory. All that previously may have seemed an advantage to him Paul now considered nothing at all for what he had gained in Christ. Old things had passed away, praise God, all things had become new.

When faced with the prospect of returning to his former estate, Paul was adamant, "I do not nullify the grace of God . . ." (Gal. 2:21). He asked of his readers, "Are you so foolish? Having begun by the Spirit, are you now being perfected by the flesh?" (Gal. 3:3). There was no compromise possible: those who choose to live in the Spirit must walk in the Spirit.

Paul warned of the danger of setting our minds on the things of the flesh. When we sow to the flesh, we reap of the flesh. The course stretches toward certain destruction, and the day of reckoning comes much before we anticipate. "For the mind set on the flesh is death, but the mind set on the Spirit is life and peace" (Rom. 8:6).

As William Barclay elaborates: "Daily it is coming nearer heaven even when it is still on earth. Daily it is becoming more Christlike, more one with Christ. It is a life which is such a steady progress to God that the final transition of death is only a natural and inevitable stage on the way."[8] All men must die, Paul observes, but those who die in Christ rise also through Him. They triumph in the end even over their traditional enemy, the grim reaper.

Paul testified to a new inner resource of power that did not fail when called upon. This power was not to be associated with any of the resources common to man. It drew from above, outside of man and yet available to him. It was the Stranger within.

Eduard Schweizer likely overstates the case in making a legitimate point: "Israel's first experience of the working of the Spirit was of a strange power breaking into everyday life in unpredictable ways, a power that could not be clearly recognized as being good or bad, divine

8. William Barclay, *The Letter to the Romans*, p. 108.

or demonic."[9] Paul identified this alien power as "the Spirit of Christ" (Rom. 8:9). There was no question but that the Spirit meant to empower the disciple for his calling in Christ.

72 Witness

Paul continues to discuss the indwelling of the Spirit: "For you have not received a spirit of slavery leading to fear again, but you have received a spirit of adoption as sons by which we cry out, 'Abba! Father!' The Spirit Himself bears witness with our spirit that we are children of God" (Rom. 8:15–16). Roman history provides an outstanding illustration of the adoption practice that the apostle had in mind. The Emperor Claudius adopted Nero in order that the latter might follow him on the throne. Nero, wishing to ensure his position, asked to marry Claudius' daughter Octavia. But this could not be done until the Roman senate passed special legislation, seeing that, upon adoption, Nero and Octavia were legally brother and sister.

We are not told how Nero felt about the matter: whether or not he felt accepted as a bona fide member of the family. That was not actually the issue, any more than it is the issue whether the individual feels accepted by God. Theodore Epp argues: "The indwelling of the Holy Spirit does not depend upon our consciousness of that indwelling. . . . Since God says this is so, it is so."[10] The Holy Spirit assures us through the Word of God that we have been adopted into the family of God. Although we ought not to presume when God does not speak, we ought not doubt what He *has* said.

The apostle Paul seems to have something more in mind when he describes the Spirit as witnessing with our spirit. Barclay reflects on another feature of Roman adoption practice: "The adoption ceremony was carried out in the presence of seven witnesses. Now, suppose the adopting father died, and then suppose that there was some dispute about the right of the adopted son to inherit, one or more of the seven original witnesses stepped forward and swore that the adoption was genuine and true. . . . So, Paul is saying, it is the Holy Spirit Himself who is the witness to our adoption into the family of God."[11] Therefore, the objective promise is reassured by an inner conviction that we are now the children of God.

---

9. Eduard Schweizer, *The Holy Spirit*, p. 10.
10. Theodore Epp, *The Other Comforter*, p. 65.
11. Barclay, *The Letter to the Romans*, p. 113.

While our confidence does not rest in a feeling devoid of promise, neither should we choke off the spirit of adoption that springs from within. We cry out "Father" at the prompting of the Spirit, the One who has witnessed the adoption ceremony. He knows better than we the relationship which has been firmly established.

The corporate dimension must be tied in, even though we are accenting the individual's experience with the indwelling Spirit. To be in the Spirit is to be in Christ, and the latter constitutes one of Paul's favorite expressions—alluded to more than two hundred times. Archibald Hunter observes that "Pauline 'mysticism' is no 'flight of the alone to the Alone.' It is a social experience. It is to have discovered the secret of true community—in Christ."[12] So might we also affirm of the indwelling Spirit: that it is no flight into seclusion but a profound experience of community—where, as brothers and sisters together in the faith, we rejoice in the promise of God and the testimonial of His people. Thereby is the individual reassured by those of like faith.

73 Heirs of God

Paul turns his readers' attention to those things that await the children of God. If we are children by adoption, we are "heirs also, heirs of God and fellow heirs with Christ, if indeed we suffer with Him in order that we may also be glorified with Him" (Rom. 8:17). The apostle says *if* one, *then* the other: if children, then certainly heirs also. We may have such confidence even in the face of the present suffering.

What does it mean to be an heir of God? It suggests that inasmuch as God does not die, neither will those who draw upon His inheritance. The inheritance is life, eternal life and abundant life as well. It is abundant life because it is life with God. God is Himself the inheritance, and the believer anticipates fellowship with the Almighty. Anything God might provide for us dims by comparison with the gift of Himself. Heaven has no richer treasure.

Michael Ramsey writes: "The Christian life as St. Paul sees it concerns not the human race alone, but the world of nature too. That world, in consequence of man's fall, is in deep frustration. Its deliverance will come when redeemed humanity reaches to the maturity of sonship, and then it too will be delivered into freedom and glory."[13] The anxious

12. Archibald M. Hunter, *Introducing New Testament Theology*, p. 96.
13. Michael Ramsey, *Holy Spirit*, p. 71.

longing of the creation for "the revealing of the sons of God" (Rom. 8:19) suggests the glory yet to be revealed to the heirs of God. Paul does not press the matter further at this point, and we shall leave the subject for a future consideration.

But the apostle adds in passing that man is saved by hope—not what is seen but what is longed for (Rom. 8:24–25). Paul was well aware of the discouraging facets of life, but he believed that the dark night of the soul would vanish with the impending dawn. As one indwelt by the Spirit, he had already experienced an earnest of what as yet remained the object of hope.

Paul concludes "that God causes all things to work together for good to those who love God, to those who are called according to His purpose" (Rom. 8:28). He does not allege that all things are good in and of themselves. Neither does he suggest that things work out well for all who are involved. His confidence is restricted to those who experience the indwelling Spirit and are sensitive to His promptings. These may be assured that God will turn all things to their eventual benefit.

74 Greater Things

We turn to Jesus' remarkable promise as to the productivity of those who experience the indwelling Spirit: ". . . he who believes in Me, the works that I do shall he do also; and greater works than these shall he do; because I go to the Father" (John 14:12)—and because He will send the Spirit to indwell and empower the believer.

On the surface, the promise seems thoroughly incredible. When one realizes the mark Jesus has left on human history, how could His disciples be imagined to accomplish anything even slightly approximating His work, let alone something still more significant? Yet, Christ obviously meant what He said.

There is no use comparing Christ's activity with our own. Even if we were to travel farther and speak to larger audiences, our work would never approximate His. The point is not that we improve on His record but build upon it. Since our work would be impossible without Jesus' intercession, we are little more than His instruments—poor instruments in the Master's skillful hand.

The works of the disciples become greater because they involve a partnership previously lacking. J. B. Phillips describes the sight from heaven as the ministry of Jesus is replaced by that of the disciples: "As they looked, in place of the dazzling light there was a bright glow which throbbed and pulsated. And then as the Earth turned many times, little points of light spread out. A few flickered and died, but for the most part the lights burned steadily, and as they continued to watch, in many parts of the globe there was a glow over many areas."[14] The one dazzling light left behind a pulsating glow which ignited little points of light around the globe, lighting up the world as never before. Phillips concludes that while his account is certainly imaginary and fanciful, it is "a good deal truer than some of our current modern thinking."

Indeed, it is. More is accomplished as a result of every disciple who links up with the Lord. This creates a conduit for the Spirit to touch the lives of others.

The work of a disciple is also greater because it casts the gospel in another setting. The nature of the setting is irrelevant. Jesus touched a certain few through His public ministry, using the means at His disposal: as, for example, a small boat thrust out from the shore so that He could be better heard by the multitude. His disciple, any disciple, adds a new set of circumstances so that men may hear the gospel. Therefore, his ministry is "greater," not by measuring it alongside that of Jesus, but by adding it end to end.

The works are likewise "greater" because they extend through subsequent history, continuing the course Jesus set in motion. They are greater in the sense of this continuation, of not leaving things as they were.

Finally, the works are "greater" because they represent the ministry of Christ in session at the right hand of the Father. "In that day you shall know that I am in My Father, and you in Me, and I in you" (John 14:20). The relationship extends back to the Father, implying the global and pervasive possibilities available to the disciple. It is global because the Father is sovereign over *all* the world; it is pervasive because He is *sovereign* over all.

It is by now evident that the notion of being indwelt by the Spirit is no trivial matter. This indwelling implies freedom from all that held men in bondage to the flesh, and suggests the glorious realization that we have been adopted into the family of God and are destined to be His heirs. It promises that we shall, rightly understood, accomplish greater things than Jesus was able to accomplish in His remarkable ministry.

John wrote: "You are from God, little children, and have overcome them; because greater is He who is in you than he who is in the world"

---

14. J. B. Phillips, *New Testament Christianity*, pp. 18–19.

(1 John 4:4). Any victory presumes a prior struggle, and this is no exception. The conflict is real, with the powers of this world contending for every foot of ground, as pressed by the children of light.

However, there are certain conditions required for success. It is not by might nor by power, but by the Spirit of God that triumph is assured (*cp.* Zech. 4:6). Otherwise, man is no match for his adversary. He would fall easy prey, were it not for the indwelling Spirit.

Our vulnerability accents the importance of the earlier exhortations to be filled with and walk according to the Spirit. We must fine-tune our wills and ways to the Spirit within if we are to succeed with our struggle against the enemy without. We are our own worst enemy, seeing the potential readily available to us. The world trembles before the advance of a Spirit-empowered believer.

75 Sanctification

We would assume from the frequency with which the term *Holy Spirit* is used that holiness (sanctification) would be a primary concern with the work of the Spirit in the life of the believer. The assumption is borne out in various contexts (1 Cor. 3:16–18; Eph. 4:28–30; 1 Thess. 4:7–8). Accordingly, Christians may be called saints (Rom. 1:7) and rebuked when their lives fail to reflect the holiness anticipated (Eph. 5:3).

The topic of holiness conjures up the stereotype of a person somehow untouched by the feelings, needs, and temptations of the rest of mankind. But this is a distortion of the worst order. The saintly man is a man of like passions, yielded to the will of God for his life. He lives in the world by the power of the Spirit.

Dietrich Bonhoeffer's comment relates to our present subject: "Man no longer lives in the beginning—he has lost the beginning. Now he finds he is in the middle, knowing neither the end nor the beginning, and yet knowing he is in the middle, coming from the beginning and going toward the end."[15] Paradise has been lost, and heaven not as yet gained. There remains only the interim, a fallen world through which the pilgrim travels.

Holiness takes a realistic outlook toward the world in which we live. It dares to face life as it is, without shading it in terms of what we wish it were, and accepts "the middle" without qualification or mental reser-

15. Dietrich Bonhoeffer, *Creation and Fall/Temptation*, p. 14.

vation. As such, it stands in sharpest contrast to the idea of detachment and withdrawal. The world is seen as the arena of action.

This likewise implies the acceptance of self as the object of God's love and grace, as well as His instrument of service. Self-acceptance is involved in being in the middle, where we are not what we might have been (were it not for the fall) or what we will be but are not as yet. Holiness starts where we are and moves out into greater possibilities through the agency of the Holy Spirit. It is not complacent for being realistic.

The restless character of holiness can best be seen against the backdrop of its struggle with sin. It resists evil inclinations and offers encouragement to the more noble aspirations, refusing compromise with the world and fostering the communion of the saints. Holiness urges the saint to follow Christ, not counting the cost of discipleship.

Christian holiness is endowed with a profound sense of humility. It sees from the middle. Such truth as God reveals, He reveals to those encumbered with the responsibilities of life. One believer has no monopoly on truth, even Christian truth—seeing that this has become a matter of common knowledge. He labors with partial insights in a world not of his choosing, plagued by ambiguity at every hand.

Some take a higher road to realism than others. Their sense of what is real incorporates the purposes and activity of the Almighty. Therefore, while there is a common respect for life as we discover it, Christians see life within a larger perspective and have reason for hope that would otherwise be lacking. Theirs could be called a sacred realism, in contrast to the more restricted secular realism.

76 Focus on Christ

Biblical holiness must always point beyond itself toward Christ. As Christ is the center, holiness consists in approaching the center. This may be thought of in both an initial and progressive sense. We have been sanctified by faith in Christ (Heb. 10:14). Here the emphasis is placed upon man's position in Christ. According to Donald Bloesch, it "means to be engrafted into the righteousness of God."[16] Thus one is clothed in the righteousness of Christ.

Sanctification is also a progressive transformation of one's life, a reaching after Christian maturity. This progression must also be seen as

16. Donald Bloesch, *Essentials of Evangelical Theology*, II, p. 41.

approaching Christ, the center. Holiness can be viewed as the cultivation of a fellowship once begun and now being enriched. This does not rule out the idea of a crisis in engendering a holy life, although it ought not to exclude the dimension of a more gradual progression.

It follows that Christian holiness should not be understood as something we have in and of ourselves. This holy life consists of abiding in Christ. It has substance only as that substance reflects the vitality of this relationship. Holiness does not stand alone, as though we could characterize it apart from Christ.

Martin Luther wisely warned us against portraying Jesus as the paradigm of the pious life. While we may gather from His life something of the character of holy living, Christ is far more than our example. He is the center, which implies a more dynamic relationship than were He simply a model we might emulate. We do not walk in His footsteps except as we walk with our hand in His strong hand.

All of this suggests a distance between Christ and ourselves. I am not Christ; my ideals are not Christ's; our consensus is not Christ's. He is the Other, who stands over and against me, both in judgment and in offering reconciliation. Only when I have come to appreciate the chasm between Christ and myself can I begin to grasp the conditions required of a holy life. It starts, if at all, with the realization that Christ is the center. We walk with Him if we would walk in holiness.

To this we add that Christ is *for* us, even when we are not for our own best interests. He resists our efforts to self-destruct, seeing some potential in us that we have despaired of ever realizing, and promoting the good without ceasing. Such is the "happy coincidence" C. S. Lewis speaks about: that the will of God and our best should turn out to be one and the same thing.

We must make the adjustment, rather than expecting Christ to do so. His way is right, and it is right for us. He does not accommodate to our sinful predilections. We must accommodate to His aspirations. But Christ does accommodate in another sense, working in a most creative way to achieve His purposes. No matter which way we turn, He enjoys opening up new possibilities for holiness—so that we meet Him at each turn of the road, pointing us toward God's way.

We have argued that the sanctified life is one *in* and *of* Christ. It is also *for* Christ. We shall develop this latter point subsequently, but it is appropriate to mention it in passing, for Christ is the focus of Christian piety in all its connections.

77 Dynamic

Holiness, as Epp observes, "is not a human accomplishment but a divine work. Sanctification is one of the great operations of the Holy Spirit in the salvation of believers. Without this work on our behalf there would be no manifestation of holy living in our personal conduct."[17] Of course, we allow that the individual must be willing to cooperate.

The first response that proves the occasion for the Spirit to work is faith. But faith should not be thought of *as* a work. Faith does not accomplish holiness; the Spirit does. Faith allows the Spirit to act on our behalf. It resembles opening all the doors to allow Him free course.

Faith allows one to press on from a prior point, without constantly returning to cover the same terrain over and over. It allows that the transaction is done, that we are the Lord's and He is ours. With faith we can take each subsequent day in confidence that He who has begun a good work will bring it to a happy conclusion. Faith transcends all that casts doubt, bringing confidence that all things work together for good for those who love God and seek to serve Him.

Our second response is hope, which is closely associated with faith. Christian hope sponsors a life of holiness. "Since all these things are to be destroyed in this way, what sort of people ought you to be in holy conduct and godliness!" (2 Peter 3:11). Hope sees that the day of the Lord will come suddenly, when it is little expected, and that we shall be called upon to give an account for how we lived in this present age.

Helmut Thielicke elaborates: "I encounter my own future and the future of 'my world' in the sense that I am called to assume responsibility for shaping it, and also in the sense that I look upward and outward towards the succession of events which transpire independently of me, and toward that future which is always coming upon me without my doing."[18] Therefore, one must account for what portends for the future, as well as for his own obligation for tempering it. The believer's duty resides in coping with the future as it breaks in on the present, and he does that through allowing the Spirit to minister to and through him.

The final response is love, which ties together the previous two. Love is faith taking hold of the promises of God to serve His purposes, and it is hope relying on the promises of God in the face of every obstacle. Love

17. Epp, *The Other Comforter*, p. 92.
18. Helmut Thielicke, *Theological Ethics*, I, p. 469.

is openness to what God has done, is about to do, and is doing. It welcomes every overture of the Spirit.

One who fails to act on behalf of another may be said not to love, but the proper motivation must also be present for an act to be called "loving." Love involves both motive and action. The two taken together foster the presence of the Holy Spirit in sanctifying the human spirit.

We do not want to give the impression that the dynamic of holiness is precisely predictable. The Spirit works in ways that surprise us, but this is because of the complex nature of life, and not because the responses of faith, hope, and love are irrelevant. It is simply that we see only the tip of the iceberg and not what is out of sight to us, yet known intimately to the Spirit. The Holy Spirit works with pliable and responsive believers to fashion saints worthy of the designation.

78 Context

Bloesch comments: "Whereas mysticism placed the emphasis on the journey inward, Luther stressed the importance of breaking out of the self into service to others. For the Reformers the road to God is the road to our neighbor's needs. Works of piety must be supplemented by works of mercy, though the latter should always be grounded in the former."[19] In other words, service constitutes the proper context in which holiness can thrive.

What is the character of such service as fosters a holy life? It is what we described earlier as service *for* Christ. The saints assume Christ's servant role: seeking not to be ministered to but to minister. They labor not out of thought of reward, or to secure their position, but from compassion for those in need. They see such selfless labor not as an imposition, but normative for the Christian life.

Service for Christ is nonetheless service. It seeks out the nature of the need before presuming that it is known, let alone offering a resolution. There are few more frustrating experiences than attempting to meet a need that does not exist or seems not readily apparent. We have to learn to listen and to respond to such needs as become evident.

Of course, there is a time to help a person see that a need exists, or that there are more pressing needs than he supposes. This is also involved in the idea of service. However, we ought not to assume that we know more about the needs of another than we actually do. We should,

---

19. Bloesch, *Essentials of Evangelical Theology*, II, pp. 53–54.

even in advancing some suggestion, not pontificate as if we were the Almighty. We do persons an injustice by playing God.

We also serve by allowing others to minister to us. Service seldom if ever flows in only one direction. Whenever we intend to give, we regularly experience that we have received more in return, and we ought not to deprive others of their opportunity to share.

Service is not strictly a matter of closing out old concerns. It can be in helping other people face new and threatening developments. Life must be kept open-ended, since the person who tries to play it safe finds the result constricting and painful. To live is to risk one's life in new adventures. We serve by exemplifying such openness in our lives and encouraging it in others.

That is not to minimize the importance of what we have previously experienced. Life should be celebrated, even in its more mundane aspects. We also serve by cultivating a rejoicing spirit in others, by helping them to appreciate their rich bounty, and by weighing the obligations that attend—for, from those who have received much, more will be required.

We have been sanctified to serve. That is the sum of the matter. Scripture charges that "the one who does not love his brother whom he has seen, cannot love God whom he has not seen" (1 John 4:20). Similarly, one cannot profess to serve God and not his fellowman. A holy people is a helping people.

Summary

We shifted our emphasis from the community to the individual, from life together to life alone, with the warning that one ought not to pursue one to the exclusion of the other. If you cannot bear to be alone, beware of community; and if you lack a feeling of community, beware of being alone. The Spirit works in both connections to further His purposes.

The first place we confronted solitude was with regard to confession. Here there can be no proxy, and here one must affirm his own faith, regardless of whether or not he is joined by others. Private prayer is another instance of life alone, as is intercession—as a special case in point—and meditation.

We also encounter God in solitude, when we stand alone in His presence and realize in the words of Saint Teresa that "there is One stronger than ourselves." On Him we depend for the necessities of life and without Him we could do nothing at all. This helps explain both our fear and our fascination with solitude, for in some unguarded moment we may meet the Almighty.

Pursuing the idea of life alone further with the notion of being indwelt with the Spirit, we first considered the freedom we experience in the Spirit, once the bondage of sin has been broken. Through this indwelling, life takes on a radically new character for those no longer in the flesh but in the Spirit. A peculiar people results from the presence of the Stranger within.

This led us to consider the witness of the Spirit, whereby we cry out "Abba! Father!" This witness comes objectively through the Word and subjectively as an assurance to faith. It ought not to be limited to one or the other, nor divorced from the community where faith is fostered, recognized, and reenforced.

Our confidence suggests that if we are sons, then we are also heirs of God. We are assured that the Almighty will withhold no good thing from us, least of all Himself. The creation, frustrated as a consequence of man's fall, anxiously longs for deliverance, and man is not only drawn by hope in the future but spurred to negotiate the present as one indwelt by the Spirit.

Thus also we accomplish things which Jesus promised would be greater than His own deeds. The point is not that we better His record, but that we build upon it. These greater works imply drawing man into a partnership, creating a conduit for the Spirit to work, casting the gospel in still other settings, and extending the ministry of reconciliation to future generations as the result of Christ's intercessory ministry at the right hand of the Father.

We concluded our discussion of life alone with the sanctification of the believer. The Holy Spirit creates a holy people in a fallen world, whereby we are not transported back to paradise or promoted to heaven, but granted grace to live in this present evil world—with confidence that the indwelling Spirit will bring the pilgrim journey to a successful conclusion.

Biblical holiness points beyond itself to Christ, not as exemplar alone, but as the center of life. Holiness consists of approaching the center, of cultivating a relationship. The sanctified life is life in, of, and for

Christ. Holiness is not man's struggle to attain some ideal on his own, but reliance on the indwelling Spirit, who may be said to work in response to man's faith, hope, and love. Yet, this does not rule out the unpredictable way in which He turns even the most difficult situations and personal dispositions to eternal gain.

Finally, we located the context of holiness in service. The Holy Spirit seeks out a people to minister—in contrast to the way of the world, where people seek their own needs to the exclusion of the needs of others. Those who qualify as saints must validate their credentials as servants.

9

The Powers

As we turn finally to the struggle between the Holy Spirit and the forces of evil, we employ for this purpose Oscar Cullmann's often-repeated analogy between the conquest of Christ and the invasion of the European continent during World War II. Cullmann likens the first advent of Christ to D-Day, and the second advent to V-Day.

79 D-Day

Cullmann's analogy suggests that the world is somehow alien territory for the people of God. It exists not to make life easy for the pilgrim, but as an adversary, one which is subject to "the prince of the power of the air" (Eph. 2:2). "For our struggle is not against flesh and blood, but against the rulers, against the powers, against the world forces of this darkness, against the spiritual forces of wickedness in the heavenly places" (Eph. 6:12).

Christians formerly walked according to the course of the world, obedient to its resident powers. But now they form a beachhead of the Spirit on the domain of Satan. They are the earnest of ultimate and complete victory over the forces assembled against the Almighty.

Modern man has difficulty with all this talk about spiritual forces in conflict. It seems strange, antiquated, and unreal, at least on the surface of things. But old beliefs tend to be revived in new contexts, as illustrated by the present popularity of astrology and the revival of spiritualism. This suggests that there may be more to this world than we have taken for granted. There are inexplicable forces at work, and man is not, strictly speaking, the master of his own destiny. At such moments as we become aware of this cosmic struggle, our Enlightenment mentality seems an ineffective protest against the spiritual character of the world in which we live.

In any case, the powers were real to the apostle Paul and those to whom he wrote. They had experienced to their own satisfaction the reality of such powers and had engaged the spirits at one point or another. In what connection? As both intermediaries and malevolent rivals. Annemarie de Waal Malefijt notes: "Spirits are usually created by the gods. However, the power of creation is of less social importance than the power to intervene in everyday human affairs: the growing of the crops, health, and other matters directly concerning human welfare. When spirits are believed to be responsible for common aspects of daily life, they loom larger in man's consciousness, and rituals in their honor are more frequent."[1] Thus the attention becomes centered on the intermediaries who might negotiate some favor for their supplicant.

The spirits exacted a high price for their cooperation, or they changed their minds due to some subsequent intervention. Some were even hateful and capricious. Man learned to live in fear of the spirits and what they might do if offended.

We can only imagine how revolutionary the gospel may have appeared to those caught up in the spirit world. Paul wrote that "there is one God, and one mediator also between God and men, the man Christ Jesus" (1 Tim. 2:5). With one sentence he swept the heavens of a warring pantheon, as well as the spirits that attended them. So also he banished the fear with which they had been regarded. This was indeed good news for a beleaguered humanity, for it dealt with life at its most critical level.

The "powers" must be understood primarily in political and religious terms, as expressing the pleasure of those from which their authority is derived. We are reminded how quickly that which is meant to serve man, whether in political or religious contexts, turns to dominate and intimidate him. This is to suggest that the basic problem persists even in

---

1. Annemarie de Waal Malefijt, *Religion and Culture*, p. 154.

secular society, where some ideal supplants religious belief and—under the pretense of serving—afflicts man instead.

The Holy Spirit may be said to stand in uncompromising opposition to the powers in their attempt to dominate man. He enters the arena in order to put the elemental spirits to flight. He asks no quarter and He gives none, nor will there be any respite until the kingdoms of this world have been subjected to Christ.

80 Triumph

The cross points us to Christ's encounter with the powers. They put Him on the cross, and He overcame them through the cross. Had they understood the wisdom of God, "they would not have crucified the Lord of glory" (1 Cor. 2:8), for this proved to be their undoing.

Paul portrays the powers as in the process of passing away. The beachhead, according to Cullmann's analogy, has been firmly planted; final victory is assured. For all of the appearance of power, the reins of government are slipping from the hands of the rulers of this world. They strike out in desperation, but their end is assured. The people of God sense their triumph through Christ, even in the midst of persecution and martyrdom.

The outcome is no longer in doubt, whether or not it ever was. When Christ "disarmed the rulers and authorities, He made a public display of them, having triumphed over them . . ." (Col. 3:15). As with the parade of those vanquished in military battle, the powers are stripped of their arms and displayed as trophies of victory, for all the world to see how those who once terrified them are powerless to do so any longer.

This helps us understand why the powers chose to fight against Christ. Albert van den Heuvel writes: "Jesus had come as their Lord, in him they were created, and in him they met their master. Since they had become independent, however, and had set themselves up as gods, they could attack Jesus. Their service structure had become a structure of domination: neither politics or religion was helping men to live according to God's will any longer."[2] On the contrary, they had enslaved men to a servitude contrary to the freedom God wanted for them. Jesus represented the ultimate challenge to their usurped authority.

All hope of pretense for the powers vanished with the cross. They had carried on their devious activity under pretense of service, while extend-

2. Albert van den Heuvel, *The Rebellious Powers*, p. 61.

ing oppression. But the cross revealed them for what they had become, totalitarian spirits who would risk anything to keep their power intact, even when it meant putting to death the Lord of glory.

The cross was not the first encounter of Christ with the powers. Herod had tried to kill Him as an infant; the adversary had tempted Him at the outset of His ministry; demons challenged Him from time to time. But Christ persisted in the Spirit through it all, bent on doing His Father's will. The cross was only the last desperate effort of the powers to snatch victory from defeat, but instead it ensured their own defeat.

We often think of the forgiveness of sin as the primary significance of the cross, but we ought not to overlook the prominent place that Paul gives to the triumph of Christ over the powers. The former is no substitute for the latter. It is rather an aspect of the victory won over the powers and principalities of this world. This is a victory so extensive, so pervasive, as to sweep all before it.

It is a tragic thing that we do in persisting to serve the powers. It bears witness against the freedom provided for us in the cross. It gives comfort to the enemy and results in every kind of wrong that Christ meant to make right.

Far better it is to realize that those born of the Spirit overcome the world in the cross of Christ. The Spirit bears witness to the truth that we are sons of God and thereby overcome the powers (1 John 5:4–7)—thus also transforming us into the image of Christ as "from glory to glory" (2 Cor. 3:18).

81 Power Encounter

All of this suggests the need of what has been called a "power encounter." It results when one reaches the point where he sets aside all in which he has heretofore put his confidence in response to a newly discovered loyalty. Such is the nature of disposing of the dethroned powers in order to follow the triumphant Christ.

The power encounter may be illustrated by the experience of a friend of mine whose father was a tribal priest. Through a series of circumstances that we need not repeat here, he became a follower of Christ. One day, many years after his conversion, he excitedly shared with me the fact that his father had finally decided to embrace Christ. The father had anticipated over the years that his son would return to seek the intercession of the spirits on his behalf, when confronted by some trial or other. But when this did not happen, he was assured that his son had discovered a truth that liberated him from dependence on the powers.

The idea of a power encounter has generally been associated with primitive cultures, but there is no reason to suppose that it should be limited to these alone. It is the nature of the gospel that it triumphs over the powers, however they may be expressed in one culture or another. One must be prepared to leave all in order to follow Christ, whether this "all" involves a sacred tree in a primitive village or the organizational image of some industrial firm.

Now let us look more closely at the dynamics of our experience of Christ in dethroning the powers. Such a power encounter obviously involves rejecting the powers as having any ultimate authority over us. They have been soundly defeated at the cross, so that we might be freed by the Spirit. We are free men from this time forward.

But we are free only in Christ. We need to affirm Christ's victory over the powers in the cross. Otherwise, there is no triumph for us. We dispel the powers of darkness by calling on the name of Christ.

Thereupon, we rely on the Holy Spirit. Helmut Thielicke discussed why, strictly speaking, ethical decisions cannot be made in advance. The argument is involved, and we do not need to repeat it for our purposes. What interests us is that Thielicke directs his attention to the guidance of the Holy Spirit in a given situation. Referring to what he calls the "improvisation of the moment," Thielicke represents this moment as a contest between the Spirit of God and the powers, wherein the individual Christian provides the focus. He reasons, "The kingdom of God 'uses' me. The Spirit himself is present to meet the assault."[3]

Thielicke assures his reader that the Christian need not be anxious when he approaches the contest with the powers, for the Spirit will speak in his stead, rebuking the powers and exercising the authority of Christ over them. The Spirit fashions our intent to dispel the powers into an actual occasion for doing so.

This suggests two things: the importance of becoming familiarized with the promises of God and maintaining an active prayer life. The Spirit does not function just any way, but in accordance with the promises explicit or implied in Holy Writ. The Christian who has not immersed himself in the Word of God is ill-prepared for spiritual warfare. There are no substitutes or exceptions.

---

3. Helmut Thielicke, *Theological Ethics*, I, p. 651.

A vigorous prayer life is also critical, seeing that we rely on the Spirit to press the claims of Christ against the powers. We cannot prevail in the flesh, and we cannot prevail in the Spirit apart from sustained prayer. The prayer vigil consists not of vain repetitions but an earnest petition that seeks first the kingdom of God and the righteousness of God. Such prayer causes the powers to retreat in disarray.

The power encounter dramatizes Christ's victory over the powers. Here we see how ineffective the powers are to intimidate the believer who puts his confidence in the indwelling Spirit. We also sense the conditions necessary to wage spiritual warfare.

82 Militancy

We need to look at the nature of the conflict in more detail. Paul admonishes his readers that henceforth they be strengthened in the Lord, which ought to set aside any impression that the Christian is simply passive in the conflict. He participates as fully in the contest as a soldier who wages war, or a wrestler who struggles with his opponent. Like them, the militant Christian must prepare diligently and be able to call upon his training intuitively when the time comes.

Paul warns his readers of the critical nature of the conflict. It is no sport for the pleasure of its observers, but a struggle of cosmic proportion. The struggle calls upon all our energies and such support as we can muster. No halfhearted effort can be expected to prevail.

This condition requires the believer to reach beyond himself. As John Calvin elaborates: "For the saints the occasion that best stimulates them to call upon God is when, distressed by their own need, they are troubled by the greatest unrest, and are almost driven out of their senses, until faith opportunely comes to their relief."[4] Only those deeply aware of their own insufficiency to meet the task are candidates for the sufficiency of the Spirit. Only they measure the situation accurately and respond appropriately.

If some lose sight of man's role in the conflict, others lose sight of the Spirit's enablement. They are prone to become obsessed with the difficulties or their own deficiencies, so that they are drawn in the opposite direction—away from Christ. This is to suggest that our need, rightly understood, is to draw near to the Lord. In this way, we recognize that

4. John Calvin, *Institutes of the Christian Religion*, III, 20, 11.

the Spirit means to cope not only with the task before us but our own disposition toward it.

The conflict is always situational. We deal not in abstractions but in concrete challenges, needs, and resources. Here we face some particular objective, the obstacles which hinder us, and the demands for accomplishing our goal. Here we call out to Christ, confident of His victory over the powers and our partnership with the Spirit. Each encounter with the dethroned powers teaches us anew the seriousness of our struggle and the conditions for experiencing triumph. We are firmly planted as a beachhead on an alien shore, precarious and yet assured.

Whether we encounter the enemy forces unmasked in the form of demon possession, or obscured in entrenched political and religious forms, they are ever around us. We must be alert to their presence, resist their endeavor, and press the cause of Christ, persuaded in the process that the Spirit within is greater than all the forces assembled without, as well as our own fears. The Christian forces the conflict, knowing that D-Day lies behind him and V-Day lies ahead.

83 V-Day

There remains to consider what Oscar Cullmann described as V-Day, the consummation of the conflict with the powers of this world. At this time of final victory, the swords may be laid down and the eternal peace brought in. All this relates to the blessed hope of the Christian in the return of Christ, the last judgment, and the final state of things.

Emil Brunner explains, "Just as He [Christ] is our righteousness and our life, so is He our future, our hope. He is the consummation, the fulfilment of the prophetic promise. On Him alone Christian hope is based; not on any apocalyptic or eschatological statements of Scripture."[5] Although this puts the matter in its most polemic fashion and requires certain qualifications, Brunner is correct insofar as the Christian hope is not in something so much as in Someone. The Christian is certain that whatever the future holds, it is secure in Christ. He need not be unduly concerned with the circumstances as such, since Christ delights in turning even the most difficult of circumstances to His good purposes. This holds true whether in terms of the result of our ministry to others or its enrichment to our own lives.

---

5. Emil Brunner, *The Christian Doctrine of the Church, Faith, and the Consummation*, p. 340.

It may be more precise to say that it is Christ's victory over the powers that gives us reason to hope. He has soundly defeated them at the cross and with the resurrection, and He continues to put them to flight upon the beckoned call of His disciples. Paul confidently concludes, "But in all these things we overwhelmingly conquer through Him who loved us" (Rom. 8:37). To which he adds: "I know whom I have believed and I am convinced that He is able to guard what I have entrusted to Him until that day" (2 Tim. 1:12). Of such was the nature of his hope and that of Christians at large.

Christ's triumph provides the objective basis of hope. The promises of God and the witness of the Spirit (that we are sons and therefore heirs of God) supply the subjective certainty. Although there is no hope for those outside the household of faith, there is no reason to waver in hope for those within the believing community. This confidence ought to be validated in the community, where the testimony is heard and verified. Here faith answers to faith. Here we learn that no one has a monopoly on hope and the riches we hold in common as believers.

But to say with Brunner that Christ is our hope, allowing such qualifications as we have added, is not yet adequate. Brunner adds that hope (or faith as hope) is "necessarily bound up with a twofold consciousness, a consciousness of Him who has already come and of Him whom we are still to expect, who has not yet come."[6] There can be no end without the beginning, and no beginning that does not anticipate the end. The Christian consciousness always hinges on this "now but not yet" reality.

The "already" experience of Christ includes His life, death, and resurrection/ascension. It involves all that we know of the life and teaching of Christ, as recalled for us by early disciples. What has been recorded is not enough to satisfy the curiosity of the reader, but rather to provide such information as piety requires. Thus, we do not know what color were His eyes, but that He had compassion on persons, regardless of their social status or religious credentials.

The cross casts a long shadow back over the life of Christ, in all of its particulars. We are never far from the impending death of Christ on behalf of a lost mankind. He would lay down His life for others, as a final sacrifice in a life of ministry.

Christ's death was followed in quick order by the resurrection, and shortly thereafter by the ascension. He shook loose from the grip of

---

6. *Ibid.*,p. 341.

death, to leave behind an empty tomb and a living faith. Thus Paul reasoned that "if the Spirit of Him who raised Jesus from the dead dwells in you, He who raised Christ Jesus will also give life to your mortal bodies through His Spirit who indwells you" (Rom. 8:11). Accordingly, we may speak of resurrection faith as a present reality for those who have passed from death to life and enjoy the presence of the Spirit in their lives.

But such consciousness and faith also point to the future, to what the Spirit intends to do in quickening our mortal bodies. There remains the "not yet" in our experience, which together with the prior confidence creates Brunner's reference to a twofold consciousness. Every effort to reduce the one to the other must be resisted. Christian eschatology (doctrine of the "last things") is inevitably inaugural in character. It concludes that what was begun in the former advent of Christ will be concluded with His second advent.

84 Crisis of Hope

The interim between the advents created what some have called "the crisis of hope." Why has the second advent been so long in coming, seeing that evil continues seemingly unabated? Why have the martyrs' cries fallen on deaf ears? Some rationale seemed called for.

The earliest Christians concluded that the unpredictable imminence of the Lord's return required extreme vigilance. They repeated Jesus' words, "Take heed, keep on the alert; for you do not know when the appointed time is" (Mark 13:33). In other words, those who have been thrust into the messianic age cannot presume from one day to the next or postpone their discipleship (Luke 14:18–21). Since there is a continuity between the *now* and the *not yet* that appears more significant than the difference, the crisis, if that is not too strong a word, seems less marked in the early community than one might expect.

There was a second reason advanced for the apparent delay, as Thielicke explains: "The certainty that the kingdom of God has drawn near rests primarily on the fact that in the person of the risen Lord the world of death has been decisively broken and the end has been anticipated. To use a metaphor of Luther's, the serpent's head has been broken. All that the time of this world can now bring is the writhing of its body."[7] What remains has little consequence in the light of Christ's

7. Helmut Thielicke, *The Evangelical Faith*, III, p. 431.

conquest over the powers. It is only the working out of this event in some particulars.

Still more obvious was the possibility this alleged delay offered to those still outside the household of faith. "The Lord is not slow about His promise, as some count slowness, but is patient toward you, not wishing for any to perish but for all to come to repentance" (2 Peter 3:9). This would suggest that we be more concerned with those who might otherwise perish than with whatever inconvenience the extension of time works on us.

But the early church did not rely on reasons alone for their confident hope. It had already received the Spirit as an earnest of their hope. The Spirit of Christ was present to bless, console, and whet the appetite for such as God might choose to add at some future time. One need not languish for the provision of the Spirit.

85 Content of Hope

There are signs that V-Day is approaching, no matter how poorly we may read them. They are of two sorts: the breaking up of the old powers and the breaking in of the new. The signs are both individual—as with the exorcism of a demon—and cosmic in character. They suggest that the powers are loosening their hold on things. Here and there something slips out of place, not in some trivial area alone but with major disruptions.

At the same time, the authority seems to be changing hands. Now and then some facet of life seems to fall into place in reference to a coming order. As the old shows signs of disintegrating, the outline of the new seems to be taking shape. While these signs may not, strictly speaking, be called the content of hope, they do anticipate what is about to come to pass.

We shall consider the content of hope proper with reference to the parousia (second advent of Christ), final judgment, and final state. This is to sketch only the broad outline of the Christian hope by way of emphasizing the role of the Spirit in the consummation of things. We do not want to get bogged down in related matters that might add to the picture but frustrate our purpose.

We contrast the first and second advents of Christ by saying that He came first as the Suffering Servant, and will then be revealed as the Sovereign King. These are interrelated, so that no absolute distinction can be made, but the contrast deserves attention. The Suffering Servant inconspicuously goes about His duties, and in the end lays down His life without a word of protest (Acts 8:32–35). The Sovereign King comes with legions of His attendants to put down such evidences of rebellion as remain. The former dawns almost without notice, the latter with such fanfare that none can miss it. The former persists in the face of opposition and hostility, the latter crushes all opposition before Him. The former concludes with a cross, the latter with a crown.

The parousia breaks with an unexpected suddenness. Like a storm over the Sea of Galilee, one moment all is tranquil and the next moment the waves are beating at the sides of the boat. It is too late to make preparation. The events fall into order before one has a chance to evaluate their meaning or accommodate to them.

What some claimed would not happen, and others hoped would not happen, comes to pass. Those who pierced Him shall look upon Him, and all the nations will lament because of Him (Rev. 1:7). This is also the moment of truth for which the martyr waited, and now the cries of anguish and joy join in a mixed refrain.

We view the parousia from the middle rather than the end. Thielicke admits that "It transcends our history insofar as this is the way from the fall to judgment and is bounded by death. The forms and categories which we have to describe it are all shaped by our being in this world."[8] But we sense it, no matter how imperfectly, through the Spirit who indwells. We sense both the terror and joy of the parousia.

We may say that the Holy Spirit provides a glimmer of dawn to come, no matter how faint that glimmer may appear in contrast to full daylight. When rejected, such light as we have leaves man in greater darkness than before, but it may also pave the way for the parousia. The Spirit cultivates the blessed hope until such time as the hope becomes a reality.

There awaits the judgment. It is not God's vindictiveness but His thorough justice that should concern men. Jesus came into the world, and men did not care to know Him. They preferred to continue on their own way, seeking to get the better of their fellowman, and turning a deaf ear to the promptings of the Spirit. Now they must stand to give an account for what they have done with the opportunities provided them.

No one boasts before God. No one expects more than he receives. The results might have been predicted sometime earlier, seeing that matters left unchecked have a way of running their course. But Paul wisely

---

8. *Ibid.*,p. 438.

counseled his readers against passing judgment before the time: ". . . wait until the Lord comes who will both bring to light the things hidden in the darkness and disclose the motives of men's hearts; and then each man's praise will come to him from God" (1 Cor. 4:5). Outward appearances shall give way to the realities we attempt to hide from others and even from ourselves.

That is not to say that all will be pleased with the outcome of the judgment. There will be "weeping and gnashing of teeth" and pain mingling with anger, as some are "cast out into the outer darkness" (Matt. 8:13). Not all sorrow leads to repentance, and it may even intensify our bitterness with life and rage toward others.

We generally think of judgment in negative terms, but it bears the idea of vindication as well. The world is quick to condemn, but not as ready as the Lord to forgive. So, in the judgment, there will be words of commendation as well as condemnation.

But, seeing that "all have sinned and fall short of the glory of God" (Rom. 3:23), blessed is the man whose hope resides in Christ. In that day he shall rejoice not in his own righteousness but the righteousness imputed to him. He shall acknowledge that his salvation is by Christ alone, through the regenerating power of the Holy Spirit.

As concerns the final state, C. S. Lewis writes: "Evil can be undone, but it cannot 'develop' into good. Time does not heal it. . . . If we insist on keeping Hell we shall not see Heaven: if we accept Heaven we shall not be able to retain even the smallest and most intimate souvenirs of Hell."[9] There occurs in the words of C. S. Lewis "the great divorce" between those who would have their sin dealt with and those content to let it continue unresolved.

Hell is not portrayed as a rehabilitation station. Matters appear to have developed beyond that point. Sin runs its course in hell. It is likely neither better nor worse than unregenerate man would make it. But it certainly leaves much to be desired when compared to what God hoped to bestow on man.

Heaven, in contrast, opens up the future to man in fellowship with God. It unfolds from glory to glory, so that the skills of service previously developed may be exercized more fully, to the benefit of all. This is in keeping with the sense of anticipation cultivated through the years of pilgrimage by the indwelling Spirit.

---

9. C. S. Lewis, *The Great Divorce*, p. 6.

86 Life in Hope

We have from time to time touched upon the impact of hope on our manner of life. Karl Barth reasons that the Christian hopes on the basis of what is past, with the resurrection of Christ, and present, with the work of the Spirit in and through his life.[10] This invites the believer to respond positively to the ongoing work of the Spirit. It amounts to saying *yes* to the prompting of the Spirit, first in one context and then another, always with the understanding that the Spirit will lead him on through progressive stages of Christian life and ministry.

This is not to suggest that saying *yes* comes easily or all at once. The Spirit sustains our intention, assuring us of its wisdom and strengthening our determination. Thereby, the Christian life from beginning to end is a recognition of the lordship of Christ.

Barth rightly accents the present with regard to the role of the Spirit in establishing the rule of Christ in the life of the disciple. This "now" may be extended from one point to another, so that the Spirit must negotiate once and again the claims of Christ over every succeeding occasion. This is a strikingly dynamic perspective from which to see the Spirit at work, one that may be said to bridge the experience of D-Day and V-Day with reference to the sovereign rule of Christ.

The Holy Spirit appears as a tireless worker in this connection. He allows no compromise, exception, or postponement. There is no stone left unturned, no avenue unexplored in order to further the kingdom of God in the affairs of men.

Life in hope and life in the Spirit turn out to be synonymous. Only the emphasis is different. Hope accents the future as it reaches back into the present; life in the Spirit stresses the present as it extends toward the future. This also helps us understand why Barth insists that V-Day is already present in D-Day.

Summary

We turned at last to consider the struggle of the Holy Spirit with the powers of this world. We assumed Cullmann's popular analogy for this purpose: D-Day and V-Day as resembling the first and second advents of Christ. We identified the former specifically with regard to Christ's defeat of the powers, and the latter with their final subjection.

---

10. Karl Barth, *Church Dogmatics*, XVI, 73.1.

This world takes on the character of alien territory in Cullmann's analogy. The powers represent malevolent intermediaries that must be put to flight. Paul advocates a revolutionary gospel to meet such a demanding task. And the Spirit takes an uncompromising stand in opposition to the powers.

Jesus appears in the analogy as the conquering general who dethrones the powers, putting them on public display. The Spirit bears witness to this victory, as the Spirit of truth. He encourages the disciple to believe in and be transformed by this divine leverage.

This introduced the idea of a power encounter, where one sets aside all in which he has previously placed his confidence in response to a new loyalty. Thus must the Christian reject the authority of the powers, affirm his victory in Christ, and rely on the Holy Spirit for whatever results. In the light of this, the believer must cultivate the diligent study of Scripture and an active prayer life, as the means of cooperating with the indwelling Spirit.

We turned at this point to consider the remaining aspect of Cullmann's analogy: D-Day. We discovered that the victory of Christ provides the objective basis of hope, and the promise of God coupled with the witness of the Spirit provide the subjective assurance. All of this ought to be validated in the fellowship of believers, so as to challenge presumption and encourage genuine faith.

The so-called crisis of hope had to do with the extended interim between the advents of Christ. The earliest Christians reasoned that this constituted an unpredictable imminence of the Lord's return, requiring extreme vigilance. Another reason advanced for the delay pointed to the decisiveness of the victory won by Christ (so that subsequent events were of relatively little consequence). Finally, the interim points to the long-suffering of God for those who might otherwise perish. In any event, the potential crisis was further allayed by the presence of the Spirit, as an earnest of the future.

We considered the content of hope with regard to the parousia, judgment, and final state. The Holy Spirit provides what resembles a glimmer of light within to signal the approaching dawn. When rejected, this light leaves man in greater darkness yet, but its acceptance primes him for the appearing of Christ. At such time no man can argue with the justice of God or suggest that, given more time, the results would have been different.

The closing comments with regard to hope tied together earlier discussions of the topic. We concluded that life in hope and life in the Spirit were synonymous except for their respective emphases. The former accents the future, the latter the present, but both are extended toward the other. Thus we concluded our discussion of the Holy Spirit with regard to His powers and work in general.

PART 3

Historical Theology

Paul Tillich writes: "A theological system is supposed to satisfy two basic needs: the statement of the truth of the Christian message and the interpretation of this truth for every new generation. Theology moves back and forth between two poles, the eternal truth of its foundation and the temporal situation in which the eternal truth must be received."[1] The latter focus is particularly the concern of historical theology, which attempts to reconstruct the historical setting as a key to understanding the theological enterprise.

Historical theology delves into the history of Christian thought.[2] It observes how biblical teaching has been understood in some connection or another, as conditioned by the perspective assumed and as tied to a preceeding tradition. This approach resembles taking a cross section of Christian thinking at some time and place, in order to appreciate more

---

1. Paul Tillich, *Systematic Theology*, I, p. 3.

2. Such works as the following are helpful resources in historical theology: Geoffrey Bromily, *Historical Theology;* T. A. Burkill, *The Evolution of Christian Thought;* William Cunningham, *Historical Theology;* Justo Gonzalez, *A History of Christian Thought;* Bengt Hagglund, *History of Theology;* Otto Heick, *A History of Christian Thought;* Bernhard Lohse, *A Short History of Christian Doctrine;* Jaroslav Pelikan, *Historical Theology*. Alasdair Heron's *The Holy Spirit* combines the biblical and historical theology perspectives in one volume.

fully what was in progress and ascertain what instruction this has for a subsequent generation of believers.

One can attempt to sweep the span of years by trying to suggest representative thinkers or movements that somehow better seem to illustrate the developments than others that might come to mind. The briefer works use broader strokes, perhaps introducing an important contribution here or there; the larger studies indulge themselves with more detailed discussion of the complex interrelationships and the views of individuals in particular. The present work is obviously of the former nature.

We have divided the discussion into three segments: the Early Church; Christendom, or the political and social establishment of Christianity; and the Modern Church. The first era comes to a close roughly with Constantine's imperial sponsorship of Christianity, and the second period closes with the rise of the Enlightenment. While one era flows into the other, these divisions provide us with a workable arrangement.

10

The Early Church

W. H. Griffith Thomas divides historical theology into two massive epochs: the Sub-Apostolic Age to the Reformation, and the Reformation to the present. He adds that the former was concerned primarily with the person of the Holy Spirit and the latter with the work of the Spirit.[1] We have chosen rather to employ a tripartite division, beginning with the early church. These classifications are associated with the diasporan church of the earliest Christians, the establishment of Christianity as the state religion, and the post-establishment era. Christians had to reason through their understanding of the Spirit in the changing circumstances of these three historical periods.

This is not to suggest a uniform approach during any one time period. There has never been a time, as nearly as we can determine, when Christians were thoroughly agreed. Although there was a common faith that most adhered to, even this resembled a kind of general consensus that repudiated the more deviant alternatives.

1. W. H. Griffith Thomas, *The Holy Spirit of God*, p. 114.

87 Diasporan Christianity

The early church was reluctant to turn its back on Jerusalem. In fact, most of the earliest Christians were Jews and may have felt that their messianic faith enhanced their Jewishness. When early controversy arose concerning the obligations for which Gentile converts should be held responsible, it seemed proper, even incumbent, to refer the issue to a council in Jerusalem (Acts 15). After careful deliberation, a decision was reached and the word circulated to the Gentile congregations.

The Christians continued to draw upon the "Jewish" Scriptures, while formulating their own set of inspired commentaries. This constantly reminded them of their roots in the Holy Land and their role as God's chosen people. To read Holy Writ was to take a pilgrimage back to their origin.

There was also an antithetical feeling among the Gentile converts concerning the Hebrew heritage. This carried over in part from the widespread dislike of the Jew then evident in the empire. It was fueled by the early persecution of the Christian faith in the Jewish community and the prolonged debate between the two groups. Therefore, their ties to Jerusalem must have appeared as a mixed blessing.

The rapid spread of Christianity further weakened its link with Jerusalem. The major growth areas were outside Israel, among "the nations." Antioch, Ephesus, Rome, and Alexandria were becoming centers of Christian influence and outreach.

Conversely, things were not going well in Israel. Rome had run out of its patience with the troublesome Jew. When, by 70 A.D., Jerusalem lay in ruins, Gentile Christianity was no longer tightly bound to its Hebrew moorings. It was afloat on a sea where the believer must sail from one port to another, facing whatever storms might arise, without thought of home. Thus, diasporan Christianity became normative.

Some would argue that Christianity is by nature diasporan—scattered—for the Christian is a pilgrim. The world is not his home; he is just passing through. No doubt that is in one sense true, but we ought not allow this fact to blind us to the historical reality we have observed. Christianity took on a distinctively diasporan character as a matter of historical record.

Although there remained a certain theological nostalgia for all that Jerusalem represented, this had undergone a not-too-subtle alteration. It had transformed the Jewish heritage into a Christian legacy. The Holy Land now belonged to the Christian, as the later Crusades would attempt to demonstrate. However, this recasting of the matter cannot be understood apart from the diasporan experience which gave rise to it.

Circumstances allowed the Christian community relatively little time to put its theological house in order. Its energy was drained through an astonishing growth period, a time of transition and overt persecution. There were other theological concerns given priority over a consideration of the Holy Spirit. This was most strikingly true as regards the development of the Logos doctrine in the writing of the apologists.

There were two theological adjustments especially worth noting in Gentile Christianity: in connection with the traditional beliefs and subsequently with Neo-Platonism. The early churches were characteristically erected on the sites of former pagan worship centers. Insofar as possible, the pantheon of gods was accommodated by saints elevated to assume their roles. As ritual practices carried over ingredients and associations from the pagan past, what resulted was something of a Christo-paganism.

By the second century, Christianity was already vigorously competing for the religious market. It discovered a certain affinity for Neo-Platonism, a congeniality which we can see in historical retrospect as seriously overdrawn. But the fact was that the Christian apologists used this philosophic vehicle effectively in winning over the intellectuals of that day, thus establishing the credibility of the faith.

Neither of these adjustments contributed in any direct fashion to a reflection on the Holy Spirit. The Spirit was assumed in the trinitarian developments, while the various Christological controversies took center stage. One must always take up the more pressing matters first, and there may not be, as in this instance, sufficient energy left over to cope with other priorities.

But we do not want to overstate the matter, as if the Spirit were of no consequence to Gentile Christianity. Gardiner Day reasons: "If you were to have asked the disciples what the Trinity meant, they would not have known what you were talking about, for the word 'Trinity' is not mentioned in the New Testament. Had you asked them about their experience of God in three Persons as Creator, as Jesus Christ, and as the Holy Spirit, their eyes would have had no difficulty in telling you about it. They knew the love of God; they knew the grace of our Lord Jesus Christ; they knew the fellowship of the Holy Spirit in their own experience."[2] In

2. Gardiner Day, *The Apostles' Creed*, p. 115.

other words, although they had not fashioned the term *Trinity*, their experience was profoundly trinitarian in character.

If Day's observation holds true so far as the Apostolic Age is concerned, it holds with modification for the Sub-Apostolic Age as well. Thomas concludes that "Sub-Apostolic Christianity was characterized by a real Christian experience without much reflection on what was involved in that experience."[3] In fact, the Sub-Apostolic Age reveals less theological and ethical vigor than the period which preceded it.

It was assumed that God had poured out His Spirit on all flesh in these latter days. Since this was a wonderful thing to behold, and still more exciting to be a part of, there seemed little urgency to work out the doctrine of the Spirit more carefully, at least for the moment, when other priorities seemed more pressing.

Had some heresy seriously challenged the faith of early Christianity in regard to the Holy Spirit, we would expect the results to have been different. Such a challenge, as represented by Gnosticism, was more indirect, less obvious, and seemed more threatening in other connections. Although diasporan Christianity responded to attack, it was content to allow other concerns to rest—so long as they seemed to be in order.

An exception, which ought not to be made the rule, occurred with regard to Montanism. According to Eusebius: "He [Montanus] raved, and began to chatter and talk nonsense, prophesying in a way that conflicted with the practice of the church handed down generation by generation from the beginning."[4] Montanus, claiming access to the Spirit, attacked the common tradition and moral laxity of the Church. But the controversy that resulted had more practical than theological effects on the church, which developed as a response to Montanism a rigidity in organization and ministry so as not to allow such disruptions to develop in the future.

88 Speculation

Without doubt, there was more ferment going on than we might surmise on the surface of things. This would inevitably be true, even if there were no indication that it was actually the case. We shall attempt to reconstruct something of the ferment as relates to the diasporan experience with the Spirit.

---

3. Thomas, *The Holy Spirit of God*, p. 78.
4. Eusebius, *The History of the Church to Constantine*, p. 218.

Diasporan Christianity was, as a matter of record, a non-people. It could be treated as a universal variety of Judaism, although it had lost its ethnic character. Its adherents spoke no common language but the language of faith.

Kenneth Scott Latourette elaborates: "It was faith in Jesus and his resurrection which gave birth to the Christian fellowship and which continued to be its inspiration and its common tie. It was the love displayed in Christ which was, ideally and to a marked extent in practice, the bond which held Christians together."[5] It was also the fruit of the Spirit manifest in the moral transformation of people, regardless of background, disposition, or status.

All of this underscores what the later experience with Christendom tended to obscure, the distinction between the Spirit and church—and the dependence of the latter on the former. As Hans Küng explains: "The Church does not *per se* and in each case represent the Holy Spirit: the Church has to prove its holiness in action,"[6] rather than assume its holiness as guaranteed.

The uncritical mingling of Spirit and church was a luxury that the diasporan fellowship could ill afford, seeing it had no ethnic foundation or cultural synthesis, but hung by the fragile cord of faith. The church had to validate its calling through attending seriously to biblical teaching and obeying its precepts. It had to rely on the enabling ministry of the Spirit to sustain the people of God in their global mission.

This distinction between Spirit and church allowed the Spirit to work *as* He would. So, to the surprise of the earliest Christians, He chose their chief protagonist—Saul of Tarsus. To the amazement of the emperors, He employed the stalwart faith of the martyrs. To the consternation of those who crucified Jesus, He elected the power of the cross to reconcile men to God. The Spirit seemed less predictable and more engaging than perhaps any time since the early centuries.

He also appeared to work *when* He willed. Paul supposed that he might minister in Asia (likely at Ephesus), but was "forbidden by the Holy Spirit" (Acts 16:6). Later on he was to enjoy what was likely his most successful ministry at Ephesus, in the good timing of the Spirit. Likewise did others during those early days of experience with diasporan Christianity.

---

5. Kenneth Scott Latourette, *A History of Christianity*, p. 107.
6. Hans Küng, *The Church*, p. 174.

The Spirit likewise selected *whom* He would, to join in some phase of the work or another. We have already mentioned Saul, who became the apostle Paul. The Spirit directed, "Set apart for Me Barnabas and Saul for the work to which I have called them" (Acts 13:2). The church at Antioch was to acknowledge the Spirit's sovereignty in the matter and support those summoned to serve. Some went as directed and others made their going possible.

We ought not to suppose that these experiences with the Spirit were, strictly speaking, limited to the early church, since their influence was felt during the subsequent rise of Christendom. Thus what resembles the earlier experience is sensed against the background of what intervened. There are similarities noted in later times but no exact replicas.

89 A Balanced Approach

We do not intend to detract from anything that has been already affirmed about the early church by mentioning its Spirit-cultivated order (1 Cor. 14:40). Community requires order, and the Christian community was no exception. Those who used the pretext of Christian freedom to push their partisan interests were severely rebuked. Any who persisted in their disregard for order were disciplined. Although Gentile Christianity embraced a great diversity, it demanded that this diversity serve the whole. One believer could not pull in one direction and another in the opposite. The Spirit was not the Spirit of confusion but of peace, understanding, and power (v. 33). He creates from a rich diversity a blend of ministry.

The diasporan church existed in the interim between the loss of its heritage in ethnic Israel and the birth of Christendom as such. This was a transitional phenomenon whose characteristics had no equal in later developments, although there were threads of similarity. It was God's answer to that time, when the Spirit blew across the extent of the ancient Roman Empire.

While there was relatively little articulated about the Spirit, there was much experienced. The experience was trinitarian from the outset, engendering the love of God, the grace of Christ, and the fellowship of the Spirit. Faith reached out to touch faith in the lives of others, creating a sense of fellowship in and of the Spirit. The fruit of love was evident for all to see, and for the Christians to rejoice in.

We can with some certainty recreate certain facets of diasporan Christianity's experience with the Holy Spirit. Much of this has to do with the sovereign work of the Spirit in calling out a people from all the nations and blending them together as a people zealous for the things of God. More particularly, the experience affirms that the Spirit works as, when, and with whom He wills, not in some arbitrary fashion, but purposefully as the agent of the kingdom of God. In this way must order be preserved, for the Spirit does not author confusion or partisan loyalties.

90 Orthodoxy

We are not leaving one clearly defined epoch and entering another when we turn from diasporan Christianity to the struggle for orthodoxy. They are actually overlapping movements. We can sketch one after another in order to gain a better perspective on the whole, but we do not strictly follow a time line.

William Hodern defines orthodox Christianity as "that form of Christianity which won the support of the overwhelming majority of Christians and which is expressed by most of the official proclamations or creeds of Christian groups."[7] He intends the term to be purely descriptive, so as neither to commend nor criticize.

It might be more accurate to speak of orthodoxies rather than orthodoxy. Certainly there were multiple divisions within Christianity from early on, and each one promoted its own brand of Christianity, rightly so-called. But there was also a central core of Christian faith that persisted in spite of—and perhaps in some sense because of—the differences. The struggle for orthodoxy concerns itself with that central core of Christian doctrine.

There is perhaps no affirmation more central to Christian orthodoxy than "that God was in Christ reconciling the world to Himself" (2 Cor. 5:19). The earliest Christians believed that the Almighty had confronted them in Jesus Christ, reconciling those who turned in simple faith to Him for forgiveness. The faith had a predominantly historical setting so long as it resided in its Semitic context.

The truth remained while the setting changed from Semitic to a more pronounced Hellenic mode of thought. Bernhard Lohse writes: "The result was that metaphysical concepts which were focused upon being took the place of concrete, biblical forms of speech. As we know, Greek thought differs from biblical thought above all in this, that for

7. William Hodern, *A Layman's Guide to Protestant Theology*, p. 1.

the latter the truth of God is revealed in history, while for the former it is grounded in metaphysical being."[8] This meant that the work of God had to be defined in metaphysical terms in order to be credible to the Greek mind.

It was no menial task. Much was at stake in translating the fundamentals of Christian faith. Nor was it easy to know precisely how to represent the truth without distorting it in some fashion or another. The struggle did not center for the most part on the Holy Spirit, but with regard to the trinitarian issue in general and Christology in particular. Such statements as were made concerning the Holy Spirit were relatively uniform, except that they often left the door open for some form of heresy to develop.

The struggle waxed and waned over the years, disrupting the pastoral and evangelistic activities of the church. Matters finally came to a head with the Council of Nicea. Emperor Constantine had interjected himself into the controversy. Having become a Christian adherent and concerned for the stability of the empire, he chose to take the initiative with regard to the Arian issue.

The Arian controversy centered on whether Christ ought to be described as of the same or like essence as the Father. The creed of Eusebius was taken as a basis and put forward by the council in a revised fashion to deal with the matter. It included a brief reference to the Father and, in conclusion, a reference to belief "in the Holy Spirit." What has come to be known as "The Nicene Creed" was not read and approved until the Council of Chalcedon in 451, as the creed of those assembled previously at Nicea and later at Constantinople (325 and 381 respectively). The trinitarian model had been worked out in some detail by that time, so that the Holy Spirit was described as "the Lord and the Life-giver, that proceedeth from the Father, who with Father and Son is worshipped together and glorified together, who spoke through the prophets." Thereafter, there follows reference to the "one holy Catholic and Apostolic Church," "one baptism unto the remission of sins," and to the resurrection of the dead and the life of the age to come. Since all of these stand in a subsidiary position to belief in the Holy Spirit, they may be said to be not simply additions but extensions of belief in the Holy Spirit's activity in these related matters.

Were we able to reverse the order of events and return the issue to its original Semitic setting, orthodoxy meant to assert (in a way similar to

8. Bernhard Lohse, *A Short History of Christian Doctrine*, p. 41.

God's being in Christ to reconcile the world to Himself) that God was in the Holy Spirit transforming people into the image of His Son, in preparation for the consummation of all things. But history does not run in reverse, and those who try to make it do so only collide with the oncoming traffic. The orthodox had to settle for the metaphysical language of hypostasis (person) and rule in favor of the deity of the Holy Spirit.

This has led some to suggest that orthodoxy was defining the nature of the Spirit in heaven—that is to say, defining the Holy Spirit as relates to His preexistent and persisting relationship to Father and Son. But that is to miss the cutting edge of the controversy, which was twofold: that *God* was active in the Holy Spirit, and acting *here* in our midst.

91 With Augustine

We pick up the struggle for orthodoxy at a rather late point, when Christendom was feeling its way with Augustine (354–430), who dominated his time as no other. His *Confessions* was a classic work in Christian piety, and *The City of God* was a landmark in the philosophy of history, but *On the Trinity* was his longest and most significant work in philosophical theology. The prestigous Bishop of Hippo began with an exegesis of relevant biblical passages, before turning in a polemical fashion on those who challenge the orthodox notion of the Holy Spirit. Building his case by way of the incarnation, the notion of hypostasis, and certain reflections regarding goodness and love, he finds intimations of the Trinity especially with reference to the psychology of man.

Augustine develops his argument: "But love is *of* some one that loves, and *with* love something *is* loved. Behold, then, there are three things: he that loves, and that which is loved, and love. . . . It remains to ascend also from thence, and to seek those things which are above, as far as is given to man."[9] We discover, as it were, a trace of the Trinity in these three aspects of love.

Such observations may not seem overwhelming in and of themselves, but their composite effect was greater than the parts taken alone. They took on still greater credibility when understood as Augustine's effort to clarify his faith, and as a defense of historic Christian orthodoxy. He speaks out of faith, and on behalf of faith. Strictly speaking, the argu-

---

9. Augustine, *On the Trinity*, III, p. 24.

ments are not the evidence for faith, although they may sort of "soften up" the candidate for conversion.

Augustine speaks elsewhere on the nature of the Holy Spirit. What he expressly states is that we should not identify the Spirit *as* God, for in so doing we give the impression of belief in three gods. But we must not give the contrary impression that we meet something less than God in the divine person of the Spirit.[10]

As it is generally known, Augustine believed that there exist two cities: the earthly and the heavenly. The earthly was subject to selfishness and pride, but was not entirely bad because it brought about peace and order out of the motive of self-interest. The heavenly city, which men may enter here and now, is governed rather by the love of God and submission of self-interests to the purposes of God. The earthly city will fade as the heavenly city takes its place.

What would bring about a transformation of the earthly into the heavenly city? Certainly not human endeavor, as Pelagius' teaching seemed to imply. Augustine knew full well from his own experience the serious limitations placed upon human effort to set and hold to a righteous course. The bishop countered with an uncompromising accent on the grace of God as encountered in the presence of the Holy Spirit. Here, with the Spirit, we see *God* at work.

But it is striking that Augustine's *The City of God* does in fact concern itself with man. As Latourette comments, "To be sure, its subject was the dealings of God with man, but its emphasis was upon what happens to man. In this interest in man, visible institutions, and history Augustine differed from the thinkers of the Eastern sections of the Catholic church."[11] In emphasizing the sovereign nature of God's work, Augustine succeeded in elevating the role of man within the purposes and enablement of God.

All of this suggests that Augustine had much more than a theoretical interest in the Holy Spirit. He meant to assure his readers that God was at work in their midst. This was especially true with regard to the transforming presence of the city of God.

92 General Trends

What we might have surmised from Augustine's work was true in regard to the theological trend in general. Lohse explains: "Neither at

10. Augustine, *A Treatise on Faith and the Creed*, III, p. 327.
11. Latourette, *A History of Christianity*, p. 128.

Nicaea nor at Constantinople was the attempt made to plumb the depth of the divine mystery or to define God's essence. The intention was, rather, to indicate that God himself encounters us in Jesus Christ, and that in the Holy Spirit God himself is present within his church."[12] The work of the Spirit was seen as being consolidated in and expressed through the church.

The church was by then no longer made up of scattered congregations that were persecuted or tolerated according to the mood of the time. It had grown out of the decay of the empire to assume an unrivaled place of power. In fact, as Augustine claimed, it appeared that the city of God was replacing the city of man.

There were still those who carried over the fear that the church would further weaken the empire and invite the barbarians to reap the spoils. The apologists had to deal with this point of view. Taking on what amounted to false allegations, they set forth a case for Christianity, not for faith alone but as a basis for political and social renewal.

This brought Christian orthodoxy into conflict with trends to the right and left. One faction advocated a more separatistic life than orthodoxy chose, one sheltered from the storms and compromises of life. The Montanists provide one such example. Montanism flourished during the latter part of the second century and persisted for more than two hundred years. It advocated a stricter code of living than did the church in general, and held a belief in the early end of the world with the return of Christ. Such emphases did not lend themselves readily to those interested in fashioning a Christian life and world view.

On the other hand, there were those who welcomed uncritically the alliance being forged between the church and society. They hastily espoused pagan ideas, ideals, and practices in order to make them their own. The distinction between church and world became more tenuous, less certain, and even of less concern. As a result, Christian orthodoxy was faced with protagonists on either side and had to struggle to steer a course between the two. This struggle became embodied in the teaching of orthodoxy on the nature of the church.

93 The Norm

It has been customary to speak of the church as being *in* but not *of* the world. That conclusion could readily be drawn from Scripture

---

12. Lohse, *A Short History of Christian Doctrine*, pp. 65–66.

alone, but the fact is that it took on a peculiar historical pattern as a result of the struggle for Christian orthodoxy. It came to imply a stand against undue separation on the one hand, and capitulation to the world on the other. As church orthodoxy became a measuring standard for subsequent times and movements, we ease over from our interpretation of Scripture into a subsequent mold with little or no awareness that we have made a transition.

Lesslie Newbigin puts matters in this way: "I have spoken of the life of the Church in terms of the words 'come' and 'go.' The Church is indeed a gathering of those whom the Holy Spirit calls into the fellowship of Christ. . . . There has [also] to be a movement of *kenosis;* one has to be willing to go, to become simply the unrecognized servant of men where they are, in order that *there,* perhaps in quite new forms, the authentic substance of the new life in Christ may take shape and become visible."[13] As a result of the struggle for Christian orthodoxy the Holy Spirit had been cast as providing a rhythm, a double movement—in and out—to which the church was expected to respond.

The Spirit bids "come." Come from our diverse backgrounds, our partisan interests, our places of security. Come to a fellowship unmarked by social status, ethnic origin, or racial castes. Come from the far country at the invitation of the Spirit.

"Go" likewise. Go to an apathetic and sometimes hostile world. Go as a lamb among wolves. Go to serve in Christ's name. Go as urged by the Holy Spirit.

Summary

Orthodoxy seems to have articulated a clearer perspective on the work of the Spirit than did diasporan Christianity. The latter skirted the issue, with a reminder of the uninhibited character of the Spirit and an appeal to order. Orthodoxy then took over center stage to describe the ebb and flow of the Spirit in transforming the kingdom of men into the kingdom of God. The struggle for orthodoxy was vigorous, demanding virtually the full energy of the church for a time. No one intended to let such an expenditure of time and energy go to waste. Orthodoxy meant to defend its hard-won victory.

We observed that the struggle for orthodoxy centered on Christology, only in a more general sense on the Trinity, and then without par-

13. Lesslie Newbigin, *Honest Religion for Secular Man*, p. 121.

ticular concern for the Holy Spirit. All sides of the issue seemed willing, even anxious, to make orthodox concessions with regard to the Holy Spirit, even though these sometimes left something to be desired and opened the door to future deviation. We might say that the orthodox definition of the person and work of the Holy Spirit came into being as a matter of default. It occurred when the parties in the church were locked in bitter confrontation and wanted to protect themselves from unnecessary attack with reference to their convictions concerning the Holy Spirit.

This might mislead us into thinking that the Spirit played a lesser role in their lives than was actually the case. Here is a classic instance where experience preceded careful theological reflection and expression. The early church fathers bore testimony to the centrality of the Spirit in their life together, even when they declined to enter into a more vigorous theological definition. Everyone agreed that the Spirit was where the action was.

Thus we found that with Augustine there was a pointedly practical turn to his interest in the Spirit. He meant to expose the work of the Spirit with regard to the church, the coming of the city of God into the city of man. He hoped to reveal the dynamic that invests all of culture with a force so persistent as to escape the ravages of time and the assaults of men.

Although it may seem paradoxical that the struggle for Christian orthodoxy should have left such a pronounced impression on our understanding of the operation of the Spirit—despite a general lack of precise theological definition—such seems to be the case. The double movement so characteristic of orthodox thinking has been passed on primarily as a testimonial to how the Spirit of God designs to work with the people of God. It appears to have touched on a biblical nerve, so that subsequent generations have been inclined to accept the verdict of Christian orthodoxy. Even among those groups which have challenged the content of Christian orthodoxy, there has been a tendency to preserve the categories it assigned to the work of the Spirit. This is perhaps the highest compliment that can be paid to the contribution of any movement.

11

Christendom

Since we have already made reference to the rise of Christendom with Constantine and illustrated its rationale with Augustine, we need now only take up the course previously anticipated—from diasporan Christianity to the "establishment" of Christianity. This introduces what was at the very least a noble experiment, a permeation of all of life with the Christian faith. When, in turn, it too would pass from the scene, there would be those who would deeply regret its demise.

94 The Establishment

Christopher Dawson is such a case in point: "This progressive extrusion of Christianity from culture is the price that Christendom has had to pay for its loss of unity—it is part of what Richard Niebuhr has called 'the Ethical Failure of the Divided Church.'"[1] Dawson saw the disintegration of the synthesis between Christianity and culture as a tragic event. While others may not share this view, they can agree with identifying the rise of Christendom as a major development in the history of Christianity.

---

1. Christopher Dawson, *The Dividing of Christendom*, p. 17.

We should consider the nature of establishment before proceeding with Christendom as a specific instance. Sociologists remind us that "Man occupies a peculiar position in the animal kingdom. Unlike the other higher mammals, he has no species-specific environment, no environment firmly structured by his own instinctual organization."[2] In a manner of speaking, man must create his own world out of whatever is available to him. He has seemingly endless possibilities open to him, what Berger and Luckmann, who are quoted above, term his "world-openness."

For man, reality is what he perceives as being true, growing out of his relationship with the world around him. This "truth" may be divided for purposes of analysis into objective and subjective reality. Objective reality is already a social product, a consensus as to the nature of life. Christendom provides one such consensus, but there are many others. Each differs from another at salient points, although there are complex similarities. Often one discovers cultural equivalents, whereby different things seem to serve similar purposes.

Subjective reality refers to how the individual sees himself in relation to what he accepts as objectively true. It consists of his complex roles in society and in what manner he thinks of himself as transcending those roles. It is the introspective side of a social process.

Christendom did not fall from heaven. Rather, it grew out of a profound response by man to the revelation of God, taking such opportunity as was available to him to fashion a sanctuary out of life, to the glory of God and the service of man. It was a noble undertaking, but nonetheless a human one.

Christendom incorporated all that we might expect of any establishment: an economy of energy, an apologetic, and maintenance of an order. It is the nature of an establishment to standardize behavior to a degree that people can function together easily. We take this service so much for granted as perhaps never to imagine what it would be like if we had to start at the beginning to negotiate even the simplest understanding.

We also find it necessary to legitimize what we are doing. Good parents are careful not only to guide their child through command, but to explain their rationale insofar as possible, so that the child understands the "why" as well as the "what." An establishment which can no longer commend itself to its constituency has its days numbered.

---

2. Peter Berger and Thomas Luckmann, *The Social Construction of Reality*, p. 47.

Of course, any establishment shows strain with the passage of time and under the pressure of change. It has to maintain itself by eliminating what has come to be a hindrance, recasting other elements to meet new challenges and introducing new features. In so doing, it must resist either an uncritical preservation of the past or an indiscriminate acceptance of what is presently in vogue. Christendom was typical of establishments in this and the previous connections.

95 The Spire

Christendom can perhaps best be illustrated by the church spire, reaching toward heaven out of a sprawl of human dwellings. It signifies that man's chief end is to glorify God and to enjoy Him without end. Whatever may be the other legitimate rights, there exists no higher priority. Thus, when conflicts of interest develop, as they must, the concerns of the kingdom come first.

Dawson reflects that in the earlier stages of Christendom the state, in our sense of the word, hardly existed: "There were a vast number of political and social units—feudal fiefs, duchies, counties and baronies, loosely held together by their allegiance to king or Emperor. There were Free Cities and Leagues of Cities, like the Lombard Commune or the Hanseatic League. There were ecclesiastical principalities like the German prince-bishoprics, and the great independent abbeys. Finally there were the religious and military orders—international organizations which lived their own lives and obeyed their own authorities in whatever country of Europe they might happen to be situated."[3] All of these were so intermingled that it would have been difficult to identify precisely what was "the state."

Christendom was pervasive as a cultural phenomenon, penetrating all aspects of life, from the most menial to the most profound. One could scrub floors to the glory of God as well as rule over a kingdom or pray at the altar. The church spire was central to all.

Of course, the ideal was only approximated. Men were regularly governed by baser motives and with worse results than would have otherwise been expected. Some received more than they deserved, while others suffered from lack of the bare necessities of life. Rivals were anxious to fight to the last drop of someone else's blood. Christendom characteristically proved to be its own worst enemy.

---

3. Dawson, *The Dividing of Christendom*, p. 25.

96 Whither the Spirit?

Thus came about the saying, "The nearer the church, the further from God." We must not confuse this with subsequent times. The critics were not doubting the truth of Christianity, but rather the faithfulness of the church. Christendom was still intact. The sense of its reality was so pervasive and deeply engrained as to survive for the time being on cultural precedent alone, were that to become necessary.

Monasticism provided a significant effort to combat the loss of vitality in Christendom. Not a recent development, monasticism enjoyed a mounting influence by the tenth and eleventh centuries. In the words of K. S. Latourette, "Here was a swelling tide seeking to deepen and make more intelligent and effective the loyalty to the Christian faith which had become nominal through the mass conversions of the earlier centuries."[4] And which Christendom had failed to compensate for during the interim.

It became evident to a large proportion of the Christians that the monastic way of life provided the means through which to pursue the Christian life most successfully. Here the Holy Spirit was at work in a distinctive fashion not available elsewhere, so as to preserve the critical aspects of the Christian heritage and extend its influence into the society at large.

But the monastic effort tended to expend its efforts on preserving its own institutions, without proper regard for others. In practice, it often became prosaic, and sometimes even corrupt. It also spawned new monastic movements out of protest against the existing ones and against the status of Christianity in general.

There was considerable emphasis placed on the efficacy of the sacraments. It had been one thing to baptize on the credible confession of faith, or even as the child of devout parents, but another thing to offer baptism as a matter of course to all registered in Christendom. The efficacy of the sacrament was often invoked to compensate for the lack of credibility in the participants, but not without increasing the uncertainty of a salvation depreciated by this expression of cheap grace.

Where was the Spirit in the midst of such seeming contradictions? How had Christendom refashioned the understanding of the operation of the Spirit? The primary focus was still on the person rather than the work of the Spirit. W. H. Griffith Thomas, as mentioned earlier, was

4. Kenneth Scott Latourette, *A History of Christianity*, p. 443.

correct in affirming that the primary concern up to the Reformation was with the person of the Spirit.

The partial answer that these early centuries of the church gave as to the person of the Holy Spirit is that He constituted *God* with us. (We repeat what was stated earlier.) Thus we are assured that God has not left us alone, with Jesus' departure, but has come to us as the Holy Spirit. He has created a divine leverage in our midst. So also the Holy Spirit means that God is with *us*. There has come into being a people of God, at the invitation of the Spirit. The church exists as the body of Christ, bent on His service, empowered by the indwelling Spirit.

Christendom primarily added to these features the focus of the Spirit's work in the world, as creating a new society endowed by Christian principles and sustained by the divine presence. While not a totally new idea, Christendom so emphasized it as to make it appear virtually new. Unfortunately, Christendom also corrupted the ideal so as to make it seem undesirable to an increasing number of sensitive persons.

There were related emphases growing out of Christendom's approach to the Spirit. Most striking was its stress on *order*. Paul had taught that things should be done decently and in order, but Christendom carried the note to an extreme—so that everything in society had its place, and one could not move one aspect without affecting the rest. This emphasis was not completely bad, since it encouraged a sense of corporate responsibility. No person was strictly on his own; every person was at least in theory his brother's keeper. It also cultivated an appreciation for the land, which was held in corporate trust. No one ought to think that private ownership implied more than responsible use.

But, as we have observed, the ideal degenerated into a static community, where some benefited at the expense of others, and to be available to God all too often meant not to be available to others. Man's perversity seems to plague his highest ideals, and Christendom was a case in point.

Another emphasis on the Spirit that grew out of the experience with Christendom was seeing life as the *occasion* for celebration. It created a disposition toward worship as a natural aspect of life, not as something that one must tack on in a belated show of piety.

If it were possible to mass-produce Christianity, Christendom appeared the most likely candidate. It carried people along until such time when, hopefully, faith would be kindled and reach out to touch eternal verities. Disbelief and impiety would seem unnatural, socially repugnant, and individually self-defeating.

Discrimination did not hold the same virtue it came to have in the wake of the Reformation. Rather, Christendom promoted faithful adherence to the church, socially responsible behavior, and personal piety. One spoke of "mother church" not as a literary device but out of a deep sense of reliance.

Christendom likewise fostered a sense of life as mystery, whereby the forces of good and evil contended together over the souls of men. The other-worldly seemed more real, more pressing than it is perhaps possible for post-Enlightenment man to appreciate. We have to search for some example in primitive society, where there exists no dichotomy between the sacred and secular, to gain a better impression of the experience of Christendom with mystery. The Holy Spirit was associated with all sorts of extraordinary events that occurred with striking frequency.

Modern life would likely seem flat to those nurtured by Christendom. People would seem oblivious to the things of the Spirit. They would appear taken up in the pursuits of this life, without a long-range goal or a sense of how to achieve even their short-range pursuits.

97 Retrospect

Christendom soon began to flounder. Latourette reminisces: "Then (with the use of Christendom) decline, slow but prolonged, had set in. In winning the professed allegiance of the peoples of the basin of the Mediterranean the process had been completed by a mass conversion which watered down the quality of living. Swamped by these millions, the Catholic Church had relaxed its discipline and in some areas had apparently all but given up attempts to enforce it."[5] The monastic effort attempted to recover the initiative, but could not turn the tide.

Christianity had taken on the sickness with which the Roman Empire was inflicted. The invasion of Moslem Arabs swept away half of the area once belonging to Christendom, and within that territory the churches dwindled under the pressure of persuasion and coercion. The remainder assumed a bastion mentality, in order to survive what Latourette entitles "the darkest hours" (500–950 A.D.).

---

5. *Ibid.*,p. 375.

Christendom never fully recovered from those dark days. There was a time of resurgence, a second recession and recovery, before the Reformation broke in its full fury. There followed the tragic Thirty Years' War (1618–1648), which discredited an already disparaged Christendom. The handwriting was already on the wall. It remained only for the Enlightenment to lay siege to Christendom. Except for its legacy, Christendom came toppling down with the beginning of the modern era.

We noted how Christendom served, like any other establishment, as a secondary environment that man spun around himself in order to sustain and enrich life. It provided a sense of objective reality as living in God's world, and a corresponding subjective reality for the individual so involved. It helped him relate to others, confirm his way of life, and adjust to changing circumstances. Christendom pervaded all of life, as a matter of faith, political design, and cultural endeavor. While falling pathetically short of its ideal, it attempted to structure all of life to the glory of God and to bring each of its parts into harmony with the rest.

What distinctive emphasis had Christendom placed on the Holy Spirit? Primarily with regard to the person of the Spirit, not simply as *God* with *us*, but in the enterprise of creating a new society of the redeemed. Related to such an imposing task, the Spirit was viewed in connection with establishing order, offering the occasion for celebration, and investing life with mystery. To that extent, we can confidently conclude that the influence of Christendom in general and accent on the Holy Spirit in particular have outlined the movement itself.

98 East and West

Christendom was never monolithic. There were differences, many of them substantial. Most pronounced was that between the Eastern and Western churches. Each developed a rather distinctive understanding of the Holy Spirit.

The great empires of antiquity were located in Asia and Egypt, but the conquests by Alexander the Great brought the center of civilization westward to Europe. Subsequently, the Roman Empire incorporated all within its borders. It extended the *pax Romana* throughout, giving the impression of a unified confederation. Bernard Ramm elaborates: "But this is a mirage, for the map fails to convey the enormous diversity that persisted in the Roman Empire. Underneath the apparent unity was a great cultural division of the East and West."[6] The cultural division persisted in spite of—and sometimes in defiance to—all efforts to reduce it.

We cannot hope to explore this profound cultural differentiation in any detail. The Hellenistic world of the East was bound together by a cosmopolitan civilization and a common language of trade. Its territory was dotted with growing cities, providing convenient centers for the surrounding districts and giving it a distinctive urban character. Its leaders were devoted to the pursuit of learning and fostered the quest of truth, beauty, and morality. This world drew upon its shadowy origins in the Nile and Tigris and Euphrates valleys. When conquered by Rome, it was said to have vanquished its conqueror, so much so that some depict Roman civilization as merely an imitation of the Hellenistic original.

But that is to do Roman civilization an injustice. The Romans had developed a rigorous practical approach to life that colored whatever they touched. Their genius lay in the fields of the practical arts: engineering, law, and government. They built virtually indestructible roads that bound the ancient empire together, and they created massive aqueduct systems to meet the needs of growing urban centers. The *pax Romana*, for all its shortcomings, was an impressive feat of jurisprudence. The Roman felt somehow obligated to rule the world by bringing his peculiar insights to bear on the affairs of all men and nations.

Rome stamped the West with its distinctive character. In addition to the general pressures on those being assimilated into the Roman Empire, there was a concerted effort to replace the provincial language with Latin, the provincial law with Roman law, and the provincial religion with Roman religion. To a certain degree, all Western Europe was standardized as a result.

Such differences as persisted between East and West were reflected within the church as well, and eventually contributed to its division. Theological differences were advanced to warrant the estrangement, but these were partial reasons at best. Underneath lay cultural distinctives that neither the *pax Romana* nor the church were able to eradicate.

99 Newer Developments

We do not want to give the impression that subsequent developments played no role in the schism between the Eastern and Western churches.

---

6. Bernard Ramm, *The Evangelical Heritage*, p. 17.

The rise of Byzantine Christianity, with its center at Constantinople, proved to be a serious threat to the primacy of Rome. The rapid spread of Islam created internal pressures within Christendom, and the Crusades further accented the alienation between East and West. The missionary movements of the respective churches into Western and Eastern Europe likewise underscored the polarity between Rome and Byzantium.

Our major interest lies with the differences being developed along theological lines. Although some have counted as many as sixty distinctives, most of these relate to secondary matters of liturgy and order. We shall limit ourselves to some of the more central concerns.

The Eastern church was more mystical in its approach. Vladimir Lossky comes to the heart of the issue: "The main preoccupation, the issue at stake, in the questions which successively arise respecting the Holy Spirit, grace and the Church herself—this last the dogmatic question of our own time—is always the possibility, the manner, or the means of our union with God. All the history of Christian dogma unfolds itself about this mystical centre, guarded by different weapons against its many and diverse assailants in the course of successive ages."[7] All else may be said to help clarify the nature of mystical theology in the Eastern church.

Theology in the Western church is meant to be understood, applied, and acted upon. It is rational, in the sense that it can be analyzed, distinguished from error, and propagated. Here is the approach to theology one would imagine to best satisfy a lawyer's disposition. It reached its zenith with Thomas Aquinas' *Summa Theologica*.

Eastern theology is no less theology for its mystical setting, but it is less concerned with precise definition. It holds that beliefs are meant to be adored as mysteries, rather than subjected to vigorous dissection, since the whole is never simply the sum of its parts. One loses something vital by trying to put things back together again, having disassembled its original.

Liturgy is central to the Eastern church. Therefore, Ernst Benz rejects the idea of comparing the Eastern church to the Western church on the latter's basis. Instead of outlining the doctrines of the Eastern church in analytic fashion, he chooses rather to begin with what one sees on visiting a church of the Eastern rite: "The orthodox believer who enters his church to attend services first goes up to the iconostasis, the wall of

7. Vladimir Lossky, *The Mystical Theology of the Eastern Church*, p. 10.

paintings which separates the sanctuary of the nave. There he kisses the icons in a definite order: first the Christ icons, then the Mary icons, then the icons of the angels and saints."[8] He then proceeds to a lectern where the icon of the saint for the particular day or feast is displayed. After bestowing a kiss, bowing, and crossing himself at the lectern, the believer steps back to rejoin the congregation.

The veneration of icons extends to the home. Each family has an icon hanging in the eastern corner of the living room and bedroom. It is customary for a guest, upon entering a room, to greet the icons first by crossing and bowing. Only then does he greet his host.

The making of an icon is considered a sacred art. The painter is expected to prepare himself for the task with fasting and penance, and the materials he will use are consecrated for the task. The icon itself is thought to be a sort of window between earthly and celestial worlds, through which one views the other.

This provides an access to what has been called "the deification of man" in Eastern theology. Lossky observes: "What must be deified in us is our entire nature, belonging to our person which must enter into union with God . . . a human nature which is deified, and a nature or, rather, divine energy that deifies."[9] So, while the West taught salvation by infusion, the East countered with deification.

The distinction is not easy to grasp. We might suggest that where salvation in the West is more concerned with man's position before God, the East reflects on his posture before God. The doctrine of grace in the West bestows on man a righteous quality, while in the East it allows the restoration of his divine image.

We observe in passing what is probably the most obvious difference: the Eastern churches have no human head. As Benz elaborates, "The master, lord and sole head of the Church is Christ. But the monarchial principle does not in practice rule the organization of the visible church. Here purely democratic principles prevail."[10] The clergy, aside from their sacramental powers, have no special rights that set them above the laity. Not even the bishops constitute the highest authority. This is reserved for the ecumenical consensus of the church—which means the general opinion of clergy and laymen taken together.

---

8. Ernst Benz, *The Eastern Orthodox Church*, p. 2.
9. Lossky, *The Mystical Theology of the Eastern Church*, p. 155.
10. Benz, *The Eastern Orthodox Church*, p. 70.

During this era of Christendom, the West promoted, with various degrees of enthusiasm, the Bishop of Rome as the duly appointed Vicar of Christ. He was thought to enjoy a primacy over the other bishops of the church, even to being able to speak *ex cathedra* on occasion—prescribing infallibly on behalf of the church. The Vicar of Christ resembles a benevolent ruler, to whom his subjects are obligated.

Such developments as we have outlined suggest how different a route the Eastern and Western churches had traveled. The rift between them continued to widen. Papal legates dramatically laid on the altar of St. Sophia, as it stood ready for the Eucharist, a sentence of excommunication of the Patriarch and his supporters. A synod returned the favor a few days later by excommunicating the legates. Efforts continued to mediate between the disputants, but to no avail. The die had been cast well in advance of this dramatic interchange; now the churches were determined to pursue their own ways.

100 Appraisal

The struggle between the Eastern and Western churches with regard to the Holy Spirit centered on the *Filioque* clause, suggesting that the Spirit proceeded from both the Father and Son. The Western church accepted and promoted this addition to the Nicene Creed, whereas the Eastern church took an uncompromising stand against it. Some have described the *Filioque* controversy as a contrived issue, but it has been treated with utmost seriousness until the present.

Theodore Stylianopoulas, speaking on behalf of Eastern Christians, asks the West to decide whether or not the teaching of the early councils is normative: "They must reflect on whether the Augustinian premise of rationally explaining the data of faith has not in part led western theology, either in its scholastic or modern liberal forms, to subtle but deep shifts away from the spirit and authority of Scripture and the Catholic tradition."[11] They must also be prepared to repudiate their stance if it fails to pass the test assigned for it.

Michael Fahey refuses to treat the issue as simply as he is called upon to do. He concludes that "Rome must have as its partner all the major churches of the West, and the East must include the churches of the Ancient Oriental traditions antedating the Council of Chalcedon. Whether the decision reached in prayer is to drop the *Filioque* or to

---

11. Hans Küng and Jürgen Moltmann (eds.), *Conflicts About the Holy Spirit*, p. 30.

retain it in some churches, what is important is a deeper comprehension of the workings of the Holy Spirit in different ages, and different traditions."[12] His answer hints that the issue may point to some larger concern related to the work of the Spirit in the world—as well it might.

We need to keep in mind such theological distinctives as represented by the Eastern doctrine of deification. Lossky observes that Pentecost is thus seen in regard to the incarnation as "its sequel, its result. The creature has become fit to receive the Holy Spirit and He descends into the world and fills with His presence the Church which has been redeemed, washed, and purified by the blood of Christ."[13] Once the work of Christ has been consummated, the work of the Spirit with regard to the believer begins.

It follows from this line of reasoning that whereas the work of Christ unifies, the work of the Spirit diversifies. The one is impossible without the other. We ought not to look for the kind of conformity promoted in the West, but a consensus among the faithful. The Spirit works with all so as to minimize the distinction between clergy and laity and to discourage the notion of one speaking authoritatively for all.

Herein lies one of the fundamental errors in the Western church, according to their Eastern counterpart: it presumes to know the secret working of the Spirit in others. It does not respect the sanctity of life expressed in the diversity of the Spirit's work. Thus, its understanding of the way of the Spirit proves too narrow.

But the problem lies more deeply, in that the West presumes to understand what escapes us all. By attempting to bring divine truths down to human forms, it loses the mystical quality of faith and the transcendent character of the Spirit as being present within us.

For the Eastern theologian, salvation means the appropriation of life in communion with God. It involves proper vision and action and begins now, so that we may say that the church is what God would have all to be. But God does not force Himself on any person. He draws through His word and by means of the Spirit such as welcome His initiative. We need make no sharp distinction at this point between the church and the world. It is enough to say that God saves through His Word and by His Spirit.

The Western theologian takes a more reasoned approach. He can define the character of the true church, even though he cannot differen-

12. *Ibid.*, p. 22.

13. Lossky, *The Mystical Theology of the Eastern Church*, p. 159.

tiate between the wheat and the tares. He wants to weigh the insights that have come from different religious communities and prayerfully reach such decisions as are thought binding.

We in the West have viewed the Spirit more in terms of His revealing and teaching capacity than as celebrant. He disciples us and, when faced by the impossible demands of the law, provides grace and forgiveness. The Spirit reminds us, more than in the East, of our secularity.[14] In Western thought, there is more emphasis on the cross, the realities of life, and the veil of tears. Our humanity lies still in bondage, and grace is still a token of things to come. God sees us in Christ's righteousness rather than our own. Although there is reconciliation made possible by the intercession of Christ, there is less prospect for restoration now, in this life.

The fullness of the Spirit is, whether in the East or West, the counterpart to how we view Christ. The East has accented the reigning Christ; the West has struggled more seriously to recall His *kenosis* (emptying). Thus, the fullness of the Spirit implies for the Eastern churchman a vision of the triumphant Christ and access to His throne of glory. It suggests deification.

Fullness of the Spirit for the Western Christian means the enablement to live out the vicissitudes of life by means of the indwelling Spirit. It requires that we risk our selves in the world, there to find His grace sufficient. It means losing life in order to gain it back again as God's gift to the pilgrim.

The respective emphases of East and West no doubt complement each other. But they may also reflect partisan positions, spawned in cultural preferences, refined for polemic purposes, and indulged in for pragmatic reasons. They suggest the complex character of Christendom as it developed, and the reason why ecumenical dialogue continues to flounder as a result. But they also remind us of the centrality of the Spirit in the life of the church, even though viewed differently within varying traditions.

101 The Reformation

The Western church was destined to undergo still another traumatic division. Its emphasis on conformity had produced mixed effects: a

---

14. The term "secularity" is used here as the inclination to relate man to his world without appeal to the Almighty or eternal verities.

striking degree of success in creating a Roman church, along with fostering resentment. The situation was fueled by the political maneuverings of the hierarchy, moral and spiritual malaise, and the insensitive promotion of religious indulgences. The discontent finally erupted with the Reformation.

The conflict assumed two levels of controversy: the issue of authority and certain cardinal matters of faith. Neither of these dealt expressly with the Holy Spirit, but both had bearing upon the matter. Almost without notice, the focus shifted in accent from the person to the work of the Spirit, so as to define the theological battleground. Although this was perhaps most evident in the writing of John Calvin, it was contributed to by others on both sides of the Reformation controversy.

102 Authority Issue

Battista Mondin introduces the Roman Catholic perspective with the observation: "The papacy can be considered in two ways: as an historical institution or as a living reality in the present exercise of its functions. Consequently the Holy Spirit can be invoked in support of the papacy in two different ways. If one looks on the papacy as an historical institution, one invokes the Holy Spirit to affirm that the papacy has a *divine, supernatural* origin. If on the other hand, one considers it as a living reality in the exercise of its functions, one will have recourse to the Holy Spirit in order to show that, in carrying out of certain activities at least, it enjoys a special form of assistance from the Holy Spirit."[15] In both cases, the Holy Spirit is considered indispensable in order to justify the Roman Catholic claim to papal authority.

It is argued that the Spirit guided Jesus in the selection of the Twelve, and in the appointment of Peter as their head. Jesus promised to the apostolic band, and to Peter in particular, the assistance of the Holy Spirit. This assistance involved a better understanding of the *truth* concerning Jesus (the significance of His life, as yet barely understood by them), and the *doctrine* of Jesus. The latter implied papal succession, along "with the memory of infallibility."

A more complex line of argument supports the work of the Holy Spirit in the exercise of the church. Mondin likens the structural (visible) and pneumatic (invisible) aspects of the church to body and soul. One is indispensable to the other. "Christ, in fact, through the action of

15. Küng and Moltmann (eds.), *Conflicts About the Holy Spirit*, p. 65.

the Holy Spirit, builds up his body by means of a plurality of ministries, which the Spirit in fact brings to birth within it in order to make it fit to fulfil its role. Charisms and ministries interpenetrate one another and mutually enfold one another: there is no ministry, even the most official, that is not also a gift of the Spirit, and there is no charism that is not also a service of the community."[16] The papacy is one of these *essential* structural elements, without which the church would not exist and the Holy Spirit could not be said to be fully operative.

This introduces a related line of thought. The pope is said to be singled out from among the pastors for the purpose of safeguarding and increasing the ecumenical character of the church. This function does not belong to a purely sociological order, but should be recognized as an extension of the work of the Spirit. To this end, the Spirit provides the Bishop of Rome with multiple gifts to fulfill his unique calling, sustains him in the exercise of all his duties, and helps him reflect the marks of the church.

Mondin turns at last to the Roman Catholic case for infallibility. He reasons that the qualified bearer of infallibility is the pope, in subordination to the Holy Spirit and by means of His constant assistance. Infallibility assumes a sacramental and visible form in the episcopal college, which can act in a corporate fashion or be represented by its head, the pope. The Holy Spirit follows no simple rule in providing assistance: it may be by such a direct intervention as a vision or, more often, as men laboriously search for the leading of the Spirit through all avenues of understanding open to them. The pope must listen attentively to the Word of God and work diligently to realize the will of God if he is to benefit for himself and the church at large from the assistance of the Holy Spirit.

Mondin has rendered us a service by making clear the role of the Spirit as seen in defense of Roman Catholic authority. We turn now to a Protestant response as to how the Holy Spirit was viewed as the divine agent in the Reformation. We will sense both similarities and dissimilarities in the alternative positions, apart from the obviously different purposes for which they were applied.

Harding Meyer thinks that Catholicism has put forward the wrong question, and therefore comes up with an answer that does not apply. The whole Catholic argument rests on the notion of church office as office of the Spirit, while it ought to be understood as office of the Word.

16. *Ibid.*, p. 68.

Meyer elucidates: "This subjection of the Word and reference to Christ, which comes to expression in it, of the work of the Spirit in and through Church and office were, in the opinion of the reformers insufficiently regarded—even disregarded—by the Roman Church. All decisions of both Church and office which do not exhibit this reference to the Word cannot therefore be regarded as being legitimized by the Spirit."[17] Since reference to the Word is lacking, we cannot conclude that the office bears the credentials of the Spirit.

To put the crux of the matter differently, only the Word legitimizes the office as office of the Spirit. The Word inevitably stands in judgment on the works of men, whether or not it is done in the name of the church. Infallibility is an idea best reserved for the Word of God, rather than applied to the people of God or their representative. It is not only human to err, but it is expected of humanity.

This is not primarily a problem of how to bridge a historical gap, as the Roman Catholic assumes, but how to overcome an existential gap. The Holy Spirit in Protestant thought is viewed as mediating between man and God rather than man and church. The church remains the medium, but not the mediator of the grace of God. Thus W. H. Griffith Thomas asserts: "Up to the time of the Reformation the characteristic and essential feature of mediaeval theology was 'through the Church to Christ,' but the Reformation reversed this method by a reinsistence on the New Testament principle of 'through Christ to the Church.'"[18] Thus, while the Roman Catholic might protest that this was not actually the New Testament principle, he would likely acknowledge it to be the fundamental issue at stake with regard to authority, and on which other issues were dependent.

103 Cardinal Principles

There were other issues, as we have suggested earlier, that contributed to the Reformation controversy. We may single out three of these, put in Protestant terms as *sola fide*, *sola gratia*, and *"sola" scriptura*. The most characteristic feature of the Reformation was *sola fide:* salvation through "faith alone." Martin Luther thus warned "against the presumptuousness of those who believe that they have access to God without Christ, as if it were sufficient for them to have believed. So they

17. *Ibid.*, p. 87.
18. W. H. Griffith Thomas, *The Holy Spirit of God*, p. 100.

want to come to God by faith alone, not through Christ but past Christ, as if they no longer needed Christ after having received the grace of justification."[19] Salvation is not accomplished by a human act—whether that be called faith of the individual or as administered corporately through the church—but by the work of the Spirit.

There is no salvation outside the church, according to Catholic teaching. The Protestant rebuttal is that there is no salvation inside *or* outside the church that is not in Christ. The Holy Spirit and He alone negotiates the existential gap between God and man, in response not to faith in the church, but faith in Christ. *Sola fide*—faith alone—is a shortened way of saying "faith in Christ alone."

Sola gratia was the natural conclusion of *sola fide*. We are saved by "grace alone." Paul taught that "by grace you have been saved through faith; and that not of yourselves, it is the gift of God" (Eph. 2:8). Catholicism seemed dangerously Pelagian to the Reformers, in that it gave too optimistic a report of man's condition and too positive an evaluation of his potential. The Reformers saw man in more desperate straits, seeing that they had stripped him of such support as the church might afford him. He stood defenseless in the presence of a holy God.

But, though defenseless, man was also the subject of grace—a gift of the Spirit, nothing more and nothing less. It is not something we may expect (as Catholic doctrine seemed to imply), much less deserve, but can only receive with thanksgiving. The Reformers were adamant in pressing their notion of grace as radically understood.

This was not to imply that the Reformers were unmindful of the proper place for good works in the lives of believers. Works would follow on the heels of regeneration, in the lives of those who yield themselves to the indwelling Spirit. The Spirit must be present in—but in distinction from—good works.

"Sola" scriptura rounds out the triad of distinctively Reformation teaching. The idea seemed to emerge as a result of a Protestant consensus, although it was not at the cutting edge of the controversy, as salvation by faith and grace alone had been. "Scripture alone" became a rallying cry of the Reformation as a growing realization of its central importance to the enterprise.

We hasten to add two related ideas: those of the primacy and perspicuity of Scripture. Both illustrate the particular Protestant perspective on Holy Writ, and the Holy Spirit as associated with it. One does not

---

19. Wilhelm Pauck (ed.), *Luther: Lectures on Romans*, p. 154.

advocate the primacy of Scripture to the exclusion of all other means of knowing God's will. The notion of Scripture alone would be misleading otherwise. But Scripture provides the norm for the rest. It was the final court of appeal, so that we might conclude that while reason or tradition might be correct as the *words of men*, only Scripture deserves to be revered as the *Word of God*.

Primacy of Scripture, once firmly established, allows substantial room for evaluating the rest. As a matter of historical record, Protestantism proved to be more open than Catholicism to new possibilities. Catholicism opened up to the world more slowly and more begrudgingly as a rule. This openness to the world was seen in the respective communities as either the fresh stirring of the Spirit or that of an unknown and presumably evil counterpart.

Perspicuity of Scripture has to do with our understanding of Scripture. Catholicism had advocated the need of an accredited office to correctly interpret Holy Writ, citing differences of opinion as necessitating official teaching. Reformers responded that Scripture could be interpreted along the lines one would interpret any other historical and literary work, *and* by means of the Holy Spirit. The two were thought to blend together in order to prepare the people of God for their task.

The Reformation took issue with the tendency to spiritualize the biblical text, ignore the more obvious meaning, and temper the Word of God with the wisdom of men. One ought to set free the Scripture from the bonds of tradition to do its work in the lives of men. The Bible is its own best advocate.

This allows the Spirit of God to assume His unique teaching ministry. The Spirit knows the mind of God and can best illuminate the Word of God. He is far more apt than any human instructor, no matter how well the latter is trained for his duties or how open to God's leading.

104 The Result

The lines were firmly drawn. Each side invoked the Spirit for its endeavor. The one explored the historical character of the church as derived from Jesus' charge to the apostles and Peter in particular—so that the Roman Catholic church alone could be said to be founded on Christ and fostered accordingly by the Holy Spirit. This stance likened the structural and pneumatic aspects of the church to body and soul, so that one might not be viewed apart from the other.

The other side attacked the issue as an existential dilemma of man's alienation from God, so that the role of the Spirit is interpreted as bridging that gap, as only He can do. It left the offices of the church not as offices of the Spirit but of the Word. The Reformers further developed the distinctive Protestant themes of *sola fide, sola gratia,* and *"sola" scriptura,* so as to support their contention concerning the nature of both the problem and solution.

The remainder is a matter of historical record. Unlike so many who dissented from the Roman Catholic church earlier, the Protestant movement not only continued to exist but to grow rapidly. Latourette writes that by the nineteenth and twentieth centuries, it "displayed a greater proportionate and numerical geographic expansion than did the rapidly spreading Roman Catholic Church. Moreover, it produced a succession of quite novel organizational and functional expressions of the Christian faith. Although seemingly the most divided of all forms of Christianity, in the nineteenth and twentieth centuries Protestants increasingly found new ways of coming together which eventually drew in not only the majority of their own ranks, but also many from the Roman Catholic and Orthodox Churches."[20] It was a movement so complex, so diversified, as to lend itself to varied interpretations.

Catholicism likewise underwent change. The so-called Catholic Counter-Reformation was only in part a response to Protestant criticism and secession. In any case, it would no doubt have come in some form, although perhaps not the one it eventually took. Reformation was in the wind for the Roman Catholic Church regardless. The uncompromising pronouncements of the Council of Trent, aimed at the Protestant defectors, obscured the move that was at foot but had to accommodate to it. History seems to suggest that Catholicism gained more from its efforts to reform than from the brutal Inquisition waged against its protagonists.

The central emphasis on the Spirit changed with the turmoil of the times from His person to His work. Previously, the accent had been on the Spirit as God with us, and (with Christendom) for the purpose of creating a new society. Now the polemic solicited diverse ways of seeing the Spirit at work—whether in regard to establishing the credibility of the Roman Catholic Church or in elevating the Word over the office—and reaching out for a genuine fellowship in the Spirit. The results of what some have called "the great schism" would be and are being felt

---

20. Latourette, *A History of Christianity,* p. 836.

throughout the far reaches of Christianity. It has, in one way or another, pressed us to look at the work of the Spirit more closely, whether to close a historical or an existential gap, through the church of Christ or the Christ of the church.

105 The Enthusiasts

The Reformation was a sort of alternative establishment to Roman Catholicism. The so-called enthusiasts were in contrast to both, in that they were skeptical about any overarching synthesis of Christianity and culture. "Enthusiasm," whether at the time of the Protestant revolt or previously, is perhaps better described as a tendency in Christianity rather than a movement or combination of movements, although it is more associated with some movements than with others.

Ronald Knox attempts to explain what is involved: "Our traditional doctrine is that grace perfects nature, elevates it to a higher pitch, so that it can bear its part in the music of eternity, but leaves it nature still. The assumption of the enthusiast is bolder and simpler: for him, grace has destroyed nature, and replaced it."[21] He takes a more radical stance, akin to what has been called the Christ-against-culture approach.

The enthusiast's predilection is virtually as old as the church itself. Paul confronted it in Corinth. Here the gospel had been planted in difficult soil, where misunderstanding and aberration might be expected. There arose divisions, libertine practices, competition with regard to spiritual gifts—to mention a partial list of the problems resulting. Some people took the gospel to mean that they were freed from the normal restraints of life together. Then they would function in some ecstatic world of their own making, until they were brought forcefully back to reality through the pointed criticism of the apostle.

Montanism qualifies as another case in point. Its adherents claimed that Montanus was the "paraclete" promised to come and bring about a fuller revelation. The oracles of this new prophecy would improve on what we find in the Scriptures. Along with the expectation whipped up in regard to the parousia, this encouraged a rigorous asceticism, an austerity that apparently required no biblical precedent nor practical purpose.

---

21. Ronald Knox, *Enthusiasm*, p. 3.

Enthusiasm had persisted with the passage of time. One of the more outstanding instances was Joachism. A product of the twelfth century, it promoted a detailed system of biblical numerology, from which was derived three ages of history. The age of the Father (dominated by married people and laymen) had given way to the age of the Son (controlled by the priests), and would shortly be supplanted by the age of the Holy Spirit (directed by monks). Thereupon, the eternal gospel would be proclaimed and a new, spiritually understood view of Scripture established, the spirit of poverty would triumph, and peace would come to the world.

The seed of dissatisfaction with the church hierarchy had been set in motion. Abbott Joachim, founder of the movement, fell into disfavor when his ideas were taken up by certain adherents who identified the Antichrist not with the emperor (as Joachim had done), but with the pope. When the announced date (1260 A.D.) for the new age arrived, a new burst of enthusiasm was represented by the Apostolic Brethren, who declared themselves as the church of the poor in contrast to the Roman church—described as "the Babylonian harlot." Rome crushed the movement, only to see new expressions of enthusiasm break out at other points.

Protestantism appeared at least as susceptible to enthusiasm as its Roman Catholic counterpart. Thomas Münzer is probably the most celebrated example. Münzer substituted the direct enlightenment of the Holy Spirit for Scripture, and spiritual suffering (the experience of the cross) for justification by faith. His position made for the most incredible applications of Scripture, which were said to turn the dead letter of the Word into living words.

Münzer became increasingly involved in the political struggles of the time. In the 1520s, he exhorted the peasants to take up arms against their princes, putting himself at their disposal as their prophetic leader. Münzer was eventually apprehended and put to death.

Luther, by contrast, repudiated the peasants' cause and called upon the princes to set down the revolt. The enthusiasts had given an extreme turn to Luther's teaching in order to accommodate it to their understanding of being free in the Spirit. Luther's attack on the peasants ranks with his most vicious assaults, and it no doubt reflects his difficulty in disassociating himself from the enthusiastic caste and the ferment of rebellion.

We might put a more positive construct on enthusiasm than we have been inclined to do so far. We could argue that enthusiasm need simply be balanced over and against an appreciation of the institutional structure of the church and society in general. As such, we would view it as straining against the inhibiting character of the status quo and probing for some creative alternative. It goes wrong, in this case, only when carried to some extreme, as with certain aforementioned instances.

106 Reconsideration

The Confession of Augsburg (1530 A.D.) seems clearly to be combating enthusiasm when it states: "The Anabaptists and others who teach that we can attain to the Holy Spirit without the bodily word of the gospel and through our own preparation, thoughts and work are condemned." Herein we can begin to pick up the thoughts associated with the Spirit in enthusiasm, and in the writings of its critics. Thus, hopefully, we can gain some further insight into the operation of the Spirit.

Inge Lonning concludes that the Augsburg Confession resists two incursions: "On the one hand, it explicitly marks off the conviction of the Reformers from the spiritualized pneumatology of the enthusiasts. On the other hand, however, it also explicitly marks off their teaching from the pneumatology of the Roman tradition with its strong emphasis on canon law. The Spirit is not, in other words, tied to the Church as a hierarchical institution, but to the bodily word of the gospel in baptism, preaching and the Lord's Supper."[22] Since we have already explored something of the difference between Roman Catholic and Reformation views of the Holy Spirit, we can proceed to tie in that of the enthusiast—of whatever derivation.

John Yoder discovers four concepts of the Spirit within the enthusiasts' thought.[23] Although these may appear as separate or in some particular grouping, they represent individually and collectively enthusiasm's contribution to our understanding of the work of the Spirit.

Some treated the Holy Spirit "as a principle of uncontrollable inspiration." This seems the tendency that Paul means to correct when he writes to urge that "the spirits of prophets are subject to prophets" (1 Cor. 14:32). One is not simply passive in being "possessed by the Spirit," but can and should behave responsibly.

This is the context in which a technical definition of enthusiasm would be most appropriate. The word is derived from *en* and *theos*

22. Küng and Moltmann (eds.), *Conflicts About the Holy Spirit*, p. 35.
23. *Ibid.*, pp. 41–46.

(god) and connotes being possessed by the divine. Enthusiasts conceive of the Spirit in such terms and profess to be under the sway of the Spirit.

Scripture counsels, "do not believe every spirit, but test the spirits to see whether they are from God; because many false prophets have gone out into the world. By this you know the Spirit of God: every spirit that confesses that Jesus Christ has come in the flesh is from God; and every spirit that does not confess Jesus is not from God . . ." (1 John 4:1–3). The Augsburg Confession thereupon protests against those who claim the Holy Spirit "without the bodily word of the gospel." The text further suggests, as a proper alternative, viewing the Spirit in reference to baptism, the sermon, and communion. So, while the confession appeals to biblical teaching, it also conveys a theological tradition.

There may be more that can be said for such an enthusiast's perspective than the summary rejection in the Augsburg Confession would imply. Taken in its most orthodox light, the enthusiast appeal can be seen not as freeing the Spirit from the Word but the Word from the office. It thus becomes an attack on the institutionalizing of Christianity, a plea for the community to stand free of its traditions to hear the Word of God as it comes alive through the teaching of the Spirit.

A second perspective growing out of enthusiasm was that of the Spirit as the seal of a new age. Thus the Spirit was thought to authenticate, through whatever means, that the final days had dawned. The effect was to provide for the faithful some previously lacking distance from life as they had experienced it, especially as it had come to be among nominal church adherents.

According to which movement we consider, the Holy Spirit would authenticate the new age by extraordinary means (visions, signs, inner assurance) or extraordinary insight into the meaning of Scripture. With the latter instance, the hermeneutics departed dramatically from the historical and literary methodology wisely advocated. This departure was attested by the testimony of the Spirit (an inner confirmation), a gestalt (where things fell into place), or a combination of the two.

Such a concept of the work of the Spirit naturally led to excesses of many varieties. It was enough to encourage the sober mainstream of Christianity that they were better off promoting the traditional tenets of their faith, and even invoking state supervision as a proper safeguard. But, problems aside, the enthusiasts had touched on an aspect of the Spirit we mentioned in regard to diasporan Christianity: the unexpected, unpredictable character of the Holy Spirit—how we ought to be open, not to *any* spirit, but to the Holy Spirit as the changeless faith enthusiastically faces changing times. There was an authentic note which had not been heard all that often in the staid ranks of Christianity.

A third perspective on the Spirit revolved around the subject of authority, which, as we have seen, was a critical concern in the Reformation controversy. The enthusiasts added still another dimension with their particular point of view regarding the role of the Spirit.

A strict congregationalism often resulted. John Yoder selects as a precedent Luther's and Zwingli's support of the local community to make "binding decisions on matters of truth, life and Church order without consulting distant hierarchs. The argument for this authority was provided by the model represented in I Cor. 14, where every member has the right to speak and all the others listen and make a critical evaluation, and the account in Acts 15, where the result of a similarly structured discussion was a consensus."[24] Thus the fellowship came together in order to sense the mind of the Lord in matters of church practice, personal deportment, and social responsibility.

These communities (unlike the churches of Christendom) found that they could survive without the support of civil power, and even in some instances in opposition to it. They had, to their own satisfaction at least, freed themselves from such entangling alliances as had compromised the church in the past. They were free from worldly concerns, so as to be the faithful company.

Enthusiasm provided no panacea with this alternative. One has to come to grips with society at some point, if not in terms of establishment then in some voluntary capacity. And the course of seeking consensus among the brethren can be a difficult, time-consuming, and even self-defeating exercise. But, at the very least, the enthusiasts provided a fresh insight into the Spirit at work for those of like faith, concern, and openness to the viewpoint of others.

The final perspective encountered in enthusiasm represented the Holy Spirit as the means of subjectively appropriating truth. The emphasis was not, as in the first instance, with the Spirit as the source of truth but as the means of appropriating truth. It implied that truth could not be imposed from without, whether through ecclesiastical or civil authority. This view demanded that persons be attentive to the Spirit in order to sense His leading.

---

24. *Ibid.*, p. 44.

Such a perspective tends to foster personal piety and reliance on the Spirit. It could also weaken the necessary checks and balances of life together, so that one could justify all sorts of individual idiosyncrasies that come to mind. Therefore, it is not surprising that it produced mixed results and conflicting evaluations.

Summary

We take our leave of the age of Christendom, having seen its expression in connection with the rise of the Christian cultural synthesis, traced some of the differences related to its division into East and West, explored the Reformation alternative, and probed the counter-Christendom movement identified as "enthusiasm." We sensed in the process that the operation of the Spirit is such a rich and varied enterprise that we had best not limit it to one partisan perspective or another. But neither should we accept a point of view indiscriminately, seeing that we are charged to "try the spirits" (1 John 4:1, KJV).

How shall we counter the seemingly incompatible contrasts between East and West, Roman Catholic and Protestant, the establishment and the enthusiast? Hans Küng's suggestion concerning how to counter enthusiasm may apply in the other tensions as well. He reasons: "The real answer must obviously be: *by concentrating on the Gospel of Jesus Christ*. Instead of negative polemics, the Gospel, the *whole* Gospel must be positively preached and positively lived. The demands of the enthusiast (or any other) which are truly rooted in the Gospel must be energetically taken up and put into practice."[25] Such as fails to accord with the gospel must conversely be repudiated in the process.

In its various forms, Christendom was a witness not only to the presence of the church in the world but its responsibility for the world. It illustrated that the Spirit of God was at work in the community of faith as a cultural catalyst. The distinctive emphases, while important enough in themselves, were more variations on a theme than anything else.

Enthusiasm presented the greater challenge to thinking of Christ as transforming culture. Enthusiasm forged anew the Christ-and-

25. Küng, *The Church*, p. 198.

culture dichotomy through its emphasis on the Spirit as the principle of uncontrollable inspiration, as heralding the zeal of a new age, as authority in the community, and as the means of subjectively appropriating the truth. It was at best a needed connective, and at worst an aberration of the faith.

If we might be so bold as to wed Christendom and enthusiasm, we would be reminded that the Spirit has vested interest in both continuity and discontinuity. What the Spirit builds, He builds to last against the ravages of time. But He continues to build, using a previous foundation to construct new improvements. Christendom erred with its efforts to perpetuate continuity; enthusiasm erred in its one-sided focus on discontinuity. Although both alike sensed something of the Spirit at work, each was tempted to one extreme or the other.

12

The Modern Era

We will assume, as has previously been stated, that the Enlightenment ushered in what we have come to call "the modern age." James Livingston writes: "Underlying this whole movement is a renewed awareness and trust in man's own capacities and appreciation of, interest in, and hope for human life on earth. Reason supersedes revelation as the supreme court of appeal. As a result, theology faced a choice of either adjusting itself to the advances in modern science and philosophy and, in so doing, risking accommodation to secularization, or resisting all influences from culture and becoming largely reactionary and ineffectual in meeting the challenges of life in the modern world."[1] Christianity was caught between two undesirable alternatives, either of which seemed to call for a compromise of its convictions in general and concerning the Holy Spirit in particular.

107 Resulting Controversy

It seemed strange that a movement given its impetus within Christendom could turn with such violence against its mentor. But circum-

1. James Livingston, *Modern Christian Thought*, p. 2.

stances had contributed to what came to pass. When the church could not solve its differences through peaceful means, it turned to the sword. The Thirty Years' War seemed to accentuate everything base, cruel, and oppressive in its previous experience. The fruit of Christendom was tainted, so far as its Enlightenment critics could determine, and it was time to cut down the tree.

This left subsequent Christians in an intolerable bind—caught between either surrendering cherished convictions or facing the prospect of an early demise. The dilemma brought on the so-called Modernist-Fundamentalist controversy between opposing points of view. The modernist or liberal chose to reach some accommodation with Enlightenment modernity; the fundamentalist or conservative decided to keep faith with the past, regardless of the cost.

108 Rise of Liberalism

Friedrich Schleiermacher set the course for those of liberal persuasion. He was hailed as "the father of modern theology," and few religious observers since that time could afford not to weigh his words, whether to agree or disagree with them. Nurtured in Moravian piety, Schleiermacher had entered avidly into the spirit of the era. He addressed his associates on religion as "its cultured despisers." Schleiermacher reasoned that religion is not essentially "knowledge and science, either of the world or of God. Without being knowledge, it recognizes knowledge and science. In itself it is an affection, a revelation of the Infinite in the finite, God being seen in it and it in God."[2] Thus he saw the despisers as allies of true religion if they would press on to recognize its incorruptible inner essence.

Religion, stripped of its outward garb, involves the feeling of ultimate dependence, without which there would be little or nothing creative on our part. For religion provides the source for that free and higher life to which Enlightenment man aspires. According to William Hodern, Schleiermacher held that "All great art and literature has a concept of the totality of the universe, and this is, whether it is recognized or not, an experience of God."[3] With this concept Schleiermacher hoped to preserve the essence of religion for modernity.

The God of liberalism was radically immanent. Pantheism qualifies as the most extreme form of immanence because it identifies God with

2. Friedrich Schleiermacher, *On Religion*, p. 36.
3. William Hodern, *A Layman's Guide to Protestant Theology*, p. 44.

the world. Although Scheiermacher stopped short of pantheism, he insisted on finding God in the entirety of life and not in some few particular events. God works by way of progressive change, through natural law, and not in the form of miracles or special acts of revelation.

Schleiermacher's view of the Spirit, with liberalism following him, conformed to this idea of an immanent deity. This basic view took on several aspects of Enlightenment thought for religious purposes, not least of which was the emphasis on autonomy. Man best serves God by being himself. We can recognize the operation of the Spirit primarily in regard to the humanization of man, so that man can break free from the religious and metaphysical times to enjoy the positivistic (scientific) character of modernity.

This appeal to the Spirit involves the release of man from his self-incurred tutelage. The Spirit repudiates on our behalf all arbitrary mandates, those we cannot readily justify by reason. He also repudiates the imposition of sanctions from the outside, whether to coerce by way of present punishment or future retribution.

This constituted a radical reversal of thinking from the time of Christendom, which had been suspicious of exception and innovation and invoked the Spirit to preserve life by way of tried and proven methods. In contrast, liberalism made virtues out of departure and novelty. It viewed the Spirit as constantly on the move to meet some new challenge with fresh insights and unique results.

The difference can also be seen in the reappraisal of the nature of faith, although the distinction is more subtle in this instance. Gabriel Vahanian argues: "When doubting no longer liberates the movement of faith or propels the movement of faith, it is quite likely that faith has become petrified and threatened with self-extinction, and that this condition threatens with extinction the cultural forms to which such rigid faith was wedded."[4] Thus, while a previous age might have commended unmitigated faith, Vahanian allows only such faith as embraces doubt.

Liberalism was driven back to consider Jesus and weigh what might be the significance of the designation "the Spirit of Christ." Here differences began to strain into divisions. The minimal interpretation viewed Jesus simply as one of those more noble men who seldom grace the world scene. The maximal interpretation approached something close to an orthodox definition of Christ. Both tended to see the Spirit as

---

4. Gabriel Vahanian, *The Death of God*, p. 13.

embodying the high moral ideals of Jesus in such a way as to make them available to His followers. The Spirit creates the Christ-like spirit, without which one ought not lay claim to being His disciple.

This "orthodoxy of praxis" has characterized liberalism, but its precise definition remains uncertain. One is meant to love, be quick to forgive, overlook differences, be encouraging, and the like. In other words, one must behave in the way Jesus did. This is not simply a matter of modeling life after Jesus' example, except perhaps in the more extreme liberal thought, but being open to what the Spirit of Christ would like to bring to pass.

Liberalism inherited a strong sense of toleration from the Enlightenment, coupled with a distrust of binding theological statements. Outside whatever boundaries people tried to set on Him, the Spirit no doubt worked with those who did not expressly confess Christ but exhibited something of His disposition. In fact, the church often seemed the least responsive to Christian faith as the liberals understood it. They wanted to help church members see that the Spirit, under various disguises, was at work in His humanizing activity, urging them to join with Him in freeing mankind from every semblance of bondage.

109 Conservative Response

The conservative had difficulty deciphering the design of Christian faith in the liberal's theological meanderings. The latter used many of the right words, but in the wrong places and apparently with the wrong intent. He seemed to pursue contemporaneity at the loss of continuity with what preceding generations of Christians had believed.

The conservative emphasized the transcendence of God, and hence of the Spirit, without denying immanence. He liked to think that this was due simply to his fidelity to biblical teaching, but it seems to have involved his struggle with modernity as well. The post-Enlightenment world proceeded to erase the former Christian landmarks where feasible, or camouflage them when this was not possible. The conservative felt increasingly alienated from his society, with the result that he increasingly emphasized the transcendent character of the Spirit.

The conservative believed it necessary to stress the personality of the Holy Spirit in the light of liberalism's spotted record in this regard. R. A. Torrey writes: "If we think of the Holy Spirit only as an impersonal power or influence, then our thoughts will constantly be, 'How can I get hold of and use the Holy Spirit'; but if we think of Him in the Biblical way as a divine person, infinitely wise, infinitely holy, infinitely tender, then our thoughts will constantly be, 'How can the Holy Spirit get hold of and use me?' "[5] It was not, in his thinking, a theoretical issue alone, but one with profound practical implication.

Torrey meant to preserve the divine leverage in his accent on the Spirit. What if man were to gain respectability with his contemporaries, and lose his hold on God? Or, to be more in keeping with Torrey's thrust, to lose God's hold on us? It would hardly be a fair exchange.

The fulcrum for God's leverage for the conservative was a remnant community which bravely stood up to modernity. I have elsewhere observed: "The modern evangelical (conservative) movement grew out of these unsettled times (following the Enlightenment), when the Roman Catholic community was feeling the increasingly impossible strain of resisting the winds of the time and Protestantism was having second thoughts about being so cooperative. Evangelicalism appeared as a remnant within the institutional church and even a smaller remnant among contemporary man."[6] It resembles "a people of God set afloat in the sea of the Enlightenment."

We may not be overstating the case to say that the conservative saw the present world on a collision course with the will of God. The Spirit served in two capacities: to resist the presumption of the age and to console the remnant—yet, not so as to condemn all that modernity had achieved by way of improved conditions, all of which ought to be employed in the service of one's fellowman.

Conservatism's teaching on the Spirit differed much less from that which preceded it. The conservative was careful to document his case with Scripture and an occasional church father. It was almost imperceptible that the accent conformed to conservativism's status as a remnant community, fighting to preserve its very existence against the tide of the times. And its views eventually gained a wider hearing, as the influence of the Enlightenment ran its course, so that old issues could be reconsidered.

110 Recasting the Issue

The controversy peaked during the first quarter of this century, just as there began new stirrings on the continent of Europe. The defeat of

5. R. A. Torrey, et al., *The Fundamentals*, II, p. 323.

6. Morris Inch, *The Evangelical Challenge*, p. 104. The conservative was also in some respects a disciple of the Enlightenment, but this is a complex issue we have opted to simplify for discussion purposes.

Germany in World War I had been a bitter setback to many of those trained in liberal theology. They felt misled by the unrealistic optimism engendered by the movement and trapped by the resilient evil that men had proved capable of afflicting on others. Such names as Karl Barth, Emil Brunner, and Friedrich Gogarten simply provide a beginning to a long and impressive list of persons estranged from their liberal heritage by the crush of the times.

Barth reminisces: "One day in early August 1914 stands out in my personal memory as a black day. Ninety-three German intellectuals impressed public opinion by their proclamation in support of the war policy of Wilhelm II and his counselors. Among these intellectuals I discovered to my horror almost all of my theological teachers whom I had greatly venerated. . . . For me at least, 19th-century theology no longer held my future."[7] The liberals had, in the words of one critic, entered so fully into the human as to lose the divine. Their faith appeared to have no higher point of reference than the destiny of their nation.

These protesters did not throw out liberalism in its entirety, but attempted to rediscover what had in their judgment been lost in the rush to accommodate the Enlightenment. This meant, first and foremost, to reestablish the thorough transcendence of God, without qualification or exception. God, Barth proclaimed, is wholly Other. His emphasis on the Spirit kept pace, so as to distinguish the Holy Spirit from the human spirit. He drove the wedge deliberately: "But the Holy Ghost who does this in time (in reference to vocation) and history is not an anonymous magnitude and force using the Gospel to accomplish it. As the Spirit of the Father and the Son He is the power of the Gospel itself to call and enlighten and sanctify and preserve man in the true faith."[8] He is the Spirit of *God*, with all prerogatives so related.

"Let God be God" was a theme Barth liked to repeat in various ways. Let the Spirit be the Spirit of God, rather than subverting Him to some human design. We cannot make progress with the notion of immanence without first treating transcendence seriously.

We must recognize a chasm between God and man, which only the Spirit can hope to bridge. When applied to Brunner's thought, this disposition produced what has been called "crisis theology." That is to say, man does not comfortably meet God in the easy flow of events, but

7. Karl Barth, *The Humanity of God*, p. 14.
8. Karl Barth, *Church Dogmatics*, IV. p. 501.

encounters Him in a leap of faith. This was thought true even in regard to reading the Scriptures. The Scripture became the Word of God in an encounter between God and man. It was the fragile, human instrument used by the Holy Spirit to confront man in his sin and offer reconciliation.

We get the impression that in the encounter the Spirit pulls more from the other side than pushes from this one. This would seem consistent with the emphasis on transcendence. For Barth, religion was the last defense man raises against God, when everything else fails, rather than the reasoning intuition of God—as Schleiermacher had described it.

All of this suggests how difficult Christianity's encounter with modernity has been. Liberalism did its best to accommodate to the new way of thinking, to make virtue out of novelty and evil from conformity. On the other hand, conservatism advocated continuity over contemporaneity, assuming a remnant psychology in the process. Eventually, there was defection on the continent from the liberal persuasion, emphasizing the transcendent character of God and His purposes over man and his movements.

These efforts were accompanied by differing perspectives regarding the Holy Spirit. The liberal identified the Spirit essentially with the humanizing process, a development he supposed was served by modernity. The conservative resisted what seemed to be a depersonalization of the Spirit. Neo-orthodoxy reacted with an emphasis on divine transcendence, so much so that the Spirit was often typecast as a mediator in a crisis capacity where man encounters God in a leap of faith.

Where does one go from there? To the recognition that the Enlightenment, significant as it most certainly was, offers only one perspective on reality. It, too, had its limitations, its blind spots, and its prejudices. We cannot afford to accept its finding uncritically.

And where do we go from *there*? To the appreciation of the fact that *the* theological question of our day is how to be a contemporary Christian. It was forced upon us by the Enlightenment and remains current partly because Christendom was reluctant to face its pressing character earlier.

How does the Spirit direct us to answer this current issue? Perhaps as we resemble the people of God moving through history, confronting one obstacle after another, but pushing ahead with confidence. In that manner, He blazes the trail before us as we take courage to encounter a set of new and sometimes overwhelming challenges, similar to what has transpired in regard to the modern missionary movement.

111 Era of Modern Missions

Lesslie Newbigin calls to our attention that the church derived its main features during a time when it had practically ceased to be a missionary religion: "Christianity was the folk religion of a diminishing minority of the world's peoples, squeezed into a smaller and smaller part of the western peninsulas and islands of the Eurasian continent. It was in this period, when the ends of the earth had ceased to exist as a practical reality in the minds of Christians, that the main patterns of churchmanship were formed. The congregation was not a staging post for world mission but a gathering place for the faithful of a town or village."[9] This also caused Christians to think of the Holy Spirit in terms of a fortress mentality, until challenged by the rise of modern missions.

William Carey (1761–1834) has been described as the father of modern missions. Of course, there were earlier rumblings of the movement. One could trace back the history of modern missions to the Pietists and Moravians, and there were three British missionary societies already in operation by the time Carey came on the scene. But Carey brought into focus what had preceded him, giving a distinctive impetus to a movement already under way. He still best represents for us what the undertaking was all about.

Some like to be even more specific and identify modern missions with the date (May 31, 1792) when Carey, preaching from Isaiah 54:2–3, expounded the missionary maxim: "Expect great things from God; attempt great things for God." These words seemed to awaken a slumbering giant. Soon thereafter, twelve ministers formed the first Baptist Missionary Society, and Carey offered himself as its first missionary. From that moment on, missionary activity reached out to embrace the globe.

Kenneth Scott Latourette enthusiastically describes the nineteenth century as "the great century" for the global expansion of Christianity. Many factors favored such growth: the modern missionary movement had by then taken firm hold on the situation, there was a general air of hope and expansion that characterized the event, there had been a great increase in wealth in areas where Christianity was strongest, com-

---

9. Lesslie Newbigin, *Honest Religion for Secular Man*, p. 102.

munication and commerce had improved strikingly, and the impact of the West had opened avenues in non-European cultures: "All of these, however, would have been of no avail had they not been paralleled by the burst of new life within Christianity itself. It was this surge of vitality which was the primary cause of the daring vision, the comprehensive plans, and the offering of life and money which sent missionaries to all quarters of the globe."[10] When we trace the origin of this impulse, we discover that it lies in a stratum as old as Christianity itself, and as recent as its recasting of the role of the Holy Spirit in the life of the Church.

Christianity would not surrender its fortress mentality easily. Carey's critics argued: "When God pleases to convert the heathen, He will do it without your aid or mine." This was as if to justify the loss of vision and the preoccupation with one's own parish. Even when the surge of missions could no longer be contained, a peculiar bifurcation resulted, in which one did his best to maintain "business as usual" here at home. Accordingly, missions activity was thought of more as an appendage of the church than all-pervasive.

112 Vision Unlimited

The modern missionary zealots would not be denied their task. They felt compelled to encompass the globe in their search for those lost and without hope. They believed this was prompted by the Holy Spirit, and that they must obey God rather than man in the matter. No obstacle seemed so great as to dissuade them, as they drew strength from one another—as though they were fagots ignited by the Spirit of God.

The first thing to strike even a casual reader concerning the impetus to missions is the ingredient of compassion. "Love" could mean almost anything, depending on the context in which it is used, but love in this instance meant concern for the lost and a willingness to assume whatever sacrifice was necessary in order to remedy the situation. The Spirit's role in this regard was to touch the lives of both those who would go and those who would stand with them, as with a flame from the altar. Thereafter, He would stand beside them in times of discouragement, in the face of obstacles, and when the task seemed too great for their resources, in order to see that the job was completed.

10. Kenneth Scott Latourette, *A History of the Expansion of Christianity*, IV, pp. 45–46.

This may sound like the recovery of primitive Christianity, but it was more than that. Reawakening is never the same as first awareness. It comes with reluctance at first and then with a freshness of the new day that has dawned. From its vantage point, the modern missionary movement could see the distant lands and countless multitudes in need. These needy were drawn from countless peoples around the globe, differing in appearance and cultural preference, but alike in lacking the gospel—which had for so long been taken for granted in Europe and America.

Love was translated early on in the movement to mean concern for *all* the needs of these distant peoples. Latourette observes that this "led to the reduction of hundreds of languages to writing and to the translation of the Bible into a thousand tongues, to the erection of hospitals and the creation of new medical professions, to the rise of educational systems for entire peoples, and to vast changes in the family system and in the status of women."[11] Ironically, this was often in contrast to a more limited concept of ministry at home and for the church at large.

Men were moved to act through the faithful ministry of the Spirit. In the early days of the movement, those who had supported Carey wavered in their resolve. How could they, ministers of poverty-stricken churches, undertake a mission so demanding and beset with uncertainty? J. Herbert Kane tells us that at the crucial moment, when it seemed as if the vision would vanish, Carey pulled from his pocket a booklet entitled *Periodical Account of Moravian Missions*. "With tears in his eyes and a tremor in his voice he said: 'If you had only read and knew how these men overcame all obstacles for Christ's sake, you would go forward in faith.' That was it. The men agreed to act."[12] Some have described missionary activity as the most difficult of undertakings. It is certainly a leading candidate. Jesus asked His disciples, "Are you able to drink the cup that I am about to drink?" (Matt. 20:22). They responded all too hastily, "We are able." They lived to reflect on how difficult it can be to follow Jesus in service—as has many a missionary after them.

This introduces the notion of sacrifice. Some complain that it should not be called "sacrifice," seeing that we are Christ's debtors, but that is a matter of semantics, nothing more. Undoubtedly, the one who goes has to leave behind things he cherishes greatly and to do without in the process. And what may be still more difficult, he must call upon others

11. Latourette, *A History of the Expansion of Christianity*, IV, p. 46.
12. J. Herbert Kane, *Understanding Christian Missions*, p. 147.

to sacrifice: the family which goes with him and those he leaves behind. But for all and in every regard, he trusts in the consolation of the Spirit.

The modern missionary depends no less on the Spirit to give him boldness in speech. When Peter and John were commanded that they should no longer speak or teach in Jesus' name, they replied, "Whether it is right in the sight of God to give heed to you rather than to God, you be the judge; for we cannot stop speaking what we have seen and heard" (Acts 4:19–20). Their fear of God left no room to fear others. They spoke boldly, and they died triumphantly.

Courage ought not to be confused with bravado. Courage in this context is more nearly associated with the willingness to accept risk in the course of pursuing the Great Commission. It has less to do with whether one wavers within, but rather with whether he has the resolve to press ahead in the face of obstacles and in confidence in the indwelling Spirit.

No one can read missionary biographies without being impressed by the zeal they exhibit. Kane elaborates: "Hudson Taylor said, 'If I had a thousand lives, I would give them all to China.' Count Zinzendorf said, 'I have one passion. It is He and He alone.' Henry Martyn, on his arrival in India, said, 'Now let me burn out for God.'"[13] They were not only called but driven, consumed by their mission.

Nothing less could have accomplished what has transpired in the history of modern missions. No halfhearted effort could have turned multitudes to believe and spawned countless ministries to the oppressed. These missionaries were not all great persons, as we are inclined to estimate greatness, but they were moved by a great sense of mission to exploits which still amaze us as we read of them. But, we might ask, ought we to expect anything less of the mission of the Spirit through people of faith?

Not all missionary activity was crowned with success, let alone immediate results. How is one to understand the role of the Spirit in this connection? His is the task of convicting those who hear the Word—of its truth and of the desperate nature of their condition—and bringing them to the foot of the cross. The missionary was meant to be faithful in sowing the Word, patient in waiting for it to bear results, and diligent in supporting the work in prayer.

Since the Spirit was thought to observe neither language nor cultural barriers, the missionary had to contend with new situations he little

13. J. Herbert Kane, *Christian Missions in Biblical Perspective*, p. 129.

understood. He witnessed to the truth he could not precisely explain, in confidence that the Spirit would turn his words to profit. This created a rewarding ministry from what often seemed an intolerable situation.

The results were not always exactly what the missionary expected. The faith of the converts, while sometimes mimicking its expression by the foreign missionaries, often took an unpredictable turn, one that seemed inexplicable to the missionary, but faithfully reflecting the convert's culture. This, too, was thought of as the creative genius of the Spirit, so as to express abiding truth in novel ways.

We have been speaking primarily in terms of the ideal, which was seriously taken and zealously pursued, rather than a consistent record. Obviously, there were some failures, and the Spirit was invoked to explain them. For instance, the movement often carved out colonial enclaves for its converts. It built structures more suitable to Scandinavia than Kenya, promoted clothing more representative of England than India, and advocated behavior more in tune with Middle America than Latin America. One could look at the matter from two perspectives: as representative of man's sinful pride, or in light of the Spirit's abiding faithfulness. The point is that in spite of all this the work was solidly planted on a thousand frontiers.

113 Particular Accent

The admonition not to quench the Holy Spirit (1 Thess. 5:19) took on new significance with the modern missionary movement. Where previously this had been thought of primarily in regard to the call of godly living, it was now seen in terms of dispersing the saints. The fields were seen as ready for harvest. Only the workers were lacking.

The major contribution of the modern missionary movement to our understanding of the work of the Holy Spirit is its integral relationship with witness. The Spirit motivates witness through love; He sustains witness through the willingness to sacrifice; He accommodates witness through courage; He underscores witness with zeal; He honors witness with appropriate results. Thus, the Spirit makes His presence known through witness, the preparation for witness, and the results of witness.

Harry Boer concludes: "Because the Spirit indwells the Church, the Church is a witnessing Church. Because He indwells the Church, He indwells every member of the Church, and therefore every member of the Church is in his nature a witnessing member."[14] The idea of wit-

14. Harry Boer, *Pentecost and Missions*, p. 213.

nessing cannot be attached to the life of the church as a rider, or delegated to some particular agency within the church, not unless we intend to quench the Spirit and draw back from our task as a witnessing people.

This implies that we must see ourselves, individually and collectively, in the light of the Great Commission to "go therefore and make disciples of all the nations" (Matt. 28:19). Vocation must be selected with this in mind. We must assume the obligations of marriage and family with this in mind. We must set our priorities with this in mind. All of this is to allow the Spirit to do His work in His way in our lives.

One does not readily grasp the world as the Spirit's parish. Man has to start somewhere, with what he sees of the world and can do provisionally in terms of witness. But an individual's vision can be broadened if he is open to that possibility, and this can lead to more extensive ministry. "Not quenching the Spirit" amounts to starting where people are and radiating out to the distant corners of the globe. The true test may be less what anyone has achieved at a particular point than the direction in which he is moving, whether with increasing concern for his own interests or to incorporate others more fully in his ministry.

It is never too soon to start. The new convert has to try his legs if he means to use them at a later date. Although he ought not to be rushed too early into places of leadership, neither should he be pampered. He is a witness from day one onward, or he faces the prospect of extinguishing the Spirit.

It is also never too late to start. This conviction was written in bold letters across the modern missionary movement. From the beginning, it faced apathy, reluctance, and even overt opposition to its hope of sharing the gospel. But things changed, a bit at first and then as if a dam had burst. It is far better that the vision come late than never at all.

This is not to commend complacency, as if we could do tomorrow what we have no disposition for today. If there was any factor that most marked the rise of modern missions, it was the sense of urgency. Man today is in a more desperate condition than we may have imagined. The Spirit is concerned and is calling into being a community of the concerned. It is no time to tarry, but to witness boldly in the power of the Spirit, for "night is coming, when no man can work" (John 9:4).

But this sense of urgency ought not to cause us to take wasteful shortcuts. There are no easy roads to effective ministry. No gospel blimps can substitute for sensitive sharing. One must approach the task deliberately, responsibly, confidently. Any alternative would be to estrange the Spirit, who takes greater care than many others in how best to bear fruitful witness.

114 Ecumenical Murmurings

The modern missionary movement contributed significantly to an increase in ecumenical dialogue, since a divided church found it difficult to succeed in its world mission. Increasingly, confessing Christians began to reconsider their relationship with those from whom they had been estranged.

The documents of Vatican II are a case in point. They lament the divisions among those who profess Christ, in opposition to His will, as a stumbling block to the world and a hindrance to proclaiming the gospel. Vatican II welcomed the movement of recent times, not limited to the Roman Catholic communion, "fostered by the grace of the Holy Spirit, for the restoration of unity among all Christians."[15]

Not all have been as positive with their estimate. Some see the ecumenical effort as preparing the way for the Antichrist, and point out the syncretistic tendencies as evidence of compromise of the faith. But, even in these circles, the pervasive ecumenical spirit seems to crop up where one might least expect it, in some cooperative venture or other.

While the concern for unity is as old as apostolic times, the current ecumenical movement is of recent vintage. Willem Visser 't Hooft dates it to the World Missionary Conference of 1910, and to its vigorous chairman, John Mott.[16] There were certainly antecedents, but this provides a convenient place to begin.

Those at the conference assumed world evangelization to be the urgent task of the Christian fellowship. Given modern technology, they could see to the ends of the world, and the sheer intensity of human need was staggering to behold. The pagan religions appeared too strong a front for a divided and bickering church to overcome. Secularism in its varied forms created still another imposing obstacle. Totalitarian regimes prostituted the church where possible and oppressed it when not. Time seemed to be running out with the proliferation of military hardware and man's apparent willingness to use it. All these factors created a powerful incentive to act with Christian unity.

The role of doctrine was ill-defined from the beginning. The task seemed too urgent and the resources too limited to squander efforts on

---

15. Walter Abbott (ed.), *The Documents of Vatican II*, p. 342.
16. Willem Visser 't Hooft, *No Other Name*, p. 103.

anything but sending out the gospel. This implied cutting back on duplication, consulting on strategy, and cooperating on many endeavors. But the doctrinal issues would not remain silent. The movement had received its initial impetus within the divided churches of Protestantism, and there had been agreement from the beginning not to push actively for ecclesiastical union. However, something short of union seemed called for. The churches needed a clearer understanding of what bound them together in a common cause.

Visser 't Hooft documents that the Affirmation of Unity of the Edinburgh Conference (1937) concluded: "This unity does not consist in the agreement of our minds or the consent of our wills. It is founded in Jesus Christ himself, who lived, died and rose again to bring us to the Father and who through the Holy Spirit dwells in his Church. We are one because we are all the objects of the love and grace of God, and called by him to witness in all the world to his glorious Gospel."[17] This preserved the original focus of the movement within an explicit theological framework.

Some of those formerly attracted to the movement interpreted such statements as a device meant to exclude certain of the churches. This was not the purpose, although it had that effect. It was a choice to affirm a Christological unity in preference to a more vague and undefined sense of oneness.

The focus of the ecumenical dialogue still seemed somehow incomplete. By assuming an introspective posture, it was in danger of minimizing its objective. There were countless immediate issues to be faced when witnessing to the world. People clamored for a more practical expression of Christian conviction, attuned to the needs of those around us. The concerns for doctrinal clarity and life application were pretty well accommodated to each other over the period of 1925 to 1935. There were a lot of loose ends left over, but the movement seemed on track from that point on.

There is always a danger of considering the movement too narrowly. The ecumenical effort seemed virtually a ground swell, allowing the kind of landmarks we have suggested. Each community seems to have developed its own peculiar response to what has been so pervasive as to influence all. It is a phenomenon we understand only in part, and which has justified its impetus as drawing from the stirrings of the Spirit. The Spirit seems to anguish over the wounds self-inflicted by the

---

17. *Ibid.*, p. 107.

church, its inability to rise to the task of world evangelism and accept the invitation to healing and enablement for the as-yet unfinished task.

115 Perspective

This perspective on the Spirit, no matter how accurate it may be judged, was a product of the time. It grew out of a vision of the church's task in world evangelism, complicated by an intimidating array of obstacles. Reaching back for a theological understanding which might satisfy the demands of the situation, it was willing to take a step at a time, while the burdens for theological clarity and life application could be worked through.

The ecumenical movement assumes something of the task of the Spirit as forged by the modern missionary movement. Even when it turns back for theological reflection or focuses in on some specific application, it assumes the working of the Spirit in global perspective. We note this fact in passing, so as to get on with the more distinctive developments concerning its understanding of the operation of the Spirit.

This trend was already a rejection of the syncretistic temptation which grew out of the Enlightenment, although some toyed with this possibility for a time, until an accommodation could be worked out between the concerns for theological definition and practical application. The position hammered out insisted on both a confessional stance and commitment to the Christian mission—granting the variety of definitions given in both instances.

Robert McAfee Brown reflects on the nature of current Roman Catholic and Protestant dialogue. He suggests that there is more to this than a common search for truth (which might be said to be the theme of the Enlightenment); it involves a joint commitment to *the* Truth (Jesus Christ). "The reason why, in this particular dialogue, we must believe that the other partner speaks in good faith is not merely because we assume that the other is a civilized man, but because we are both servants of Jesus Christ."[18] Christian dialogue makes progress on the basis of a common confession of Christ.

There are subtle nuances which have contributed to the ecumenical dialogue, for example, the willingness of Vatican II to recognize different levels of dogma. As a result, not all theological issues have the

18. Robert McAfee Brown, *The Ecumenical Revolution*, pp. 70–71.

same priority or concern. This opens the door to getting on with the first things, those which pertain to the universal task of the church, allowing that those who differ from us do so at less critical points than a common allegiance to Christ.

The Spirit, as viewed from the ecumenical perspective, is seen as directing our attention in two complementary directions: toward Christ—"the author and finisher of our faith" (Heb. 12:2, KJV)—and toward our common task. These are the most critical considerations, more important than those introduced by our respective traditions, and without which our task will necessarily falter and fail.

Look to the world and realize our need of Christ in order to minister to it; look to Christ and recognize that He calls us to serve the world in His stead. Either way we look, our attention is projected in the other direction as well, so that only in this manner can we escape the partisan concerns which separate the body of Christ and frustrate the Great Commission.

How, then, are we to understand the dynamic of the Spirit at work? When we are driven by whatever order of fortuitous circumstances to look back at Christ or to see our task more clearly, we may imagine that the Spirit has a hand in the matter. This is what He delights in doing.

But the ways in which the Spirit chooses to accomplish His purpose never cease to amaze us. He seems so thoroughly unpredictable in the matter, turning up in some unexpected context, in an unfamiliar role, to reap some astonishing result. He continues to defy the neat categories we assign to Him, in favor of some creative alternative or another.

This suggests a bifurcation in the Spirit's ministry, thereby to help us accept what had previously appeared unacceptable and reject (if necessary) what we had uncritically accepted concerning the Christian's stance in the world. He encourages us to weigh new possibilities as likely avenues for enriching our ministry; to take a fresh look at things, along with those who had seemed unlikely associates—with all that implies for a new beginning. Imagine that the Spirit may be working in such a fashion, for this we may expect of Him.

Also be prepared to lay aside whatever proves too heavy a burden to bear in the process. Let the stereotypes go, along with the security they provide. Be content with the thought that whatever truth resided in these former things will show up in some new context, for the Spirit may be said to lead us from truth to truth, without substitution for the Truth.

This would further suggest that the Spirit creates a certain dissatisfaction with things as they are and an urgency to get on with the common task. He wages war on apathy, indifference, and indolence. He calls persons to serve this present age, without delay, as empowered for a purpose.

The Spirit also elicits the longing for accord among the estranged members of the body of Christ. In all of Christ's disciples the Spirit arouses the desire to be peacefully united under the lordship of Christ. So, while the understanding of what it means to be united with Christ as Lord may vary, the longing persists at the impetus of the Spirit in the hearts of the faithful. One must not rush ahead uncritically into an unholy alliance, but neither can one sit complacently secure apart from others or deride those who seek common cause.

We cannot easily avoid the issue of conscience in connection with the dynamic of the Spirit as conceived in ecumenical terms. Each of us must be true to his own conscience, while realizing that it may not be in objective conformity to God's will. He who violates conscience is at risk to his own integrity and in defiance of the will of God as he understands it.

However, we can improve on our understanding of God's will. This we do in part by recognizing the communal aspect of the Christian faith. To believe in the Spirit is in some sense also to believe in the church, and to accept life together. This helps curb excessive individualism and cultivates sensitivity to the Spirit, as we are corrected or encouraged by those of like faith and commitment.

In the pilgrimage of conscience, Charles Curran says, "Reality is complex. The problems of conscience are complex. Frequently there are no easy solutions. After prayerful consideration of all values involved, the Christian chooses what he believes to be the demands of love in the present situation."[19] One does not do this lightly, but deliberately—in confidence that God is prepared to forgive our failure to act *properly*, but not to condone our failure to act.

We cannot proceed far with ecumenical deliberation without realizing how much new ground there is to research and how uncertain we are of the outcome. Timid souls are inclined to turn back, and the self-assured to blunder ahead—endangering us all in the process. An appreciation of the Spirit as undergirding the task seems indispensable if we are to maintain continued sensitivity to its tenuous nature.

---

19. Samuel Miller and G. Ernest Wright (eds.), *Ecumenical Dialogue at Harvard*, p. 272.

The Holy Spirit also cultivates our willingness and ability to hear what others have to say, even when this reveals what we would rather not know or seems to give comfort to a protagonist. He helps us keep dialogue in perspective, as a means to better understanding God's will rather than creating another alliance to frustrate His purposes.

The Spirit likewise fashions that resolute determination whereby we are willing to stick to our convictions in the face of every demand to relinquish them. Ecumenical dialogue, rightly understood, does not constitute the surrender of cherished distinctives. That would not be a worthy outcome for such noble aspirations. We give up nothing, least of all our integrity.

116 Crossroads

Martin Marty portrays the ecumenical movement at something of a crossroads. It came into being out of an impetus created by a survey of the global mission of the church. The dialogue has struggled with the twin concerns of adequate theological foundation and relevant application. In the process, it has devised a distinctive outlook on the operation of the Holy Spirit with relationship to the universal commission of the church—an outlook that points back to Christ as the source of the church's commission and outward to the task itself. This involves a willingness to consider new possibilities, but not at the expense of cherished convictions. It fosters a holy dissatisfaction with things as they are, the extent of our present ministry, and the lack of accord among Christians.

Marty sees the current ecumenical movement under fire from two directions: for failing to take the world seriously and for its ineffective manner in representing the faith of the church. He criticizes the pleas to "unite in hope that we shall agree," in favor of "Let us unite insofar as we have agreed; let us unite for the sake of mission."[20] In other words, while the movement may be said to be lacking in one or both directions, we ought not to disparage what has already come into being. Many diverse communions have come together to talk, pray, share strategy, and work together. These, Marty concludes, are ways in which unity has already been discovered by "those in whom the Spirit of Christ is formed."

---

20. Martin Marty, *Church Unity and Church Mission*, p. 138.

117 Charismatic Renewal

While the modern missionary movement was an effort to reach outward, and the ecumenical movement a means of closing ranks for the difficult world mission, charismatic renewal has been an endeavor to fine-tune the church's experience with the Spirit. The modern Pentecostal movement dates to the turn of the century, although adherents would be quick to point out that it does not, in their thinking, constitute a religious innovation but rather a renewal of first-century practice. They employ the term *Pentecost* not simply as a reference to a past event, but as the continuing norm for Christian experience. The term *charismatic* has become preferred by some Neo-Pentecostals, many of whom have opted to remain within old-line denominations and rejected some of the excesses associated with the movement in its early days.

The key to charismatic renewal revolves around its hope to recover the power of the early church for our present time. Robert Culpepper allows that "The contrast which the charismatics highlight between the tremendous power of the early church and the relative powerlessness of many churches and Christians today is not to be passed off lightly. It was said of Paul and his companions that they had turned the world upside down (Acts 17:6), but most Christians today hardly create a ripple in the water."[21] Jesus' promise that "you shall receive power when the Holy Spirit has come upon you" (Acts 1:8) ought to apply to succeeding generations as well as to the earliest Christians.

Charismatics discover a relative dearth of evidence that such power existed from the post-apostolic times. J. Rodman Williams' comments are characteristic: "What, we may ask, is the record of the church following the New Testament period? One can only answer that almost immediately there was a spiritual decline. For example, the letters of the post-apostolic Fathers bear little trace of the original spiritual vitality, and the free sway of the Spirit's rule and life is greatly diminished. . . . Thus despite occasional outbreaks such as Montanism in the second century, the picture is largely one of increasing officialism, institutionalism, sacredotalism—and diminishing spiritual vitality."[22]

The *Filioque* controversy was felt to add little to the experience of the community. The Middle Ages showed minimal improvement. The Reformation was deficient in failing to recognize the uniqueness of the

---

21. Robert Culpepper, *Evaluating the Charismatic Movement*, p. 74.
22. J. Rodman Williams, *The Pentecostal Reality*, pp. 33–34.

Pentecostal event for the ongoing life of the church. Williams added that the enthusiasts, "however exaggerated some of their ideas and actions, were seeking a more radical New Testament renewal. They represented an attempt to make some further headway toward overcoming the formalism and institutionalism of the past."[23] But seeking is not the same as finding, and an attempt cannot be equated with success. The enthusiasts were simply a glimmer of the approaching dawn.

There were other precursors, such as the Quaker focus on inner light and the Holiness emphasis on sanctification. But these stopped short of the needed renewal. The revivalists also stirred people to appreciate the need for power from "on high" for effective evangelism. Williams concludes that the Pentecostal movement added the notion of enduement with power to the emerging streams of holiness and revivalism. It was a fuller recovery of the primitive dynamic of the Holy Spirit with empowering the people of God for their calling.

The idea of recovery inherently implies a situation different from an earlier one. We cannot help but wonder what were the critical circumstances surrounding the charismatic renewal. The charismatics' selection of antecedents is no doubt significant. It opts for the enthusiasts' alternative to a more institutionalized understanding of the operation of the Holy Spirit. Its teaching likewise suggests an affinity.

We ought also bear in mind the struggle through which the church was going in response to the Enlightenment. It found itself out of place in a post-Enlightenment world of reality, where still-repeated dogmas had lost their earlier impact. Charismatic pioneers seem to have imposed the malaise they were experiencing on preceding generations, so that the past was seen through their trauma with the present.

But the gospel still worked, perhaps in a less pervasive way than during Christendom, but not in a trivial fashion. This could be recognized in its inner manifestation by the holiness of life and in its outer manifestation by mass evangelism. Both the sense of need and the potential for recovery had been set for the charismatic renewal.

118 Analysis

We turn to a more systematic and detailed analysis of the charismatic perspective on the operation of the Spirit. Its emphasis, as we mentioned earlier, rests with the notion of being endued with power. Power

---

23. *Ibid.*, p. 41.

for what? The biblical context suggests that it is power to witness. This may be understood in one of two ways: the inner resolve to witness or the credibility of that witness. The charismatic accents the latter, although not excluding the former.

The Enlightenment had created something of an apologetic crisis for the church. Nils Bloch-Hoell recreates the dilemma: "The defenders of Christianity in the last century were in the main unsuccessful. Their basic mistake seems to have been the acceptance of the demand for scientific verification of the truth of Christianity, although this belongs to a sphere where nothing can be proved or disproved, either by pure logic or by experimental research verifiable to the senses."[24] The early charismatics hit upon an alternative mode: with an experiential verification of Christian faith through a recovery of the miraculous gifts of the Spirit—primarily associated with speaking in tongues. This would convince those experiencing the gift and be highly persuasive to those witnessing the phenomenon.

It is difficult to appreciate the singular significance that charismatics apply to speaking in tongues without filling in the apologetic purpose to which it was and is put. It provides for its adherents and sympathizers a bridge to Christian reality, a bridge that illustrates the maxim "we believe in order that we might know."

The apologetic value of tongues tends to erode under more careful scrutiny, a fact about which thoughtful charismatics are well aware. They introduce extended considerations to bolster their apologetic when deemed necessary. These include the rapid growth of adherents, their social concern, and their sense of transcendence.

The last of these additions to the charismatic apologetic deserves special attention. The transcendental dimension of life received a critical blow with the Enlightenment. People attempted to do without it. Some even thought man would do better as a result. Others felt the loss keenly, and the sense of loss seemed to build with the passing of time. All this came to a head with secular theology (a theology of radical immanence), but it had been a long time coming. It was popularized in an extreme expression of the movement with the God-is-dead spin-off. Man was fighting to keep alive his sense of the Other, and the charismatics generated this sense of the Spirit as being present in our midst. This brought solace to those reaching out for transcendence and a rebuke to those who had prematurely written it off.

---

24. Nils Bloch-Hoell, *The Pentecostal Movement*, p. 99.

The charismatic intended to reestablish for himself and others a continuity with biblical times, strained by the Enlightenment to the point of breaking. He refused to combat his protagonist on the other's ground: with a better but still ineffective logic. The charismatic would claim the experience of the earliest Christians for himself and let the Spirit accomplish the vindication of faith.

However, he did not want to repeat the mistake of some earlier enthusiasts, who had in their exuberance all too often divorced the Spirit from the biblical text and put Him in competition with Christ. The results had been thoroughly disastrous.

In contrast, as Bloch-Hoell comments: "Everywhere and all the time the Pentecostal Movement has been biblicistic. The Movement often underlines this by emphasizing that it has no declaration of faith except the Bible."[25] This was true even when its interpretation seemed questionable or too much was obviously taken for granted.

The charismatic renewal has generally been Christ-centered. It reasons that the Spirit points us to Christ, just as Christ directs us to the Spirit. It resists the temptation to put the Spirit in competition with Christ, even though there are instances of failure.

We need to recall that charismatics view Pentecost not as simply an event but a norm for succeeding times. Accordingly, they stress the coming of the Spirit upon those present as though it were a continuing experience. They allow that the Spirit is already present, but not necessarily in power—and for the latter purpose, the disciples must await His coming.

Charismatics view the work of the Spirit in more of a corporate manner than many. Michael Green suggests: "The charismatic movement is a corporate movement, designed to let the different limbs in the body of Christ express their several gifts in harmony. It is the very antithesis of the ministerial exclusivism which afflicts churches of all denominations, where nothing can be done without the minister, and where the conduit of worship is a responsibility shared between him and the organist."[26] Since the movement means to allow room for every gift that has been imparted to be exercised for the benefit of all, the congregation is thought of not as audience but as participant.

Of course, such an emphasis may violate the order proper to serious worship or promote the eccentricities of some few. But this is a calcu-

---

25. *Ibid.*, p. 95.
26. Michael Green, *I Believe in the Holy Spirit*, p. 206.

lated risk, seeing the charismatics' commitment to life together. And it provides a check on all sorts of rugged individualism that would minimize the body of Christ.

Charismatics foster expectancy on behalf of their adherents and spontaneity to what is understood as the prompting of the Spirit. This may, as Culpepper observes, create an unfortunate mix: "The sense of spontaneity, coupled with the expectancy that God will make himself known in new ways, sometimes leads to an unwillingness to make plans without specific effort to find the leading of the Spirit. In this effort, there is always the danger of attributing to God decisions that come from one's own subjective consciousness."[27] There is indeed such a danger, although the author does not mean to suggest that this is inevitable.

The charismatic renewal likewise promotes uninhibited worship. Adherents are encouraged to extend their hands in supplication, clap, shed tears, or give a resounding "Amen." All this may be justified as being intoxicated by the Spirit.

The charismatics have not taken the demonic less seriously because of their triumphant spirit. Quite the reverse, says Bloch-Hoell: "Satan and his kingdom have a place in the Pentecostal message on supernatural healing, in the appeal for the winning of souls and the holiness preaching."[28] Their emphasis is laid on current deliverance, so that some would teach that physical healing is assured in the atonement.

119 Ambiguities

Seldom has a movement created such pronounced ambiguities as the charismatic renewal, which has created deep divisions in the Christian community on the one hand, while fostering ecumenical growth on the other. It seems capable of moving in either direction, or going in both directions at the same time.

Likewise, the movement seems restricted at times to little more than proselytizing of other Christians, only to pioneer in evangelism on other occasions. What manner of movement is this that seems capable of shifting from moment to moment? It is certainly not a simple phenomenon, nor easy to get in clear focus.

Although charismatic renewal contributes primarily to fostering a deeper spiritual life, it is not devoid of social awareness. The difference

27. Culpepper, *Evaluating the Charismatic Movement*, p. 160.

28. Bloch-Hoell, *The Pentecostal Movement*, p. 111.

lies perhaps more in what is sensed as the proper order than in the breadth of concern, so that one should not suppose that he can do God's work without God's enablement.

Finally, there is the curious approach of the movement to Christian dogma. Charismatics have perhaps emphasized Christian experience to the neglect of Christian content, but the movement has also acted as an impetus to Bible study and devotion to the Christian faith. Some of this seems dependent on the particular tradition involved, or what seems lacking in it at a particular time. But in any case, it further illustrates the ambiguity of the movement.

We can probably relate this ambiguity to an effort to cope with the post-Enlightenment age. The charismatic renewal invokes power from on high, in order to provide inner assurance and demonstrate to others the credibility of Christianity. It also asserts the vertical dimension of life when all is seemingly being reduced to the horizontal. Perhaps we should not expect a less ambiguous response, seeing the complex task the movement undertook.

But, within understandable limits, there emerges a charismatic perspective on the Spirit, one that revolves around being endued by the Holy Spirit as an experiential apologetic for these times. Charismatic renewal also reflects a general commitment to the authority of Scripture and the centrality of Christ. All this is coupled with an emphasis on the corporate nature of the Christian faith, the blending of expectancy and spontaneity, the uninhibited expression of a joyful Christian life, and the struggle with the demonic forces—now thought to be in retreat from the victorious Christ.

Summary and Prospect

No final word with regard to the Holy Spirit ought to be considered final. In a manner of speaking, we are always attempting to discover what He has been up to lately. We may easily bypass the more significant developments in favor of what seems at the moment more striking, relevant, or legitimate. But the topics discussed are at least illustrative and to a degree representative. When taken together, they provide something of a mosaic—simplified, to be sure—of the time and trend.

Our discussion has been organized into a tripartite division: the Early Church, Christendom, and the Modern Era. We dated the last of these with the rise of the Enlightenment, which proved to be a serious challenge to the Christian faith and brought the virtual demise of Christendom. The Enlightenment Age gave rise to the Modernist-Fundamentalist controversy, thus drawing off the energies of the church into the struggle over how best to accommodate to the spirit of the times. It likewise provided a persisting point of reference, for subsequent developments: the modern missionary movement, ecumenical dialogue, and charismatic renewal. Each of these was also interrelated in such a way as to gain unique perspectives on the operation of the Spirit.

How may we say that the Spirit is at work in today's world? Certainly in a manner consistent with the past, but also so as to meet the current challenges. The Holy Spirit faithfully represents the unchanging truth of God to a new generation, lifting our horizons to the global mission of the church, impressing us with the need for cooperative endeavor, as well as the need to edify the church through a sensitive exercise of the gifts of the Spirit. He works in these ways and many more.

Much remains that we cannot predict. We are perhaps more impressed by this fact than at any time in history. The Spirit seems poised to work in still new and exciting ways. Thus we conclude that the saga of the Spirit provides no substitute for our experience of the Spirit. It is rather an invitation.

Bibliography

Abbott, Walter. *The Documents of Vatican II*. New York: Guild, 1966.

Ackroyd, Peter. *Exile and Restoration*. Philadelphia: Westminster, 1968.

Anderson, Gerald (ed.). *The Theology of the Christian Mission*. New York: McGraw-Hill, 1961.

Anderson, Gerald, and Stransky, Thomas (eds.). *Mission Trends No. 3*. Grand Rapids: Eerdmans, 1976.

Anderson, Ray. *On Being Human*. Grand Rapids: Eerdmans, 1982.

Archer, Gleason. *A Survey of Old Testament Introduction*. Chicago: Moody Press, 1964.

Augustine. *On the Trinity*. *In the Nicene and Post-Nicene Fathers*. 14 vols. (Philip Schaff, ed.), Grand Rapids: Eerdmans, 1956.

———. *A Treatise on Faith and the Creed*. *In the Nicene and Post-Nicene Fathers*. 14 vols. (Philip Schaff, ed.), Grand Rapids: Eerdmans, 1956.

Barclay, William. *The Gospel of John*. 2 vols. Philadelphia: Westminster, 1956.

———. *The Letter to the Romans*. Philadelphia: Westminster, 1957.

Barth, Karl. *Church Dogmatics*. 4 vols. Edinburgh: T. T. Clark, 1956.

———. *Dogmatics in Outline*. New York: Harper and Row, 1959.

———. *The Humanity of God*. Richmond: John Knox, 1960.

Barth, Marcus. *Ephesians 4–6 (The Anchor Bible)*. Garden City: Doubleday, 1974.

Benz, Ernst. *The Eastern Orthodox Church*. Chicago: Aldine, 1963.

Berger, Peter, and Luckmann, Thomas. *The Social Construction of Reality*. Garden City: Doubleday, 1966.

Blaiklock, E. M. *Layman's Answer*. London: Hodder and Stoughton, 1968.

Bloch-Hoell, Nils. *The Pentecostal Movement*. Copenhagen: Scandinavian, 1964.

Bloesch, Donald. *Essentials of Evangelical Theology*. 2 vols. San Francisco: Harper and Row, 1978–79.

Boer, Harry. *Pentecost and Missions*. Grand Rapids: Eerdmans, 1961.

Bonhoeffer, Dietrich. *Christ the Center*. New York: Harper and Row, 1966.

———. *Creation and Fall/Temptation*. New York: Macmillan, 1959.

———. *Life Together*. New York: Macmillan, 1971.

Bromily, Geoffrey. *Historical Theology*. Grand Rapids: Eerdmans, 1978.

Brown, Colin (ed.). *The New International Dictionary of New Testament Theology*. 3 vols. Grand Rapids: Zondervan, 1975.

Brown, Robert McAfee. *The Ecumenical Revolution*. Garden City: Doubleday, 1967.

Brunner, Emil. *The Christian Doctrine of the Church, Faith, and the Consummation*. Philadelphia: Westminster, 1962.

———. *The Christian Doctrine of Creation and Redemption*. London: Lutterworth, 1952.

———. *Revelation and Reason*. Philadelphia: Westminster, 1946.

Brunner, Frederick. *A Theology of the Holy Spirit*. Grand Rapids: Eerdmans, 1970.

Budge, E. A. Wallis. *Egyptian Religion*. New York: University Books, 1959.

Bullock, C. Hassell. *An Introduction to the Poetic Books of the Old Testament*. Chicago: Moody, 1979.

Bultmann, Rudolf. *Theology of the New Testament*. New York: Scribners, 1955.

Burkill, T. A. *The Evolution of Christian Thought*. Ithaca: Cornell, 1971.

Burrows, Millar. *The Dead Sea Scrolls*. New York: Viking, 1955.

Calvin, John. *Institutes of the Christian Religion*. 2 vols. Grand Rapids: Eerdmans, 1962.

Carley, Keith. *Ezekiel Among the Prophets*. Naperville: Allenson, 1975.

Childs, Brevard. *The Book of Exodus*. Philadelphia: Westminster, 1974.

Conzelmann, Hans. *An Outline of the Theology of the New Testament*. New York: Harper and Row, 1969.

Craigie, Peter. *The Book of Deuteronomy*. Grand Rapids: Eerdmans, 1976.

Cullmann, Oscar. *Christ and Time*. Philadelphia: Westminster, 1964.

Culpepper, Robert. *Evaluating the Charismatic Movement*. Valley Forge: Judson, 1977.

Cunningham, William. *Historical Theology*. 2 vols. London: Banner of Truth Trust, 1960.

Dawson, Christopher. *The Dividing of Christendom*. Garden City: Doubleday, 1967.

Day, Gardiner. *The Apostles' Creed*. New York: Scribner, 1963.

De Waal Malefijt, Annemarie. *Religion and Culture*. New York: Macmillan, 1968.

Eckstein, Yechiel. *What Every Christian Should Know About Judaism*. Waco: Word, 1984.

Edwards, Jonathan. *The Distinguishing Marks of a Work of the Spirit. In The Works of President Edwards* (vol. VIII), 533–594.

Eichrodt, Walther. *Theology of the Old Testament*. 2 vols. Philadelphia: Westminster, 1961.

Epp, Theodore. *The Other Comforter*. Lincoln: Good News, 1966.

Eusebius. *The History of the Church to Constantine*. Baltimore: Penguin, 1965.

Fife, Eric. *The Holy Spirit*. Grand Rapids: Zondervan, 1978.

Flynn, Leslie. *19 Gifts of the Spirit*. Wheaton: Victor, 1976.

Foerster, Werner. *From the Exile to Christ*. Philadelphia: Fortress, 1976.

Gammie, John, et al. (eds.). *Israelite Wisdom*. Missoula: Scholars Press, 1978.

Gonzalez, Justo. *A History of Christian Doctrine*. Nashville: Abingdon, 1970.

Gottwald, Norman. *All the Kingdoms of the Earth*. New York: Harper and Row, 1964.

Gowan, Donald. *Bridge Between the Testaments*. Pittsburgh: Pickwick, 1976.

Graham, Billy. *The Holy Spirit*. Waco: Word, 1978.

Green, Michael. *I Believe in the Holy Spirit*. Grand Rapids: Eerdmans, 1975.

Guthrie, Donald. *New Testament Theology*. Downers Grove: Inter-Varsity, 1981.

Hagglund, Bengt. *History of Theology*. St. Louis: Concordia, 1968.

Hamilton, Kenneth. *Words and the Word*. Grand Rapids: Eerdmans, 1971.

Hassel, Gerhard. *Old Testament Theology: Basic Issues in the Current Debate*. Grand Rapids: Eerdmans, 1975.

______. *New Testament Theology: Basic Issues in the Current Debate*. Grand Rapids: Eerdmans, 1978.

Heick, Otto. *A History of Christian Doctrine*. Philadelphia: Fortress, 1966.

Heinisch, Paul. *Theology of the Old Testament*. Collegeville: Liturgical, 1952.

Heron, Aladair. *The Holy Spirit*. Philadelphia: Westminster, 1983.

Herschel, Abraham. *The Prophets*. New York: Harper and Row, 1962.

Hertz, J. H. *The Pentateuch and Haftorahs*. London: Soncino, 1938.

Hertzberg, Arthur (ed.). *Judaism*. New York: Braziller, 1962.

Heuvel, Albert van den. *The Rebellious Powers*. Naperville: SCM, 1966.

Hinson, David. *Theology of the Old Testament*. London: SPCK, 1976.

Hodern, William. *A Layman's Guide to Protestant Theology*. New York: Macmillan, 1968.

Hunter, Archibald M. *Introducing New Testament Theology*. Naperville: SCM, 1957.

Hyatt, J. Philip. *Prophetic Religion*. New York: Abingdon-Cokesbury, 1947.

Inch, Morris. *The Evangelical Challenge*. Philadelphia: Westminster, 1978.

______. "Manifestation of the Spirit," in *The Living and Active Word of God* (Inch and Youngblood, eds.), 149–155.

______. *Understanding Bible Prophecy*. New York: Harper and Row, 1977.

Inch, Morris, and Youngblood, Ronald (eds.). *The Living and Active Word of God*. Winona Lake: Eisenbrauns, 1983.

The Interpreter's Bible. New York: Abingdon-Cokesbury, 1952.

Jacobs, Edmond. *Theology of the Old Testament*. New York: Harper, 1958.

Jeremias, Joachim. *The Central Message*. New York: Scribners, 1965.

———. *New Testament Theology*. London: SCM. 1971.

Jewett, Paul. "Holy Spirit," in *The Zondervan Pictorial Encyclopaedia of the Bible* (Tenney, ed.), 183–196.

Johnston, George. *The Spirit-Paraclete in the Gospel of John*. London: Cambridge University, 1970.

Josephus, Flavius. *The Antiquities of the Jews (The Complete Works)*. Grand Rapids: Kregel, 1974.

———. *The Wars of the Jews (The Complete Works)*. Grand Rapids: Kregel, 1974.

Kaiser, Walter. *Toward an Old Testament Theology*. Grand Rapids: Zondervan, 1978.

Kane, J. Herbert. *Christian Missions in Biblical Perspective*. Grand Rapids: Baker, 1976.

———. *Understanding Christian Missions*. Grand Rapids: Baker, 1974.

Kaufman, Gordon. *Systematic Theology: A Historical Perspective*. New York: Scribner's, 1968.

Kline, Meredith. *Treaty of the Great King*. Grand Rapids: Eerdmans, 1963.

Knox, Ronald. *Enthusiasm*. New York: Oxford, 1950.

Kummel, Werner. *The Theology of the New Testament According to Its Major Witnesses*. Nashville: Abingdon, 1973.

Küng, Hans. *The Church*. New York: Sheed and Ward, 1967.

Küng, Hans, and Moltmann, Jürgen (eds.). *Conflicts About the Holy Spirit*. New York: Seabury, 1979.

Ladd, George. *A Theology of the New Testament*. Grand Rapids: Eerdmans, 1974.

Lamb, Harold. *Cyrus the Great*. New York: Doubleday, 1960.

Lampe, G.W.H. *God as Spirit*. Oxford: Clarendon, 1977.

LaSor, William. *Israel: A Biblical View*. Grand Rapids: Eerdmans, 1976.

Latourette, Kenneth Scott. *A History of Christianity*. New York: Harper and Row, 1953.

———. *A History of the Expansion of Christianity*. 7 vols. New York: Harper, 1937–.

Lehman, Chester. *Biblical Theology*. 2 vols. Scottsdale: Herald, 1974.

Lewis, C. S. *The Great Divorce*. New York: Macmillan, 1946.

Livingston, James. *Modern Christian Thought*. New York: Macmillan, 1971.

Lohse, Bernhard. *A Short History of Christian Doctrine*. Philadelphia: Fortress, 1966.

Lossky, Vladimir. *The Mystical Theology of the Eastern Church*. Cambridge: James Clarke, 1973.

Maimonides. *The Commandments*. London: Sancino, 1967.

Martens, Elmer A. *God's Design: A Focus on Old Testament Theology*. Grand Rapids: Baker, 1981

Marty, Martin. *Church Unity and Church Mission*. Grand Rapids: Eerdmans, 1964.

Maves, W. Curry. *The Holy Spirit*. Grand Rapids: Baker, 1977.

McKenzie, John. *A Theology of the Old Testament*. Garden City: Doubleday, 1974.

Mickelsen, A. Berkeley. *Interpreting the Bible*. Grand Rapids: Eerdmans, 1963.

Miller, Samuel, and Wright, G. Ernest (eds.). *Ecumenical Dialogue at Harvard*. Cambridge: Harvard University, 1964.

Montague, George. *The Holy Spirit:* Growth of a Biblical Tradition. New York: Paulist, 1976.

Morris, Leon. *I Believe in Revelation*. Grand Rapids: Eerdmans, 1976.

Moule, C.F.D. *The Holy Spirit*. Grand Rapids: Eerdmans, 1978.

Myers, J. M. *Grace and Torah*. Philadelphia: Fortress, 1975.

Nachmanides. *Commentary on the Torah: Genesis*. New York: Shilo, 1971.

Neill, Stephen. *Jesus Through Many Eyes: Introduction to the Theology of the New Testament*. Nashville: Abingdon, 1976.

Newbigin, Lesslie. *Honest Religion for Secular Man*. Philadelphia: Westminster, 1966.

Orlinsky, Harry. *Biblical Culture and Bible Translation*. New York: KTAV, 1974.

Pannenberg, Wolfart. *Human Nature, Election, and History*. Philadelphia: Westminster, 1977.

Pauck, Wilhelm (ed.). *Luther: Lectures on Romans*. Philadelphia: Westminster, 1961.

Payne, Barton. *The Theology of the Old Testament*. Grand Rapids: Zondervan, 1962.

Pelikan, Jaroslav. *Historical Theology*. New York: Corpus, 1971.

Perdue, Leo. *Wisdom and Cult*. Missoula: Scholars Press, 1976.

Phillips, J. B. *New Testament Christianity*. New York: Macmillan, 1956.

Pittenger, Norman. *The Holy Spirit*. Philadelphia. United Church, 1974.

Ramm, Bernard. *The Evangelical Heritage*. Waco: Word, 1973.

Ramsey, Michael. *Holy Spirit*. Grand Rapids: Eerdmans, 1977.

Riggan, George. *Messianic Theology and Christian Faith*. Philadelphia: Westminster, 1967.

Robert, Andre, and Feuillet, A. *Introduction to the Old Testament*. New York: Desclee, 1968.

Rust, Eric. *Salvation History*. Richmond: John Knox, 1962.

Ryrie, Charles. *Biblical Theology of the New Testament*. Chicago: Moody, 1959.

———. *The Holy Spirit*. Chicago: Moody, 1965.

Sanders, Oswald. *The Holy Spirit and His Gifts*. Grand Rapids: Zondervan, 1974.

Schaff, Philip (ed.). *The Nicene and Post-Nicene Fathers*. 14 vols. Grand Rapids, Eerdmans, 1956–.

Schleiermacher, Friedrich. *On Religion*. New York: Scribner, 1964.

Schultz, Samuel. *The Old Testament Speaks*. New York: Harper and Row, 1960.

Schweizer, Eduard. *The Holy Spirit*. Philadelphia: Fortress, 1980.

Stauffer Ethelbert. *New Testament Theology*. London: SCM, 1955.

Streng, Frederick, *et al.* (eds.). *Ways of Being Religious*. Englewood Cliffs: Prentice-Hall, 1973.

Tacitus. *The Annals and the Histories*. New York: Twayne, 1965.

Tenney, Merrill (ed.). *The Zondervan Pictorial Encyclopaedia of the Bible*. 5 vols. Grand Rapids; Zondervan, 1975.

Thielicke, Helmut. *The Evangelical Faith*. 3 vols. Grand Rapids: Eerdmans, 1974–82.

______. *I Believe*. Philadelphia: Fortress, 1968.

______. *Theological Ethics*. 2 vols. Philadelphia: Fortress, 1966–.

Thomas, W. H. Griffith. *The Holy Spirit of God*. Grand Rapids: Eerdmans, 1976.

Tillich, Paul. *Systematic Theology*. 3 vols. Chicago: University of Chicago, 1951.

Torrey, R. A., *et al. The Fundamentals*. 4 vols. Grand Rapids: Baker, 1972.

Vahanian, Gabriel. *The Death of God*. New York: Braziller, 1961.

Visser 't Hooft, Willem. *No Other Name*. Naperville: SCM, 1963.

Von Rad, Gerhard. *Wisdom in Israel*. London: SCM, 1972.

Vos, Geerhardus. *Biblical Theology*. Grand Rapids: Eerdmans, 1948.

Vriezen, Th. C. *An Outline of Old Testament Theology*. Newton: Branford, 1970.

Walvoord, John. *The Holy Spirit*. Grand Rapids: Zondervan, 1954.

Williams, J. Rodman. *The Pentecostal Reality*. Plainfield: Logos, 1972.

Wood, Leon. *Distressing Days of the Judges*. Grand Rapids: Zondervan, 1975.

______. *The Holy Spirit in the Old Testament*. Grand Rapids: Zondervan, 1979.

Index